IN THE FOOTSTEPS OF
KING DAVID

REI   4   ATAVLA

IN THE FOOTSTEPS OF
KING DAVID

REVELATIONS FROM AN ANCIENT BIBLICAL CITY

Yosef Garfinkel | Saar Ganor | Michael G. Hasel

Scientific editor: Dr. Eyal Meiron

To Madeleine Mumcuoglu

In the Footsteps of King David © 2018 Thames & Hudson Ltd, London

Text © 2018 Yosef Garfinkel, Saar Ganor,
Michael G. Hasel

Designed by Mark Bracey
Translated by Alan Paris

A version of this book was published in Hebrew in 2012
by Yedioth Books

First published in 2018 in the United States of America
by Thames & Hudson Inc., 500 Fifth Avenue, New York,
New York 10110

www.thamesandhudsonusa.com

Library of Congress Control Number 2017959861

ISBN 978-0-500-05201-3

Printed and bound in Slovenia by DZS-Grafik d.o.o.

CONTENTS

PREFACE

In 2007 the name Khirbet Qeiyafa was unknown to both professional archaeologists and the public. In 2008 it became world-famous when the *New York Times* dedicated a full page to a description of the site, its excavation, and the preliminary results. This dramatic turn of events is entirely due to the figure of King David, who is so well known from the biblical tradition but is a very elusive figure from the archaeological or historical point of view. Nowhere else had an archaeological layer that can be related to this king been identified, not even in Jerusalem, which according to the Bible was David's capital city. For the first time in the archaeology of Judah, a fortified city from the time of King David had been uncovered. The date of the site was obtained by accurate radiometric measurements conducted on samples of burnt olive stones or pits. Its location in the Elah Valley, just one day's walk from Jerusalem, positions it in the core area of the Kingdom of Judah. Moreover, it is exactly in this area and this era that the biblical tradition places the famous combat between the inexperienced and unknown young shepherd David and the well-equipped giant Philistine warrior Goliath. Khirbet Qeiyafa, identified by us as biblical Shaaraim, has become the meeting point between archaeology, biblical studies, ancient history, and mythology. In the current state of research, characterized by postmodern approaches and a strong biblical minimalist movement that denies the historicity of the Bible, the site has also become the meeting point between solid data and wild interpretations, between science and science fiction, and has aroused strong feelings and reactions.

Our excavation project is remarkable for the amount of attention it has received from scholars, media, and the general public worldwide. The results have direct and far-reaching implications for the disciplines of archaeology, epigraphy, biblical studies, and ancient Near Eastern history. Over the years we have shown a large number of archaeologists around the site, as well as study tours from departments of biblical studies from various universities. The international media that have covered the excavations include the *New York Times*, *National Geographic*, *Los*

Angeles Times, Washington Post, Haaretz, and countless others from all over the globe. Many TV channels, among them PBS and CNN in the United States, and the BBC in the UK, have reported on the excavations. Following the seventh and last excavation season in 2013, we were interviewed by many reporters, including three from different television channels in Brazil. The general public has followed the results of the excavations by attending popular lectures delivered on numerous occasions, visiting the site in their hundreds each week, and buying over eight thousand copies so far of the popular book in Hebrew: *Footsteps of King David in the Valley of Elah.* This was published while we were still excavating the site, and thus presents only part of the complete picture we have today, after seven excavation seasons. Now, this English-language version appears after the conclusion of the fieldwork, and after most of the different categories of finds have been analyzed. This enables us to present an updated picture of the fascinating site of Khirbet Qeiyafa and the dramatic figure of King David.

The results of the excavations have also been shown to the public in a few museums. First, in 2011 to 2013, the Lynn H. Wood Archaeological Museum of Southern Adventist University staged the exhibition "The Battle over King David: Excavating the Fortress of Elah." In 2016–17 the Bible Lands Museum in Jerusalem displayed "In the Valley of David and Goliath." In November 2017 this exhibit moved to the new Museum of the Bible in Washington, D.C.

To understand the importance of the discoveries, we devote the first part of this book to a survey of the current scientific dispute involving archaeology, history, and the Bible. We will examine the development over the past generation of the school of thought known as "minimalism," a European trend that has succeeded in captivating a number of Bible scholars, archaeologists, and historians. Today, after new discoveries and objective analysis, it is clear that the authority of this trend lies in its reliance upon an absence of data and a sensational rejection of the biblical tradition. It is not surprising, therefore, that discoveries such as the Tel Dan inscription (see p. 27) or the excavation at Khirbet Qeiyafa have succeeded in refuting the minimalist approach.

We have attempted to present the reader with the data in a user-friendly fashion, incorporating numerous illustrations including plans and photographs of structures and finds. In the story of Khirbet Qeiyafa

Fig. 1 Teams at work at Khirbet Qeiyafa: the excavation was conducted in 5 × 5 m squares, leaving an unexcavated vertical section or balk on each side of the square. The shades above protect the excavators from the sun.

it is important to emphasize our methodology (Fig. 1), the accumulation of information from one season to the next, the thought processes involved, and not merely our final conclusions. For readers wanting further information on various aspects of the site, we have appended a few footnotes to each chapter. Those interested in more details should consult the scientific reports on the site, both published and forthcoming.

While this book is devoted to a city from the period of King David, another important layer of settlement was uncovered at the site dating to the time of Alexander the Great of Macedon, also an outstanding historical personality who to this day fires the imagination of millions.

Silver coins bearing his image were found in the excavation. In order to give the reader a fuller picture of the history of the site, including during the time of Alexander, we have therefore included an Appendix that examines the main finds from that fascinating period.

ACKNOWLEDGMENTS

We wish to thank all the members of our staff who excavated at the site. In the framework of the Hebrew University of Jerusalem expedition, excavation area supervision and other responsibilities were filled by Sang-Yeup Chang, Gwanghyun D. Choi, Haggai Cohen-Klonymus, Ethan Fichter, Adam Fraser, Michael Freikman, David Geldman, Peter Hagyo-Kovacs, Soo-Keum Ji, Hoo-Goo Kang, Kyle Keimer, Igor Kreimerman, Eythan Levy, Jeremy G. Lobbezoo, Ahiad Ovadia, Alla Rabinovich, Dean Rancourt, Hillel Silberklang, Katharina Streit, Amanda Thompson, Shifra Weiss, Itamar Weissbein, Alexander Wiegmann, and Peter Zilberg.

The Southern Adventist University area supervisors and staff included: Patti Anderson, Scot Anderson, Annalee Beagle, Michael Dant, Roland Dell'mour, Harald Fredheim, Heather Holloway, Martin Klingbeil, Donn Leatherman, Kenneth Mathews, Josh McGraw, Justo Morales, Marcella Morales, Thomas Olsen, Daniel Perez, Clay Perez Garcia, Kenneth Philips, Dean Scott, Lucas Simonds, Celeste Voigt, Harold Leroy Wanamaker, Travis Wichman, and Joel Willis. Other expedition members were: G. Hasel, A. Alvarez, G. Junn, A. Turner (graphics), D. Perez, S. Anderson, M. Dant, R. Delmour, T. Olsen, D. Scott, L. Wanemaker (surveying).

Other staff members participating in various scientific, logistic, and technical field roles include Prof. David L. Adams, Prof. Silvia Schroer, J. Rosenberg, Yoav Farhi, Sagi Klein, Zur Sofer, Oz Ginzburg, Tamar Shapira, Uri Davidovich, Dr. Paul Bauman, Orna Cohen, Miriam Lavi, Olga Dubovsky, Alexander Pechuro, Yinon Shivtiel, and Salama Abu Sayach.

Deep thanks go to the hundreds of volunteers who arrived from various continents and countries: the USA, South Korea, the Czech Republic, Germany, Colombia, Britain, France, Switzerland, Finland, Russia, Belgium, Italy, Bulgaria, and Israel. There was successful cooperation with the Oakland University headed by Profs. Michael Pytlik and Richard Stamps, Virginia Commonwealth University headed by Prof. Jonathan Waybright, Trinity International University headed by Prof. John Momsen, and the Charles University in Prague headed by Prof. Filip

Capek. The expedition stayed at the Ramot Shapira Hostel at Moshav Beit Meir, where they were graciously received. Without the volunteers, the staff, and the administrators, it would not have been possible to successfully uncover the secrets of this city.

Aerial photographs are by Sky-view and the artifact and site photography by Clara Amit, Gabi Laron, Tal Rogovskey, Yosef Garfinkel, and Amir Biberman. The maps were created by J. Rosenberg and the artifacts were drawn by Olga Dobovsky.

The Khirbet Qeiyafa project received support over the years from a large number of friends: Joseph (Joey) Baruch Silver, the Nathan and Lily Silver Foundation, the Curtiss T. and Mary G. Brennan Foundation, Benjamin Eisin, Jeffery and Michel Barak, Prof. Jonathan Waybright, Daniel Mintz, Meredith Berkman, Samuel D. Turner, Esquire, Varda Zinger, the Berman Center for Biblical Archaeology at the Hebrew University of Jerusalem, the National Geographic Society (2009), Sheila T. Bishop and the Foundation for Biblical Archaeology, The McKee Foods Corporation, Ellsworth and Sharon McKee, Ed and Ann Zinke, Doug and Christy Zinke, Grace M. Carpenter, Danny and Sandra Houghton, Don and Esther Latour, Kenneth and Cheryl Mathews, Richard and Patti Miller, Ronald Reece, Joan Taylor, The Burton and Dorothy Keppler Endowment for Archaeological Excavation and Publication, ASI International, Foundation Stone, the Israel Antiquities Authority, and the Israel Exploration Society.

1

THE CURTAIN RISES ON THE SOREK AND ELAH VALLEYS

STORIES OF LOVE, WAR, AND BRAVERY
Beneath the tranquil pastoral green landscapes of the Sorek and Elah valleys lies a dramatic story about the region in ancient times. Draining the western slopes of the Jerusalem Hills, the two valleys at first cut deep, narrow courses through the mountainous region before opening out when they reach the foothills, in the area of the Shephelah. The Sorek Valley, the northernmost of the two, begins in the vicinity of Ramallah and descends toward Beth Shemesh—today, the old Jerusalem to Tel Aviv railway line passes through it. The Elah Valley originates in the proximity of Bethlehem, and the road leading to Jerusalem from Mount Gilo runs next to it (Fig. 2). The two valleys meet near Ashdod, before reaching the Mediterranean Sea.

During the Late Bronze Age, Canaanite period (*c.* 1550–1200 BCE), no powerful city-states developed here. From a diplomatic archive uncovered at Tell el-Amarna in Egypt, which includes several hundred letters sent by Canaanite kings to the king of Egypt during the 14th century BCE, we learn that the two important Canaanite cities at this time in the Shephelah were Gezer (in the Ayalon Valley) and Lachish (in the Lachish Valley). However, in the subsequent biblical period two powerful Philistine city-states were located in these valleys: Ekron (Tel Miqne), next to the Sorek Valley, and Gath (Tell es-Safi) in the Elah Valley (Fig. 3). Biblical, historical, and archaeological data together indicate that at the beginning of the 12th century BCE, the Philistines established five city-states in the southern part of the Land of Israel. In addition to two in the Shephelah—Ekron and Gath—three were constructed along the Mediterranean coast—Ashdod, Ashkelon, and Gaza.

Fig. 2 A view into the Elah Valley from Khirbet Qeiyafa.

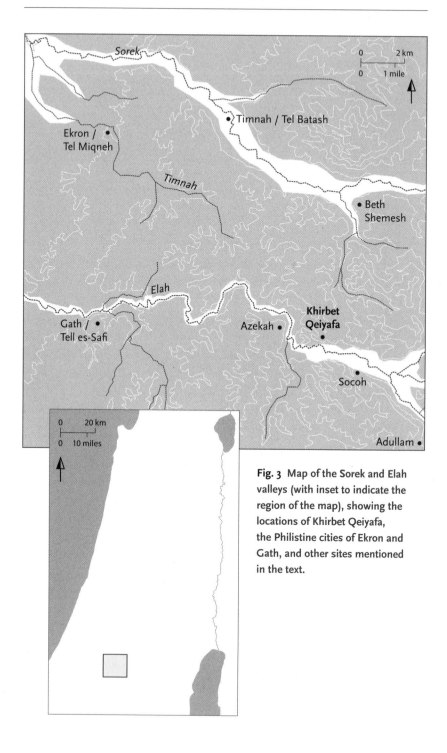

Fig. 3 Map of the Sorek and Elah valleys (with inset to indicate the region of the map), showing the locations of Khirbet Qeiyafa, the Philistine cities of Ekron and Gath, and other sites mentioned in the text.

According to biblical tradition, the Philistines were an immigrant population from "Caphtor," possibly Crete or another part of present-day Greece. Archaeological research has reached similar conclusions based on the style of pottery vessels and other finds from the ancient occupation layers of the Philistine cities, as well as inscriptions of the Egyptian pharaoh Ramesses III, which mention the Philistines as one of the "Sea Peoples," and analysis of the linguistic characteristics of the Philistine names known to us (such as Achish, a Philistine ruler of Gath, and Goliath).[1]

Archaeological excavations show that in the 12th–11th centuries BCE (Iron Age I), Ekron was an important Philistine center, extending over an area of 20 hectares (almost 50 acres). Public buildings and dwellings attest to a developed culture. This large city was destroyed at the end of the 11th century BCE, survived as a relatively small site during the 10th–9th centuries BCE (Iron Age IIA), before expanding again in the 8th–7th centuries BCE into a central site of the same extent as previously. Gath, on the other hand, was a relatively small site in the 12th–11th centuries, but grew to become the major site, with an area of some 40 hectares (almost 100 acres) during the 10th–9th centuries BCE. This giant city was destroyed around 830 BCE by Hazael, king of Aram-Damascus, the same ruler who left the inscription found at the site of Tel Dan in northern Israel that mentions the "House of David" (see p. 28). Thus we learn from the Bible: "At that time King Hazael of Aram went up, fought against Gath, and took it" (2 Kings 12:18). The two cities, located close to each other, present a mirror image in terms of the course of their histories.[2]

It is interesting that there is a correspondence between the biblical tradition and settlement archaeology in the Sorek and Elah valleys during the periods in question. In the Book of Judges and at the beginning of 1 Samuel, which reflect the Iron Age I period, two traditions have been preserved concerning this region, and both are situated in the Sorek Valley. The first relates to the legendary Samson, last of the Judges, who kills the lion and obtains honey from its corpse, attaches burning torches to the tails of foxes, and carries the heavy gates of Gaza upon his shoulders (Judges 13–16). Samson lived with his family at Zorah (Tzorah), adjacent to the Sorek Valley, and he twice married Philistine women from the valley. His first wife was from Timnah, generally identified with Tel Batash (located next to the modern village of Tal Shahar). His second wife was Delilah. While the Bible does not mention where she lived, it notes that: "...he fell in love with a woman in the Sorek Valley." After several attempts, Delilah succeeded in discovering the secret of Samson's tremendous strength: his long hair, which had not been shorn since his birth. She cut Samson's hair while he slept, rendering him powerless, so that the Philistines managed to overcome him, gouged out his eyes, and incarcerated him. As a final heroic act that resulted in his death, Samson pulled down the columns of the temple of Dagon in Gaza, killing 3,000 Philistines. His brothers collected his body and brought it for burial in the tomb of their forefathers, between Zorah and Eshtaol. Each tale about Samson has legendary content, but it should be noted that in terms of geography, his activities are mainly centered around the Sorek Valley.

The second tradition relating to the Sorek Valley tells of the Ark of the Covenant, which was kept in the Tabernacle at Shiloh in the Samaria Hills and was sent with the Israelite army into battle against the Philistines. After one victory over the Israelites, the Philistines captured the Ark and took it to various cities, where it caused grave damage to temples and people (1 Samuel 5–6). At Ashdod, for example, the statue of Dagon breaks, and its head and hands were severed and found lying at the threshold of the temple. The Ark finally arrives at Ekron, causing death and serious illness. After seven months, the Philistines decide to return the Ark to the Israelites, with compensatory offerings of gold, in the hope that they may thus assuage the anger of the God of Israel. Having placed the Ark in a cart pulled by two cattle, they traveled directly up the Sorek Valley to Beth Shemesh.

Traditions connected to the Elah Valley are preserved in the books of Samuel and Chronicles, which relate to Iron Age IIA. It is at a place called Ephes-dammim, between Socoh and Azekah in this valley, that the young David kills Goliath with a single sling-stone (1 Samuel 17), as described below. Later, David finds refuge with Achish, king of Gath, a city identified with Tell es-Safi in the Elah Valley, and then in a cave at Adullam in the same valley.

Some of these traditions may sound like gross exaggerations to the reader today. But modern research is less interested in the precise content of the events described and more in the basic and fascinating correspondence between the location of the important Philistine centers that emerges from archaeological-historical research and the geographical location of the biblical traditions. As noted above, during Iron Age I, in the 12th–11th centuries BCE, Ekron, which is located very near the Sorek Valley, was the dominant Philistine center, and the biblical tradition accordingly places the narrative concerning the Philistines in that valley. On the other hand, during Iron Age IIA, the 10th–9th centuries BCE, Gath in the Elah Valley became the dominant Philistine center and the biblical tradition recounting the border disputes between the Philistines and the Israelites accordingly shifts from the Sorek Valley to the Elah Valley.

The archaeological picture provides us with deeper insight concerning the way in which the ancient biblical tradition was shaped: border disputes between the two different populations, reflecting a historical process that continued over hundreds of years, were condensed into a folk tale with legendary elements, in which each of the two population groups is represented by a single main character: Samson or David and, opposing them, Delilah or Goliath. At night, around the campfire, when the elders of the tribe told the younger generation about history, hundreds of years were shrunk into a brief episode that lasted for a few years or even a single day. In order to keep their listeners entertained, a layer of legend was added to the events: the enormous strength of Samson or the incredible height of Goliath. Modern research cannot ignore these traditions and regard them simply as baseless legends. It is obliged to analyze them, and must attempt to distill from them the complex historical processes that extended over hundreds of years.

A BOY WITH A SLING

Khirbet Qeiyafa is located at the western edge of the high Shephelah, in the Elah Valley, between Socoh and Azekah (see Fig. 3). In ancient geo-political terms, it is situated on the border between Judah and Philistia, dominating the main road leading from the Coastal Plain to the hill country and the cities of Hebron, Bethlehem, and Jerusalem. It is in precisely this location that the biblical tradition sets the battle between David and Goliath. Furthermore, the city of Khirbet Qeiyafa, radiocarbon dated to the end of the 11th and the beginning of the 10th century BCE, existed during the period to which the biblical tradition attributes this battle. The question then arises if and how the excavation at Khirbet Qeiyafa contributes to our understanding of this tradition.

Hidden in the biblical story of the battle between David and Goliath is valuable geographical-historical information. The Bible relates that the Philistine army penetrated the Elah Valley and camped near Socoh. At the beginning, it is not stated where this army originated, but Goliath the Gittite (from the city of Gath) later emerges as a central figure, and after the battle the Philistines retreated to Gath and Ekron. We can infer from this that the main force involved in the war came from Gath, and they were joined by the inhabitants of Ekron. Gath was destroyed at the end of the 9th century BCE by Hazael, the Aramean king of Damascus, and Ekron was destroyed in 603 BCE by the Babylonians. If the story was written at the end of the 7th century BCE, during the Persian or Hellenistic period, when these cities no longer existed, its author would probably have noted Ashdod, Ashkelon, and Gaza as the cities from which the Philistine forces originated. It is thus clear that the biblical author had access to historical information originating in the 10th and 9th centuries BCE.

Facing the Philistine army is King Saul, his general Abner, son of Ner, and the Israelite warriors. They gather between Socoh and Azekah, at the place referred to as

Fig. 4 The biblical tradition of the valiant young shepherd boy David killing the giant Philistine warrior Goliath in battle in the Valley of Elah has attracted the attention of many artists, as seen in this engraving by Julius Schnorr von Carolsfeld (1794–1862).

"Ephes-dammim," or, in another tradition, "Pas-dammim." Various battles in which David's heroes were involved (1 Chronicles 11:13) occurred at this place. The name Ephes-dammim does not appear in the list of the cities of the tribe of Judah, or in traditions later than the time of David. Recently, David Adams, who has worked at Khirbet Qeiyafa, has proposed understanding the word "Ephes" in this context as the border, while "dammim" means blood in Hebrew. He therefore explains the name as meaning the "border of blood," in other words, the bloody battle zone.[3] However, the Elah Valley was an area of border conflicts only in the 10th and 9th centuries BCE, and after the destruction of Gath entirely lost its earlier geopolitical significance. In the second half of the monarchic period, the main population and military center of the Shephelah moved southward to the city of Lachish. Once more, the author of the biblical tradition was using real historical information concerning the line of the western border of the Kingdom of Judah in the 10th and 9th centuries BCE.

For 40 days Goliath, the Philistine giant, armed with the finest weaponry of his day, went forth to goad and curse the Israelites, proposing a duel with one from among their army. Given his size and strength, no Israelite warrior was prepared to take up this challenge. This changed with the arrival of David, a shepherd boy, the youngest of seven brothers, who had been sent by his father from Bethlehem to take food to his three elder brothers serving in Saul's army. Without the slightest hesitation, David, the faithful shepherd, who had already killed a lion and a bear that had attacked his flock, volunteered to face Goliath. Refusing to wear a helmet and armor or carry a sword, as he had no experience of using them, he faced his opponent armed only with five pebbles collected from the streambed of the Elah Valley. In the combat against the heavily encumbered giant, David had the advantage of lightness of foot, and ran quickly toward the Philistine, hitting him on the forehead with a sling-stone. Goliath fell down upon his face and David decapitated him with a sword (Fig. 4). His head, it is said, David took to Jerusalem. After Goliath was killed, the Philistines fled on the road to the city of Shaaraim, with Saul's army pursuing them right up to the gates of Gath and Ekron where they then killed them.

Before us is a soldier's tale, recounted at night by the light of a fire, set in the area of the Elah Valley. During times of crisis, when the army assembled for battle and soldiers were fearful of their fates, such tall tales as this one about a shepherd boy who succeeded in overcoming a trained killer armed with the finest weaponry certainly offered comfort and hope. The message is clear: with courage and clever tactics it is possible to overcome a larger and well-armed foe.

The story includes a detailed description of Goliath's weaponry: a copper helmet, a coat of mail, a spear, a javelin, and leg guards. Goliath's equipment has never been found in an archaeological context, and a large number of articles have attempted to establish the date of composition of the tradition based upon this weaponry. Some date it to Iron Age I (11th–10th centuries BCE), others to the 7th century BCE, and yet others to the Persian period (5th–4th century BCE).[4] In fact, such equipment was deployed by land forces for centuries until the invention of gunpowder and the use of guns. Does the fact that Crusader armies fought with such equipment indicate that the story of David and Goliath was composed in the Middle Ages? In our view, the main criterion for dating this tradition is the geographical and geopolitical reality that it reflects, which can be examined objectively using archaeological and historical tools.

There are, in the biblical tradition, several stories about battles in the vicinity of the Elah Valley, and David and his heroes always smite and kill the Philistines at every opportunity. But the reality was certainly much more difficult, and on occasion the Philistines were undoubtedly the victors. We read, for example, of Philistine incursions into the hill country, to Michmash in Benjamin (1 Samuel 13:23), and the Rephaim Valley near Jerusalem (2 Samuel 5:17–22). It was in one of these border disputes that the city at Khirbet Qeiyafa was conquered and destroyed. This episode, which was certainly a great disaster for the site at that time, froze and preserved the settlement, enabling us today, 3,000 years later, to appreciate directly the building skills, administration, and organization found in this region in the time of King David.

2

IN KING DAVID'S FOOTSTEPS: BIBLE, HISTORY, AND ARCHAEOLOGY

DAVID: FROM OUTLAW TO NATIONAL HERO

King David is one of the central figures of human history and pivotal for biblical tradition (Fig. 5). For 3,000 years he has fired the interest and imagination of hundreds of millions of people. The Bible tells his life story in great detail. As a young man David is called upon to play his harp to soothe King Saul, a troubled ruler who suffers from periods of deep depression. David, a faithful and handsome shepherd, protects his flocks from lions and bears, and, in a glorious moment of courage and faith, kills Goliath the Gittite, a Philistine giant armed with fearsome weaponry. Thrust on to the central political stage, David marries Michal, the king's daughter, but Saul's jealousy of his popularity with the people causes him to flee the palace. He is relentlessly pursued as a fugitive by Saul and even cooperates with the Philistine enemies of his people.

After Saul's death, David himself becomes king and establishes a new royal dynasty in Hebron. He finally defeats the Philistines in battle, bringing to an end decades of antagonism and conflict. Seven years into his reign, he conquers Jerusalem and turns it into the capital of his kingdom, a city that over the generations would become sacred to the three great monotheistic faiths: Judaism, Christianity, and Islam. David galvanizes the twelve tribes and controls all of the Land of Israel and a considerable portion of Transjordan, founding a United Monarchy that would last almost a century. His family, including numerous wives and a large number of offspring, is wracked by violent conflicts: rape, rebellion, and murder. Despite a life filled with dangers and surprising twists, David survives to a ripe old age in his palace and dies a natural death.[1] His legacy lives on through his dynasty, the "House of David,"

Fig. 5 David playing the harp, by Nicolaes de Bruyn (1581–1656).

which continues to rule over Jerusalem until the city is destroyed in 586 BCE by Nebuchadnezzar, king of Babylon.

The Bible without David would have to be completely rewritten. No other person is mentioned more frequently throughout the Old and New Testaments, from the first references in Ruth to the final chapter of Revelation. To him are attributed half the Psalms that are still recited or sung in synagogues and churches around the world. Without him there would be no capital in Jerusalem and no temple built by his son Solomon. Most importantly for both Jewish and Christian traditions, David through his father Jesse becomes the progenitor of the Messiah. Christian tradition includes him in the family tree of Jesus, son of Joseph of Nazareth.

Until around 1980, modern research accepted the biblical tradition of King David as reflecting an accurate historical memory. In the first part of the 20th century, numerous studies were written about his conquests and building activities. Burnt structures and destroyed fortifications found in archaeological excavations at various sites were connected to David's conquests, and the construction of other buildings and fortifications were attributed to his reign. A clear picture emerged of complementary biblical traditions and corresponding archaeological discoveries that pointed to the existence of a United Monarchy during the reigns of David and his son Solomon.[2] Based on the evidence, particularly the biblical lists of the kings of Judah and Israel and the years of their reigns, along with inscriptions left by kings of Egypt, Assyria, and Babylon, modern research was able to date the relevant biblical periods, from several hundred years before David to the destruction of the First Temple.

Archaeologists tend to divide this time between two main archaeological periods: the Late Bronze Age and the Iron Age (referring to the metals that tools were mostly made from in each). The Late Bronze Age is associated with Canaanite culture. A number of "city-states," each an independent political entity ruled by a king, dominated the area at that time, including Hazor, Shechem, Lachish, and Gezer. The Iron Age begins at the time of the Israelite settlement and the period of the Judges, and ends with the destruction of the First Temple. These periods create the chronological framework, the timeframe, in which David lived (Table 1). The absolute chronology of the kings of Israel and Judah, i.e., the dates

Date (BCE)	Period	Biblical tradition	External sources
c. 830–586	Iron Age IIB–C	First Temple period; Kingdoms of Judah and Israel	Inscriptions of kings of Assyria and Babylonia. Inscription of Mesha, King of Moab. "House of David" inscription from Tel Dan. Inscriptions of Egyptian King Shoshenq I / Shishak.
c. 1000–830	Iron Age IIA		
		David and Solomon	
c. 1200–1000	Iron Age I	Settlement period and Judges	The name "Israel" appears in an inscription of Egyptian King Merenptah, c. 1209 BCE.
c. 1550–1200	Late Bronze Age	Canaanite period	Inscriptions by Egyptian kings. Correspondence from el-Amarna in Egypt.

Table 1 The chronological framework of the periods discussed (the order reflects the deposition of strata in an archaeological tell, the earliest at the bottom, with subsequent periods above it).

of their reigns, once fraught with problems and perceived contradictions, has been largely established thanks to the research of several comprehensive studies.[3] The lengths of the reigns attributed to David and Solomon, exactly 40 years each, aroused suspicions, although each was probably active for a good number of decades. Accordingly, David began his reign around 1000 BCE in Hebron, where he remained for seven years before conquering Jerusalem and establishing it as his capital. Solomon succeeded him in c. 970 or 960 BCE. We shall follow this chronology here, while acknowledging that there is still debate about details.

According to the Old Testament, following Solomon's death the kingdom split into two separate political units: the Kingdom of Israel in the north, with its capital at Samaria, and the Kingdom of Judah in the south (Fig. 6), centered on Jerusalem. The northern kingdom was destroyed by the Assyrians after several waves of military campaigns, which resulted in the final destruction of Samaria in 722 BCE. The Kingdom of Judah was destroyed by the Babylonians after a series of invasions, which culminated in the destruction of Jerusalem and the First Temple in 586 BCE.

Given the centrality of David in the biblical story, it is perhaps surprising that in recent years there has been a growing trend to refute the

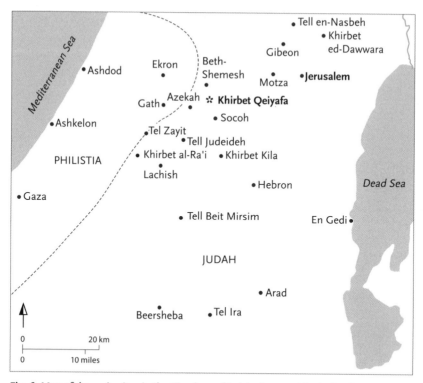

Fig. 6 Map of the main sites in the Kingdom of Judah discussed in the book.

Bible's narrative of the first kings and challenge the ideas of previous generations of scholars. Those advocating such views are popularly known as "minimalists." The interpretations of the minimalists are not uniform and encompass considerable variety, but, for the sake of clarity, we shall present this position somewhat schematically. According to the leading scholars of this approach, from the University of Copenhagen in Denmark and the University of Sheffield in the UK, rather than being historical figures, David and Solomon were purely imaginary literary creations. Biblical tradition should therefore essentially be set aside and modern research should instead base its conclusions only on extra-biblical, historical documents. Thus, for example, on the basis of an inscription left by the Assyrian king Shalmaneser III that mentions Ahab, king of Israel, at the battle of Karkar in 853 BCE, and the inscription of Mesha, king of Moab, which describes his war against the son of Omri, king of Israel, around 850 BCE (or several years later), these scholars propose that the

Kingdom of Israel (rather than the Kingdom of Judah) developed first, at the beginning of the 9th century BCE. The Kingdom of Judah, which is mentioned with certainty for the first time in an inscription of the Assyrian king Sennacherib at the end of the 8th century BCE, developed, in this view, into a kingdom only after the destruction of the Kingdom of Israel (Fig. 7).[4]

In effect, the minimalist views entirely eliminate the period of the United Monarchy, and delay by some 200 years the creation of the Kingdom of Judah. It should be emphasized that these views were based purely on extra-biblical corroboration for the biblical kings Ahab and Omri and on the corresponding absence of such evidence for David and Solomon. Such a position not only presupposes that such data will not be found in future excavations, but is also a historical fallacy in that "evidence must always be affirmative. Negative evidence is a contradiction in terms—it is no evidence at all."[5]

This was demonstrated on July 21, 1993, when the fragmentary Tel Dan stela was discovered in northern Israel. On it was carved an inscription, written in Aramaic, which refers to a battle and the subsequent defeat of the king of Israel and the king of the "House of David" at the hands of Hazael of Damascus (Fig. 8). The inscription demonstrates

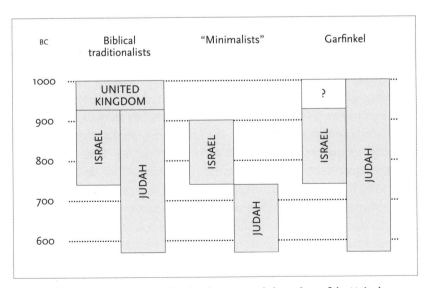

Fig. 7 Different views concerning the development and chronology of the United Monarchy, the Kingdom of Judah, and the Kingdom of Israel.

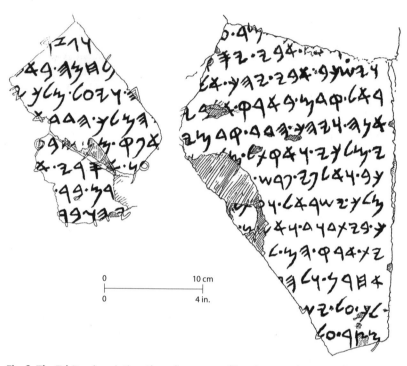

Fig. 8 The Tel Dan inscription: three fragments of basalt preserving part of a royal inscription in Aramaic. The inscription was apparently left by King Hazael of Damascus, who ruled in the second half of the 9th century BCE and boasts that he killed 70 kings, including the king of Israel and a king of the House of David.

unequivocally that by the 9th century BCE there was a memory of the existence of the founder of the dynasty named David, referring to his kingdom as the "House of David" in precisely the same way as in the Bible (1 Samuel 20:16; 2 Samuel 3:1–6; 1 Kings 12:19–26; 2 Chronicles 10:19).[6] Subsequent studies have shown that the same phrase, "House of David," also appears on the Mesha inscription from ancient Moab (see Fig. 10).[7] Following these significant developments, it was no longer possible to rule out entirely the existence of David as king. Consequently, scholarship was forced to address various questions concerning the nature of his rule: was he the head of a city-state or of a tribal alliance; what was the geographic extent of his influence; what were the main sites under his rule; what was the level of administrative organization, etc? How and where could such questions be answered?

Jerusalem, the capital of the kingdom, would naturally be the key site to investigate in search of answers (Pl. ii). But Jerusalem is a particularly difficult city for archaeological research for three main reasons. First, the modern city covers nearly all of the City of David, limiting archaeological excavation to very small areas. Secondly, the nature of construction on such a hilly site meant that in many periods builders removed all previous structures when creating new ones and built directly upon bedrock, so that remains of buildings of certain periods are entirely absent. And thirdly, during the First Temple period life in the city extended uninterrupted over a 400-year period until the Babylonian destruction, and buildings therefore remained in continuous use for a considerable time. This extended period of tranquility was good for the ancient inhabitants, but has left archaeologists with few of the destruction levels that create chronological anchors and little for them to excavate.

Despite these difficulties, several large architectural structures have been uncovered in Jerusalem, attesting to monumental construction early in the First Temple period. The first is the "Stepped Stone Structure" in the City of David. As early as 1923–25 an expedition headed by archaeologists R. A. S. Macalister and John G. Duncan exposed a portion of this impressive structure. Since then, additional sections have been uncovered by several archaeologists working in the city: Kathleen M. Kenyon (in 1961–67), Yigal Shiloh (1978–85), and, more recently, Eilat Mazar (2000–present). One of the most impressive construction projects from the First Temple period, this sloping wall consists of 55 stone steps that have been exposed to a height of 18 m (almost 60 ft). Other parts of the structure exposed nearby indicate that its full height was nearly 30 m (98 ft). Its stepped structure would mean it could be easily climbed, indicating that it was not part of the city's fortifications. It is therefore generally interpreted as a supporting wall to allow the construction of large buildings at the top of the steep eastern slope of the City of David.[8]

A second building is the "Large Stone Structure," which was exposed on the eastern slope of the City of David, above and north of the Stepped Stone Structure, in excavations conducted by Eilat Mazar from 2005 to 2007. She dates it to the beginning of the 10th century BCE and has proposed identifying it as David's palace.[9]

To these two buildings should be added the towers of the Ophel (Hebrew: rise, climb), the area via which one ascended from the City of

David to the Temple Mount, located outside the present Old City and south of the Temple Mount. In the area of the Ophel adjacent to the southeastern corner of the Temple Mount, approximately 100 m (330 ft) north of the Stepped Stone Structure and the Large Stone Structure, massive stone towers were uncovered, preserved to a height of 12 m (40 ft). These had been discovered by Charles Warren in 1867–70, and they continued to be exposed over the years. Then, in Eilat Mazar's excavations in 2009–10, pottery fragments typical of the second half of the 10th century BCE were found at the foot of the towers. Should these massive walls be dated to the time of King Solomon, based on these pottery sherds?[10]

The date of these three monumental buildings in Jerusalem is very problematic, as they are not associated with settlement strata rich in the pottery finds that can enable the archaeologist to determine their time of use, and no organic finds appropriate for radiocarbon dating were discovered. Consequently, various suggestions have been made for dating these structures. Some scholars claim that one or more of them were built several generations before King David, while others date them to the time of David or Solomon, and yet others state that they were built generations later. It is therefore not possible to say unequivocally that a monumental building dating to the time of David has been discovered in Jerusalem.[11]

Over the past thirty years several proposals have been put forward in an attempt to understand the chronology of the beginning of the monarchy in Judah. One proposal, known as the low chronology, maintains that urbanization, i.e., the transition from a rural society (the periods of the Settlement and Judges: Iron Age I) to an urban society (the period of the monarchy: Iron Age II) occurred only at the end of the 10th century BCE, and only in the north, in the Kingdom of Israel.[12] In this scenario, David must be regarded as a local tribal chief at most.

SEARCHING FOR DAVID'S KINGDOM

Our knowledge of the Kingdom of Judah is based on three main sources: archaeological excavation, archaeological surveys, and the biblical tradition. We shall briefly examine the information that each of these provides, and explore their reliability and relative advantages, as well as their limitations.

Archaeological Excavation: The first of these, archaeological excavation, is the best way to discover the history of a site. For over 150 years, excavations have been carried out at many sites in Judah, including Jerusalem, Beth Shemesh, Azekah, Gezer, Tell en-Nasbeh, Tell Beit Mirsim, Arad, Beersheba, Lachish, Hebron, Gibeon, and Tel Goded.[13] Some of the sites, such as Lachish (Pl. iii), are *tells*—ancient mounds that have been abandoned for thousands of years. Tells consist of layers of settlement largely superimposed one upon the other (for example, at Beth Shean and Hazor remains of 18 consecutive settlements were found, one on top of the previous one), so that it is often necessary to uncover finds from later periods first, in order to reach the earlier ones below, a time-consuming and costly undertaking. At various tells, layers from the beginning of the period of the kings of Judah (e.g., Strata V–VII at Beersheba or Level V at Lachish) have been excavated in only limited exposures, in small test pits representing a tiny fraction of the total area of the sites. This creates a major problem, in that the information available concerning the character of the settlement in those levels, so important to our understanding of the Kingdom of Judah, is quite limited.

Another problem arises from the excavations conducted at the beginning of the 20th century by the pioneers of archaeological research. European and American scholars visited the major locations in Israel hoping to illustrate the biblical narrative and identify various sites with places mentioned in the Bible. Since archaeological techniques were then in their infancy, the methodologies used were often lacking in precision, and early excavators did not correctly differentiate between the various strata and attributed finds from different periods to the same one. Consequently, the information we have is confusing and it can be unclear what is characteristic of each of the different biblical period levels at key sites such as Gezer, Tell en-Nasbeh, or Beth Shemesh, and the dating of individual buildings and fortifications remains uncertain. Recently renewed excavations at Gezer, Beth Shemesh, and Lachish are trying to resolve these problems.

In the Kingdom of Judah both Hebron and Jerusalem served as capitals at different times. Both sites today are covered with modern cities, making the ancient remains largely inaccessible and severely limiting the work of archaeologists. Information about both these central sites is therefore fragmentary and inconclusive. A similar situation affects Tyre and Sidon on the Lebanese coast, which in antiquity were the great centers of the neighboring Phoenician culture. There too, the ancient cities are located beneath modern ones and the possibilities for archaeological investigation are restricted.

Alongside the large, stratified archaeological tell sites are so-called *ruins* (Arabic, *khirbah*; Hebrew, *horvah*). Such sites were settled for limited periods of time and did not develop into deep, multi-layered tells. Here, ancient remains are often visible on the surface, making it possible to excavate large areas of a single settlement stratum and gain a better picture of the nature of the settlement. Thus, for example, at Khirbet Qeiyafa we exposed 5,000 sq. m (54,000 sq. ft) or around 25 per cent of the settlement in seven seasons of excavation.

Interpreting the various finds from an excavation, such as pottery, stone vessels, metal tools, figurines, jewelry, and coins requires care: those from a particular layer of occupation reflect mainly the final phase of habitation in that layer—in other words, the final days, a moment before the destruction or abandonment of a settlement. But what if a settlement was established a hundred or two hundred years prior to the destruction? How can we ascertain that? This is a difficult problem and the result is that many excavators erroneously tend to compress periods of tens or hundreds of years into brief periods of a few years.

Related to this is our ability to determine archaeologically when a given period begins and ends. For example, the transition between the period of Settlement and Judges (Iron Age I) and the monarchy (Iron Age II) occurred historically at a specific point in time. It seems obvious to us that with the transition between two periods, people's culture and way of life changed, and this would find expression, for example, in the type of cooking vessels they used, the nature of the weapons they fought with, the style of decorations they employed, the kinds of places they lived in, and numerous other characteristics that archaeologists refer to as "material culture." But did the inhabitants of settlements that existed in a given period suddenly change their way of life and culture at the transition between periods, or did this happen gradually, over decades, until the new material culture consolidated? In our opinion, a historical event does not generally change the way of life immediately; rather, a process begins and its effects can often be seen only decades later.

Archaeological Survey: Archaeological survey is a method of research that does not involve excavation, but collects finds from the surface of a site and then analyzes them to identify the period(s) during which the site was inhabited. Researchers systematically pass over a predefined area, document the surface finds, and plot them on a survey map showing where each object was found. Occasionally, a survey allows us to define the size of a site in a particular period on the basis of the distribution of finds and any visible construction remains.[14]

By its very nature, a survey depends on what is found on the surface of a site. But what are these finds, and how do they reach the surface? It is generally accepted that objects buried in a site are exposed as a result of natural phenomena (animals, rain, wind, erosion, etc.) or human activity (construction or the excavation of pits). The main finds collected by surveyors from the surface are sherds, but occasionally also coins, stone vessels, tools, and metal implements are encountered, which are often useful for dating and therefore make it possible to ascertain during which historical periods a site was inhabited.

Unlike archaeological excavation, which requires years of work, a survey can provide rapid results over a broad area, and is a very important tool for identifying the distribution of settlements in a region in a particular period, and thus for obtaining an estimate of population size. Systematic archaeological surveys have been conducted in Israel, with the country divided into a 10 × 10 km (6 × 6 mile) grid.

Some limitations of archaeological surveys should, however, be noted. First, if a site consists of a number of strata, more finds from the upper layers that lie closer to the surface will be found than those from the deeper strata. Second, one may reasonably assume that periods of extensive settlement at a site will "release" larger numbers of sherds, which will find their way to the surface, as opposed to periods of limited settlement that may not yield any sherds. As a result, surveys will fail to identify the latter's existence and a distorted picture of a "gap in settlement" will result; in other words, the surveyor will falsely conclude that during a certain period there was no settlement at a given site.

A number of surveys were conducted in the 1970s and 1990s in the area of the Kingdom of Judah—in the Hebron Hills, the Benjamin region, the Jerusalem Hills, and the Judean Shephelah. These identified scarcely any sites of the 10th and 9th centuries BCE, and some researchers proposed that the Kingdom of Judah did not exist in the 10th century BCE. However, the excavations at Khirbet Qeiyafa, conducted after the surveys, demonstrate that the reported results were misleading. If, as here, a survey failed to identify a fortified site of the 10th century BCE, with exposed walls and gates, it seems likely that this same period was missed at many tells where 10th-century BCE remains lay buried under a large number of later settlement layers. The same situation is found at the site of Khirbet al-Ra'i, 3 km (almost 2 miles) west of Lachish. In our recent excavations there, a rich 10th-century BCE level was uncovered that had not been recognized in earlier surveys.[15] The conclusion based on such surveys that there were no settlements in Judah during the 10th century BCE and that a centralized kingdom did not exist at that time is therefore essentially flawed.[16]

The Biblical Tradition: Just as we encounter difficulties in evaluating the data from archaeological excavations and surveys, there are also problems when we analyze the historical evidence that emerges from the biblical tradition. This is due, in part, to different schools of thought, methods, and assumptions in approaching the biblical text. In order to demonstrate the difficulties we can take as an example the book of 1 Samuel that describes the rise of David and his famous battle with Goliath, of great relevance to our story. Analysis of the account given in the biblical tradition raises at least four problematic areas of scholarship.[17]

1. **Contradictory traditions?** Some scholars have suggested that the Bible preserves two different traditions for the slaying of Goliath. The famous account in 1 Samuel 17 connects David, who later becomes king, with the death of Goliath, but in 2 Samuel 21:19 it seems that Elhanan, son of Jaare, smote Goliath the Gittite. So who did kill Goliath the Philistine: David, son of Jesse, or Elhanan, son of Jaare? Others have described this as a simple problem of scribal transmission, since a parallel account to 2 Samuel 21:19 in 1 Chronicles 20:5 records the correct rendering of the story as "Elhanan the son of Jaare killed Lahmi the brother of Goliath the Gittite." Recently, a fresh look at these traditions emphasized that the mighty figure of Goliath is actually created from a combination of a few short episodes in 2 Samuel 21.[18]

2. **Lack of consistency?** In 1 Samuel 16, the boy David arrives at the court of Saul to play for the king, who is in a deep depression.

Immediately afterward, in Chapter 17, which describes the battlefield in the Elah Valley, King Saul and Abner, the commander of his army, ask David who his father was. Some have interpreted this as indicating that Saul and Abner did not know David. But others suggest that, after his victory, Saul and Abner simply want to discover the name of David's father. In the Bible people were known by their lineage or ancestry; as David was a lowly musician in the court, Saul may not have known whose son he was, but after his defeat of Goliath this detail became important. Still other commentators explain this apparent inconsistency by suggesting that the biblical narrative is not providing a chronological account of events, but instead emphasizes significant elements.

3. **Anachronism?** After the battle it is written that David took Goliath's head to Jerusalem. However, according to the Bible, Jerusalem was only conquered at a later time, when David was already king, and not during the reign of Saul (2 Samuel 5:5–9). Recently, however, James K. Hoffmeier has suggested that this may have taken place *before* Jerusalem was conquered by David to serve the inhabitants notice that they would be next. It would have been a kind of challenge, and a warning of what David would accomplish some years later when he becomes king.[19]

4. **Awkward editing?** In Chapter 17 of 1 Samuel, large portions of the text seem to be repeated. Some modern scholars have suggested therefore that two versions of the same story were combined, without deleting the repetitions. Various dates have been put forward for the composition or editing of Chapter 17.[20] For instance, it is proposed that the description of Goliath reflects the image of a Mycenaean or Philistine warrior, typical of the Late Bronze Age or Iron Age I. Other scholars, however, think that the chapter was written in the 10th century BCE, shortly after the time of David. Another approach dates the writing to the end of the 7th century BCE, while a third points to the Persian period, the 5th–4th centuries BCE, since Bible scholars believe it was then that the biblical text was consolidated. Finally, there are some who think the text received its final form as late as the Hellenistic period, the 3rd–2nd centuries BCE.

Today, there is no consensus concerning the date of composition of the story of the battle between David and Goliath, or when it took on its

Fig. 9 Fragment of an inscription of the Egyptian pharaoh Shoshenq I (or Shishak) from Megiddo, c. 925 BCE. In the temple of Karnak in Egypt a royal inscription of this pharaoh lists the cities he conquered in his military campaign in the Levant.

present form. In fact, there is no unanimity about the date of the composition of most of the books of the Bible, and disagreement extends to much smaller details, such as when specific chapters and even individual sentences were composed. After an exhaustive review of scholarly discussions on this subject, the biblical scholar John Van Seters concludes that, in the minds of some, "the number of editors and revisers has proliferated to the point of absurdity."[21] We must also remember that the dynamic hypotheses of identifying various sources, redactors, and editors of the biblical text are "constructions of modern scholarship"[22] and that they continue to evolve and change.

One must accept, then, that modern scholarship has no clear and objective tool for dealing with the dating of the writing of the different biblical traditions. In the current state of our knowledge, with the evidence available, the process of formation and transmission of the texts remains unresolved, as does the time and manner in which they took on their present form. In our view, instead of entertaining ourselves with speculation concerning when the final redaction of one text or another occurred, it is more productive to look at the deeper historical question: does the text before us preserve some historical memory, even if it was composed or edited to arrive at its present form after the period it describes? In order to answer this question, we shall apply the approach of the minimalist scholars to a hypothetical question dealing with a more familiar historical period.

Let us assume for a moment that we know nothing about the Roman Empire. We do know, however, that the English playwright William Shakespeare wrote a play at the end of the 16th century CE about the murder of the Roman general and politician Julius Caesar, who lived in the 1st century BCE. According to the minimalist method, two main conclusions may be drawn from this: first, that the Roman Empire should be dated to the 16th century, and second, that Julius Caesar is a purely literary character—both of which are patently absurd.

Clear evidence for the fact that the biblical author(s) potentially had reliable historical data at their disposal takes the form of royal inscriptions from the Near East that relate to the First Temple period and for which there are generally biblical parallels: the inscription of the Egyptian pharaoh Shoshenq (Shishak) I at Karnak and at Megiddo (Fig. 9); the inscription of the Moabite King Mesha (Fig. 10); the Aramaic Tel Dan inscription (see Fig. 8); and inscriptions of the kings of Assyria and Babylon that refer to battles and campaigns of conquest (Table 2). It appears therefore that the Bible contains historical information that was passed from generation to generation, which could be used by the writer of the text and perhaps by later copyists and editors. In our view, the great challenge of modern scholarship is to reveal those traditions that preserve history, and not to categorically reject the entire biblical tradition as tendentious later fiction, lacking in any factual basis.

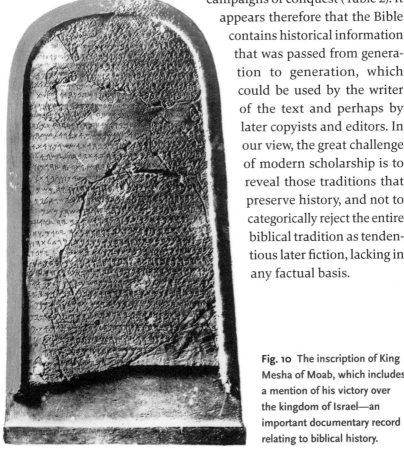

Fig. 10 The inscription of King Mesha of Moab, which includes a mention of his victory over the kingdom of Israel—an important documentary record relating to biblical history.

Table 2: Royal inscriptions of the First Temple period and parallel information preserved in the Bible.

Date (approx.)	Event	Biblical description	Royal inscription
925 BCE	Egyptian military campaign to the Land of Israel	1 Kings 14:25–26	List of cities in the Shoshenq inscription from Karnak temple in Egypt[23]
mid-9th century BCE	Battle of Karkar	*	Inscription of Assyrian King Shalmaneser III[24]
mid-9th century BCE	Military expedition to Moab	2 Kings 3:4–27	Mesha inscription (Fig. 10)[25]
around 840 BCE	Murders of the kings of Israel and Judah	2 Kings 9:21–24	Tel Dan inscription (Fig. 8)[26]
732 BCE	Assyrian campaign of conquest to the Kingdom of Israel, conquest of Galilee and crowning of Hoshea	2 Kings 15:29	Inscription of Assyrian King Tiglath Pileser III[27]
722 BCE	Conquest of Samaria, capital of the Kingdom of Israel	2 Kings 17:5–6	Inscription of Assyrian King Sargon[28]
701 BCE	Assyrian King Sennacherib's campaign to Judah and the conquest of Lachish	2 Kings 18:13–16	Inscription of Assyrian King Sennacherib[29]
681 BCE	Murder of King Sennacherib by his sons	2 Kings 19:37	Babylonian Chronicle[30]
605 BCE	Battle of Carchemish between Egyptian and Assyrian armies, on the banks of the Euphrates River	2 Kings, 23:29	Babylonian inscription[31]
597 BCE	Campaign of Nebuchadnezzar, King of Babylon, to Jerusalem: exile of Jehoiachin and coronation of Zedekiah	2 Kings 24:10–17	Inscription of Nebuchadnezzar, King of Babylon[32]

*This event is not mentioned in the Bible. The inscription describes a covenant between various kings who united and fought against the Assyrian King Shalmaneser III, with King Ahab of Israel at the head of a powerful army. It appears that the biblical tradition, which presents Ahab in a particularly negative manner, virtually ignores his military and political prowess.

GETTING DOWN TO WORK

The non-archaeologist might think that the excavation of an archaeological site is a simple matter: the excavator takes a trowel in hand and removes the layers of earth, carefully documents the finds, and interprets their meaning. What could be more straightforward? However, 150 years of archaeological research in the Land of Israel have taught us that the success of an excavation depends to a large extent on advance planning and careful consideration of the complexities, long before clearing the first shovelful of earth from the site. The excavation at Khirbet Qeiyafa emphasizes this necessity. Our research methodology and considerations in selecting the site, determining the extent of the excavation, collecting finds and data, and relating them to the biblical traditions are based upon the following major considerations.

Khirbet Qeiyafa was selected for excavation because it is not a tell that was settled continuously over thousands of years and therefore made up of numerous layers or strata, but a ruin that mainly consists of a single-level, biblical period city. It stands exposed with its walls and gates, and, relatively speaking, has suffered less from the severe destruction that generally affects settlement strata at tells that were inhabited over many successive generations.

In order to understand cultures of the past, and in particular to investigate their behavioral–anthropological aspects, it is necessary to expose a significant portion of an ancient settlement. Excavation of broad areas makes it possible to obtain the complete plans of a number of buildings, determine their interrelation, and understand the similarities and differences in their organization and in the finds uncovered in each. At Khirbet Qeiyafa we therefore favoured a large, horizontal exposure strategy, and over seven excavation seasons have excavated 5,000 sq. m (54,000 sq. ft) or around 25 percent of the site. At tell sites with multiple layers, a number of periods are studied simultaneously. If, for example, we had excavated seven seasons at a tell with a sequence of ten superimposed cities, and we wanted to examine all of them, we would have been able to expose approximately 500 sq. m (5,400 sq. ft). of each stratum.

The quantity and quality of data that we exposed at Khirbet Qeiyafa allow us to consider a variety of questions, and particularly ones relating to aspects of urban planning, the manner in which cities were built, and the social organization of the local population, questions that an excavation over a limited area cannot possibly answer. This information will assist us in learning about the way of life of the inhabitants, the cultic rituals practiced, and a variety of other aspects.

When our excavations descended between the walls of buildings and reached the destruction layer of the 10th century BCE, we sifted the excavated earth using special screens in order not to miss tiny finds that might otherwise escape notice (Fig. 11). This work takes considerable time, as every pail of earth removed from the destruction layer and the floor passes through the screens. Such sifting mainly yields ordinary finds such as pottery sherds or animal bones, but on occasion unusual objects are found, including scarabs, seals, and beads.

In the past, when archaeological science was in its infancy, excavations were managed by archaeologists alone, and they examined the finds and analyzed their significance. Since then, the situation has changed completely: working alongside the archaeologists are specialists from a wide variety of fields, who ensure all possible information is obtained from the excavation. Some specialize in studying pottery, others in art objects, in Egyptian artifacts, such as scarabs, in coins (numismatists), in metals (metallurgists), etc. Sixteen different authors contributed to the writing of the excavation report for the first two seasons (2007–08). The second report, for the 2009–13 seasons, had forty contributors.[33] The amount of information accumulated during the excavation seasons was so great that a further six volumes are planned.

Our expedition decided from the beginning that publication was a priority. The weakest link in archaeological research, in Israel and around the world, is frequently the lengthy time that elapses between excavation and publication of the results. Archaeological excavation destroys what it excavates. It is therefore a scholarly and scientific obligation to publish all of the data on the excavation procedure and the findings for other scholars and the public at large. Although Israeli law requires publication of archaeological findings within ten years of the completion of an excavation, it is quite common for an expedition to work at a site for ten or even twenty years without publishing a scientific report for a single season of excavation. The damage caused is great: over the years, important data are forgotten, excavation notes and finds are lost, the excavator sometimes dies, and often there are no staff to continue to work on the publication.

Fig. 11 A volunteer sifts earth during the excavation. All of the earth from destruction layers was sieved in this way, revealing small finds such as scarabs, seals, and beads.

Making publication of the excavation a primary objective of the expedition dictates certain aspects of the fieldwork. In 2013, we completed the investigation of all buildings in which excavation had begun in prior seasons, in order to be able to publish a coherent architectural plan of entire buildings rather than just individual walls or parts of rooms.

ARCHAEOLOGY VS. THE BIBLE—A COMPLEX INTERRELATIONSHIP

The founding generation of modern archaeological research dated archaeological strata or buildings on the basis of biblical traditions. Thus, for example, Yigael Yadin dated the gates discovered at the biblical cities of Hazor, Megiddo, and Gezer, which had similar architectural plans (three chambers on each side of a central passageway), to the days of King Solomon.[34] This interpretation was based on a single biblical passage: "This is the account of the forced labor that King Solomon conscripted to build the house of the Lord and his own house, the Millo and the wall of Jerusalem, Hazor, Megiddo, Gezer" (1 Kings 9:15). Scholars who support the low chronology have insisted that the gates date to King Ahab, a proposal with no supporting evidence, whether biblical, archaeological, or radiocarbon dating. In our view, archaeological finds should be independently dated; only then may attempts be made to connect them with historical/biblical figures, periods, or events. In this case, accurate research must first date each of these gates separately and scientifically; it will then be clear whether they were constructed at the same time by one king or, perhaps, at different times by different kings. At the moment, neither proposal cited above for dating the gates has such corroboration.

Fortunately, we were able to ascertain the date of Khirbet Qeiyafa by the radiocarbon method, as discussed in the following chapter. This is the first site in Judah from the beginning of the monarchy to be dated using this scientific technique. The results unequivocally demonstrated that the city was established at the end of the 11th and beginning of the 10th century BCE. If the dating of Khirbet Qeiyafa relied simply on an assessment of the pottery found, scholars would be able to propose raising or lowering the age of the site by hundreds of years, in accordance with views arising from historical considerations. But as soon as a dating based on the radiocarbon method was obtained, the age of the site became largely beyond dispute.

It also became clear from the excavation, as discussed below, that the city exhibits urban planning typical of Judah and that its inhabitants refrained from eating pork and displaying human or animal figurines in their cult places. Taken together, we believe this shows that the site cannot have been Philistine or Canaanite, and we concluded that Khirbet Qeiyafa was inhabited by a population belonging to the Kingdom of Judah.

In examining the kingdoms of Judah and Israel it is necessary to look at each of the two geographical regions individually: Judah in the south and Israel in the north. Scholars who attempt to apply findings from northern sites to the situation in Judah and Jerusalem are committing a methodological error. Likewise, we should not draw conclusions about the north of the country based on our findings in Judah. Therefore, despite having made significant and important discoveries attesting to the existence of a kingdom in the time of David, we refrain from using the term "United Monarchy," which implies the existence of a kingdom that also included the north of the country. Instead, we shall use here the term "Kingdom of Judah."

A second widespread methodological error is the concept of "all or nothing"—in other words, that either the United Monarchy existed during the 10th century BCE and ruled from Jerusalem over Judah and Israel, or there was no central government until the development of the Kingdom of Israel in the north at the beginning of the 9th century BCE. However, we should not exclude the possibility that a central administration emerged in Judah early in the 10th century BCE with a direct sphere of influence over Judah only, and that later, during the course of the 9th century BCE, the Kingdom of Israel evolved independently.

THE WAR OF PARADIGMS

The researcher's worldview or paradigm is a comprehensive model that incorporates the various data within a specific field. The data are like pieces of a mosaic that can be combined in different ways to form different images; the pieces themselves do not change, but the images they form can be modified. Here we briefly summarize five of the conflicting paradigms regarding David's kingdom, and their development.

The biblical paradigm: The founding generation of researchers accepted the biblical tradition as a reflection of historical reality, and they defined and dated the archaeological data using the Bible. Their premise was that David and Solomon ruled a large and United Kingdom from Jerusalem, and they dated different building projects to their time. According to this approach, the basis for dating archaeological finds is historical information, and discoveries were directly related to the Bible.

The mythological paradigm: From the beginning of the 1980s on, it was claimed by some that the Bible should not be used as a historical source. Instead, only royal inscriptions and other external documents from the ancient Near East should be relied upon. Consequently, as no external historical sources confirming the existence of the United Monarchy had then been found, the scholars supporting this paradigm deduced that the kingdom had never existed. All of the colorful biblical descriptions of the days of David and Solomon were regarded as nothing but myths and literary creations. David and Solomon were no longer historical figures. Likewise, it was claimed that the northern Kingdom of Israel was established first (rather than the Kingdom of Judah), since the earliest kings mentioned in extra-biblical inscriptions are Omri and Ahab, whose capital was in the city of Samaria. The Kingdom of Judah, first referred to in inscriptions of Assyrian kings in the late 8th century BCE was, according to this view, established only after the Kingdom of Israel had been destroyed and some of its inhabitants had emigrated southward. The Tel Dan Inscription, which provides evidence that around a hundred years after the time of David he was known as a historical figure and the founder of a royal dynasty, clearly challenges this paradigm.

The chronological paradigm: In 1996, following the discovery of the Tel Dan inscription, the low chronology paradigm was put forward by Israel Finkelstein of Tel Aviv University. He proposed that the process of urbanization in the First Temple period began around 900 BCE, in other

Fig. 12 Khirbet Qeiyafa: a diagonal aerial photograph at the end of the fifth excavation season in 2011. The city wall surrounding an area of 2.3 hectares is clearly visible.

words a century after the time of King David, in the northern Kingdom of Israel, and that again Judah became a kingdom only in the late 8th century BCE. This approach reiterates the mythological paradigm in terms of chronology, and essentially reflects the same idea. Thus, despite David having been a historical figure who founded a royal dynasty, he was not a king who ruled over a kingdom with fortified cities, but instead acted as a regional leader, a kind of Bedouin sheikh who lived in a tent. It should be noted that when this proposal was made, it was not based on any new archaeological data, excavation projects, or radiometric dates. In fact, it utilized the biblical historical narrative of kings and events as its interpretative paradigm, but simply transferred to Ahab and the Omrid dynasty the archaeological evidence assigned to Solomon. In other words, like the biblical paradigm, the Bible is used as a basis for dating archaeological finds.[35]

With our excavation of the fortified city of Khirbet Qeiyafa, dated to around 1000 BCE, it is no longer possible to maintain that the wave of urbanization began in the northern Kingdom of Israel at the beginning of the 9th century BCE, and in the Kingdom of Judah only at the end of the 8th century BCE. Rather, it is now clear that there were fortified cities in Judah in the time of David.

The ethnic paradigm: Almost immediately after the publication of the new data from Khirbet Qeiyafa, Nadav Na'aman, a Tel Aviv University historian, proposed first that the inhabitants of this site were Philistines, and later changed his opinion and argued for a Canaanite population.[36] In this view, even if the urbanization process began around 1000 BCE, it was not connected with Judah, and King David can still be regarded as a Bedouin sheikh living in a tent. This approach again reiterates the conclusions of the mythological and chronological paradigms, but here using arguments related to the ethnic identity of the population of Khirbet Qeiyafa. In the same way Zvi Lederman and Shlomo Bunimovitz, both of Tel Aviv University, have proposed that Khirbet Qeiyafa was a Canaanite site.[37]

Another possibility, put forward by Finkelstein and Alexander Fantalkin, suggests that the city of Khirbet Qeiyafa was built by King Saul and later destroyed by the Egyptian pharaoh Shoshenq I.[38] Khirbet Qeiyafa's political association would then be with the northern Israelite Kingdom of Saul. Saul, however, is a much more elusive biblical king than David; he is not mentioned in the Tel Dan inscription, or any extra-biblical source. This hypothesis also completely ignores the radiometric dating of Khirbet Qeiyafa that indicates the city was destroyed decades before Shoshenq I, who reigned in the later 10th century BCE.

A further possible ethnic affiliation, suggested by Gunnar Lehmann and Hermann Michael Niemann, is that the inhabitants of Khirbet Qeiyafa were a local population of the Shephelah.[39] This population had been described as "autonomous–rural kinship groups" and Khirbet Qeiyafa, along with some other later fortified cities in this region, were designated as "modest villages of the Shephelah." However, the heavily fortified city of Khirbet Qeiyafa, with its planning and public spaces, suggests a centralized urban social organization rather than a dispersed rural population.

We believe Khirbet Qeiyafa is a Judahite site for six main reasons, which we summarize briefly here as they will be examined in detail in the following chapters. The first is the plan of the site, including the case-mate wall (a wall built of two parallel walls with the space between them divided by perpendicular walls into long narrow rooms called casemates). Houses adjoining the wall incorporate the casemates as rooms. This plan is known today from four other sites, all in the Kingdom of Judah.

The second reason is related to the diet of the site's inhabitants and their methods of food preparation. The tens of thousands of animal bones found at Khirbet Qeiyafa were studied by zoologist Ron Kehati. They include bones of goats, sheep, and cows, but no pig bones.[40] Pig bones were, on the other hand, found at Philistine sites in some quantity and at the Canaanite city of Lachish. Also, a large clay bowl used as a baking tray was found in every house at Khirbet Qeiyafa. It was placed on the fire and foods could be baked on top, a cooking technique not utilized at Philistine sites.

The third reason is connected with cult practice. Philistine cult sites, such as the temples excavated at Tell Qasile in Tel Aviv and Nahal Patish near Gilat in the Negev, are characterized by a wealth of cultic artifacts that include images of humans and animals. Canaanite temples likewise contain an abundance of unique cultic objects.[41] Clay figurines depicting a naked woman, known as a "Mother Goddess," are quite common in private houses. Cult paraphernalia found at Khirbet Qeiyafa includes standing stones, basalt altars, libation vessels, and temple models. The rich Canaanite or Philistine iconography, however, is unknown, as are Mother Goddess figurines. It appears that the inhabitants of Khirbet Qeiyafa obeyed the commandment: "Thou shalt not make unto thee any graven image" (Exodus 20:4).

The fourth reason is the extensive use of iron tools. Recently, Yulia Gottlieb of Tel Aviv University has studied the evidence for metalworking in Iron Age I, IIA, and IIB in Israel.[42] A comparative analysis of material from northern valley sites and the Beersheba Valley reveals that by early Iron Age IIA, the iron industry in the south was already fairly well developed, while in the north iron remained largely ignored and smiths continued to work in bronze. An interesting case was Tel Masos in the Beersheba Valley, a relatively large site with urban characteristics, where there is extensive evidence of copperworking. This analysis indicates that in the early Iron Age the use of iron was not common outside Judah. The metal industry at Khirbet Qeiyafa fits the pattern observed at Arad stratum XII and Beersheba stratum VII.

The fifth reason is the geopolitical location of Khirbet Qeiyafa. The site sits on the border between the Judean Shephelah and Philistia, on a main road leading from the coastal plain to the hill country. This location is of importance only if there is a kingdom in the Jerusalem–Hebron area.

The final reason for identifying Khirbet Qeiyafa as Judahite, and not Philistine or Cannanite, relates to the inscription found at the site. According to epigrapher Haggai Misgav, the inscription on a sherd of pottery was clearly written in a Semitic language, probably Hebrew. This is because of the distinctly Hebrew expression "Thou shalt not," as well as the root of the Hebrew word meaning "to do," which was not used in the Canaanite or Phoenician languages.

The Kingdom of Judah paradigm: This is the paradigm supported by the present writers in view of the information that has emerged from the excavations at Khirbet Qeiyafa summarized above. If we first separate the question of the existence of the United Monarchy in the 10th century BCE from that of the establishment of the Kingdom of Judah at that time, we can look at the evidence from Judah itself independently. And once we establish that there is evidence that a kingdom arose in Judah at the end of the 11th century BCE, then further research can be conducted to ascertain its relationship with the northern Kingdom of Israel. These two phenomena should not be confused.

ISRAELITE, JUDAHITE, HEBREW, AND JEW

In this book we use the term Kingdom of Judah, together with various other terms such as "Judahite city plan." Other names appear in discussions of the period in question and we shall briefly explain the terms here. The Bible speaks of two kingdoms: the Kingdom of Israel in the north and the Kingdom of Judah in the south. These are two independent political units that existed in parallel for a considerable period of time. From these are derived the terms: "Israelite," which serves to describe the population and other characteristics of the realm of the Kingdom of Israel, and the term "Judahite," which describes the population and other characteristics of the realm of the Kingdom of Judah.

The term "Hebrew" is familiar from the Bible, where it is used to describe populations particularly during the Patriarchal period. Thus, for example, Joseph is described as a "Hebrew" while in Egypt (Genesis 39:14). In modern usage this term is not applied in describing population groups, but it is used for the language in which the Bible is written, the Hebrew language. Thus in this book we discuss the discovery of the Khirbet Qeiyafa inscription and the proposal that it is written in the Hebrew language, which, if correct, would make it the earliest known Hebrew inscription.

The term "Jew" entered into use only at the end of the First Temple period and appears primarily in the biblical books dealing with the Second Temple period. It appears, for example, in the Book of Esther, which mentions Mordechai the Jew (Esther 2:5). Therefore, in modern research it is customary to use this term only in describing populations from the Second Temple period onward.

To summarize: the mythological, chronological, and ethnic paradigms are in reality variations of the same minimalist approach. The justifications are modified in the light of new evidence emerging from archaeological excavations, but there is no real innovation. When the Tel Dan inscription mentioning the "House of David" was found, scholars of the minimalist school made claims to the effect that the inscription was a forgery, that it had been misinterpreted, etc.[43] Something similar can be seen in the case of Khirbet Qeiyafa, with various articles questioning different aspects of the excavation, and proposing that the city was constructed during the Hellenistic period,[44] that it was a Philistine site,[45] or was constructed by 1050 BCE.[46]

The original minimalist approach, as expressed in the mythological paradigm, was a consistent worldview that maintained that the history of ancient Israel should only be based on extra-biblical data. Both of the approaches that followed, the low chronology paradigm and the ethnic paradigm, were variations that attempted to solve questions that the previous paradigm could not answer. Our excavations at Khirbet Qeiyafa have produced sound data on which to base our proposals, including radiocarbon dating that undermines the low chronology paradigm, despite attempts to argue otherwise. Scholars of the minimalist model, on the other hand, base their arguments on an absence of data and the negation of the biblical tradition as a source of information for the time period in question.[47]

KHIRBET QEIYAFA AND THE CAIAPHAS FAMILY:
AN URBAN LEGEND

In the summer of 2011, Israeli archaeologists Boaz Zissu and Yuval Goren published the discovery of an inscription engraved on an ossuary (a small stone chest for holding the bones of a dead person) that mentions "Miriam daughter of Yeshua son of Caiaphas, priest of Maaziah from Beth Imri."[48] A high priest from the family of Caiaphas is mentioned in the New Testament in connection with the trial and crucifixion of Jesus at the end of the Second Temple period. This discovery created great excitement and interest, with scholars immediately wanting to know where the ossuary had been found. Unfortunately, it became clear that it had been illegally excavated by looters, then reached antiquities dealers and so is of unknown provenance.

An examination of the earth found adhering to the ossuary showed it to be terra rossa, a type of red soil found over large areas of the Land of Israel, but not, as erroneously stated in the article, in the area of the Elah Valley. On reading the article, however, it might be thought that the ossuary could have originated in the Elah Valley. Christopher Rollston suggested therefore that there could be some connection between the Arabic name Khirbet Qeiyafa and the name of the family of priests, Caiaphas, known from the New Testament, and that perhaps the family had a rural estate in the area of the Elah Valley, a memory of which is preserved in the Arabic name of our site.[49]

A tempting proposal, indeed, as it connects Khirbet Qeiyafa not only with King David but also with the story of the life of Jesus of Nazareth. But there is serious cause for methodological caveats. First, it is a find from the antiquities market and we have no idea if it is genuine or fake. Even the most precise scientific testing can misidentify a particularly skillful forgery and therefore, as a rule, only finds from legitimate archaeological excavation should form the basis for historical identifications. Secondly, terra rossa is extremely widespread and not limited to a specific region, making its geographical source difficult to identify. And thirdly, in the Elah Valley itself, contrary to what is written in the report on the ossuary, the soil is not terra rossa but rather a type known as rendzina. We thus regretfully reject this tempting proposal, and base our conclusions only on the finds that have been uncovered in the excavations at Khirbet Qeiyafa.

3

KHIRBET QEIYAFA IN THE PERIOD OF KING DAVID: CONSTRUCTION AND URBAN PLANNING

FROM OBSCURITY TO CENTER STAGE

Khirbet Qeiyafa is located in the western part of the Upper Shephelah of Judah, at the top of one of the hills rising to the north above the Elah Valley.[1] Other archaeological sites in close proximity include Tel Yarmouth, about 2.5 km (1½ miles) to the north, Azekah some 2 km (1¼ miles) to the west, and Socoh approximately 2.5 km (1½ miles) to the southeast. Situated in the Mediterranean climatic zone, Khirbet Qeiyafa receives around 500 mm (20 in.) of rain annually, which falls in the winter; the summers are hot and dry. The vegetation at the site reflects this seasonal cycle. In the winter and spring the ground is covered in greenery and colorful wildflowers including cyclamens, poppies, chrysanthemums, flax, knapweed, and many other varieties, and in February the almond trees are covered in white blossom. The flowers attract numerous butterflies and bees, making this the ideal time to visit the site. During the dry summer months, the vegetation dries up and the predominant color of the landscape becomes yellow-brown. The beautiful landscape of the fertile Elah Valley, extensively cultivated to this day, extends from the foot of the site.

The geopolitical importance of Khirbet Qeiyafa is clear, as the road leading from Philistia and the Shephelah of Judah to the hill country—and the cities of Jerusalem and Hebron—passes through the Elah Valley. This has served as the main route through the ages, as attested by preserved sections of Roman road and the modern road ascending from the Elah Valley to the hilltops toward the small town of Zur Hadassah.

Fig. 13 Aerial view of Area B, with the gate at the top and the casemate wall.   53

Approximately 12 km (7½ miles) west of Khirbet Qeiyafa is Tell es-Safi, Philistine Gath. As mentioned in Chapter 1, in the 10th and 9th centuries BCE Gath was a large, central city with an area of over 40 hectares (almost 100 acres). It was the nearest Philistine political entity to Judah, and undoubtedly looked to extend its control eastward to the Shephelah and the hill country. Any central administration in Judah would have had to give clear priority to the fortification and defense of the Elah Valley route, even before that of other sites such as Lachish, Beersheba, and Arad.

Prior to our excavation, visitors to Khirbet Qeiyafa could see a massive wall surrounding the upper part of the hill—the exposed parts stood to a height of 2–4 m (6½–13 ft), encircling an area of 2.3 hectares (5½ acres). Since the topography here is hilly, the outer side of the wall remained visible, creating a terrace that covered the inner face, which was buried under an accumulation of earth and the ruins of the site. At its base, the wall was formed of particularly large boulders, while its upper part was built of medium-sized stones. Within the site, the line of the wall rises above the surface, and it served as the enclosure of an olive and almond orchard planted here in modern times.

Khirbet Qeiyafa was visited by several explorers during the 19th century. The first of these was Victor Guerin, a French traveler who wrote a number of books describing the sites he encountered in the Holy Land.[2] One of these was Beit Natif, an Arab village on the northern edge of the Elah Valley, and Guerin noted that on a nearby hill was a place known as Khirbet Qeiyafa. From his description it appears that he never actually visited the site, but merely recorded information he received from local residents. Some 20 years later, Claude Reignier Conder and Horatio Herbert Kitchener, surveyors for the British Palestine Exploration Fund (PEF), describe Khirbet Qeiyafa as "a pile of stones."[3] During the 20th century it seems the place was forgotten and it is not referred to in the writings of the "fathers" of geographical-historical research in the Holy Land.

At the end of the 20th century, within the framework of a comprehensive survey of the Shephelah region, Yehuda Dagan examined the site and proposed to identify it with the biblical city of Adatayim, which appears in the list of cities of the Tribe of Judah (Joshua 15:36). Dagan noted that the site consisted of a massively fortified upper city and a lower city, with a total area of 140 dunams (1 dunam = 1,000 square meters) (Fig. 14).[4] Contrary to the findings from our excavation, Dagan's survey did not identify the

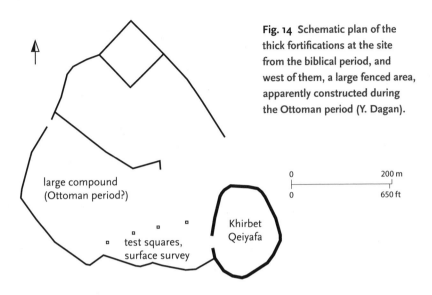

Fig. 14 Schematic plan of the thick fortifications at the site from the biblical period, and west of them, a large fenced area, apparently constructed during the Ottoman period (Y. Dagan).

large compound
(Ottoman period?)

test squares,
surface survey

Khirbet
Qeiyafa

intensive settlement of the site at the beginning of Iron Age IIA, but mistakenly dated it as 9th to 6th centuries BCE. In 2001 another survey was carried out at Khirbet Qeiyafa by Zvi Greenhut, in relation to the planning and development of an expansion of the city of Beth Shemesh. This work documented the general outline of the site's fortifications.[5]

THE STORY OF OUR EXPEDITION

In the course of his work for the Antiquities Robbery Prevention Unit of the Israel Antiquities Authority, one of the present authors, Saar Ganor, visited Khirbet Qeiyafa for the first time in 2003, after looters had used metal detectors at the site to hunt for valuable ancient coins. The battle against antiquities theft requires a good understanding of archaeology and an in-depth familiarity with an area, both at daytime and at night. Thanks to his intimate knowledge of the local topography and the archaeological sites on the outskirts of Jerusalem and in the northern Shephelah, Ganor gradually realized that this site was different from other ruins in the Elah Valley, and included architectural elements not encountered at them. His recognition that an Iron Age city existed at the site changed things dramatically. During 2003, Ganor visited the site with the late Shuka Dorfman, the director of the Israel Antiquities Authority at the time, outlining his opinion of the importance of the remains, and noting the massive fortifications and the biblical context of the area. Then, in 2005, during his MA studies at the Hebrew University of Jerusalem, Ganor participated in a seminar on biblical archaeology led by Yosef Garfinkel. During this seminar he shared his thoughts about Khirbet Qeiyafa, and proposed a fieldtrip.

Thus, early in the morning on February 2, 2006, we (Garfinkel and Ganor) met in Jerusalem and drove toward the Shephelah of Judah. During the excursion, we visited Mount ha-Yaaran, which offers a panoramic view of the Coastal Plain and the hills of Judah. From there, we crossed the Beit Natif hills in rain and deep mud, and after a few hours reached the western side of Khirbet Qeiyafa. The visit to the site itself lasted several hours, during which we discussed various aspects of the ruin, the massive nature of the fortifications, and the outer line of the city wall. We soon noticed something peculiar and somewhat perplexing about Khirbet Qeiyafa: bedrock was exposed in large parts of the center of the site, suggesting a paradox. On the one hand, the place was massively fortified, while on the other, a densely inhabited city had not developed there. This was cause for hesitation: an archaeologist who looks at a site and finds bedrock exposed will quickly leave, as it is clear that there is nothing to excavate there. At Khirbet Qeiyafa, however, the situation was different, and despite the exposed bedrock, the ruin was impressive, and its location at the entrance to the Elah Valley significant. It seemed clear that there must have been a key site of the Kingdom of Judah here. What city and when it existed it was not possible to say based on the landscape alone. On the ground, which was then entirely covered with dense winter vegetation, no sherds were visible that could help establish the age of the ancient settlement. We left the site with more questions than answers.

That short visit was not sufficient to decide whether it would be worthwhile to embark on a full excavation of the site. Such a project entails a long-term and complete commitment. Therefore, in 2007 we decided to conduct a two-week trial excavation aimed at examining the nature and state of preservation of the site, in order to determine whether a large-scale excavation of the site would be justified. At the end of August that year, we began an archaeological campaign in the Elah Valley, never imagining how significant it would be—for us, for the archaeology of the Land of Israel, and for biblical studies.

The test excavation made it clear that the site had been settled for a relatively brief period, and that it had two main building phases. The upper layer dated to the end of the Persian period and beginning of the Hellenistic period, while the lower layer dated to the biblical period and was constructed on bedrock. (Since then, evidence has been discovered for other periods of settlement at the site, but this consists of isolated structures rather than settlement layers covering significant areas of the site.) Even from this limited work, it was apparent that the biblical period layer was the more impressive, with a casemate wall consisting in places of enormous boulders. In addition, we ascertained that the biblical period layer reflected a relatively brief settlement episode: no evidence was found for the sorts of changes or repairs to structures and fortifications that naturally occur when human settlement extends over a significant period of time. We realized that the biblical period layer had been destroyed suddenly, as shown by broken pottery vessels found on the floors.

In view of these conclusions, our doubts vanished and we felt compelled to excavate Khirbet Qeiyafa. But enthusiasm aside, such an excavation project can last for several years and tends to become a bottomless pit consuming major economic resources. The excavators must

Fig. 15 The test probe conducted in 2007. At the edge of the excavation, a peripheral wall constructed of small stones is visible. Its upper portion is higher than the exposed surface of the site. In view of the test results, we decided to begin extensive excavation at the site from 2008 on.

hire a staff, provide transportation, obtain excavation equipment, arrange living quarters for the excavators, and take care of countless other practical issues. To extensively excavate a site like Khirbet Qeiyafa would require a large team of volunteers and professional staff. Often partnerships are established with other universities in order to achieve a broad range of support. In 2007 the professional meetings of the American Schools of Oriental Research were held in San Diego, California. Garfinkel and Ganor presented their preliminary conclusions from the first two weeks of test excavation that previous summer. They then approached Michael Hasel from Southern Adventist University and asked whether he would be willing to become a senior American partner in the project. Garfinkel had worked closely with Hasel at the Philistine site of Tel Miqne/Ekron in the early 1990s while both were still doctoral students. Now independently established as professors at two different institutes of archaeology, in the United States and Israel, they had participated in and directed many other projects. Hasel was intrigued by the prospect, but still had commitments at Hazor, the large 10th-century BCE site in northern Galilee; he promised to take the proposal back to his advisory board.

In the summer of 2008, at the conclusion of all the administrative preparation, the organization of excavation staff, and preliminary discussions among the excavation directors concerning where and how to excavate, a six-week season was conducted in which approximately 30 volunteers participated, mostly from abroad, with a group of Israeli youth and several people from a neighboring village.

With his commitment to the Hazor excavations completed, Hasel joined with his staff and students for the next six-week excavation season in the summer of 2009. Participation increased to some 50 volunteers, and then during each of the two following seasons, in 2010 and 2011, we excavated for six weeks with a growing team of approximately 90–100. Associated schools during this period included Oakland University, Virginia Commonwealth University, and Charles University in Prague. In 2012–13 the excavations lasted four weeks as final questions were answered and remaining buildings were excavated.

Fortunately for us, the idea of excavating the site at Khirbet Qeiyafa was turned from dream into reality thanks to the generosity of Joseph Baruch Silver, known to his friends as Joey. Joey Silver was born in Toronto, Canada, but his family emigrated to Israel when he was still a teenager. Joey went on to study Islamic art and Far Eastern studies at the Hebrew University of Jerusalem. His mother was a collector of ancient glass, exposing him while still a child to the archaeology and history of Israel. He later completed the Israel Tourism Ministry's course for tour guides, where he met Tal Ilan, Yosef Garfinkel's wife. A personal connection was thus established between the two families that has continued for nearly 30 years.

One evening, in the autumn of 2007, we sat together at dinner and among the topics discussed was the test excavation carried out at Khirbet Qeiyafa. Joey immediately expressed interested in the new excavation and asked to visit the site. Toward sunset, as a soft golden light played upon the ancient walls and the almond and olive trees, creating a magical tableau in the Elah Valley, Joey was thoroughly enchanted. Looking around, he unexpectedly asked how much a season of excavation here would cost. Upon hearing the reply, he announced that he was prepared to fund a major portion of the excavation seasons for a period of up to 10 years. And so it was.

Since archaeological excavation is in effect a destructive process, recording strategies are crucial, and one of the goals of the team from Southern Adventist University was to develop a cutting-edge cyber-archaeology system for recording the excavation data. Using the latest computer technology, a database was developed by Scot Anderson and Thomas Olsen from the School of Computing at the university. This database was tested and improved upon during subsequent seasons. Aerial photography and digital plans for each excavation area using ArchGIS software provided a daily record system, and professional animators made three-dimensional reconstructions of certain buildings of the site.

Lodging the expedition members proved a complex task as there was no suitable accommodation in the immediate vicinity of the site, and the team therefore stayed at a hostel at some distance away, in the Jerusalem Hills. A typical day for the excavators began very early—rising around 4:00 a.m to get organized to depart for the field. Two buses left every morning at 4:40 a.m., carrying, in addition to the excavators, water containers and food for the day. Fieldwork began at first light, at 5:15, and continued until 1:00 p.m. Three breaks punctuated the excavation day: at 7:00 a.m. for coffee and cake, 9:00 a.m for breakfast, and at 11:00

a.m for a treat of watermelons, a welcome relief in the scorching heat. Only on Sundays did the day's routine change: the team assembled at the youth hostel in the late morning, ate lunch in the dining hall and then set out to excavate until 8:00 p.m. On those days we often enjoyed watching the amazing sunsets from the site.

HOW DO WE EXCAVATE?

Those not familiar with archaeological excavation may find a description of some of the methods used enlightening. At Khirbet Qeiyafa we first divided the area to be excavated into 5 × 5 m (16½ ft) squares. An archaeology student supervisor was then appointed to each such square, and three to four volunteers placed in his or her charge. The square supervisor is key to the excavation: under his or her supervision, the work of digging the earth, collecting it, and removing it is carried out. The square supervisor documents the remains uncovered in that square.

Each square is excavated separately, leaving earth partitions (called "balks") on all four sides. These balks, in which different types of earth, building remains, burnt strata, etc. are visible, are of great importance—equal to that of the pottery and the buildings uncovered in the excavation. The professional archaeologist looking at the accumulation of archaeological layers reads the site's story like an open book. The balks are documented by photography and drawings, and are later dismantled in order to connect up the architectural remains to form complete rooms and structures. The excavation area and the excavators are protected from the sun by tent-like shades; for photography, we sometimes take them off temporarily.

The earth and stones extracted are removed from the excavation area. Sometimes, when a particularly heavy stone is encountered, several strong diggers are called from other squares to help move it, demanding resourcefulness and improvisation. We sometimes wonder if this is how the site's builders worked when they raised building stones to the tops of walls. All of the earth accumulated from destruction layers undergoes careful sifting in order to retrieve small finds such as beads or seals. Finds of entire pottery vessels (jars, bowls, plates, cooking pots, etc.), metal objects, or other special artifacts are a cause for celebration.

From 2007 to 2013, we excavated seven different areas at the site, some only partially and others very extensively.[6] Below are brief descriptions of the main findings in each these excavation areas, designated by letters of the alphabet, from A to F, and W, as is customary in archaeological excavations, before individual features are discussed in greater detail later.

AREA A: WHAT HAPPENED AT THE TOP OF THE SITE?

Area A is located at the center of the site, at its highest point. Important remains of a large rectangular building were visible here even before the excavation began, measuring 43 × 37 m (140 × 120 ft) at its greatest. At the center of the building was a large open courtyard, in parts of which leveled bedrock was exposed. An ancient cistern was cut into the bedrock, the opening of which was covered by a cast concrete frame during the 20th century. The complex is closed on its eastern, southern, and western sides by a row of rooms, and on the northern side by a massive wall. It became clear from our excavations that this building, probably a fortified farmstead, dates to the Byzantine period (4th–6th centuries CE).

A less encouraging discovery in the vicinity was a lime kiln. Lime was essential for mortar used in construction in ancient times and its production requires burning limestone at a temperature over 830 degrees Celsius (1,526 degrees Fahrenheit). Such temperatures can only be reached inside a kiln, not in an open fire. During the Islamic period, these kilns were frequently constructed at ancient sites, and stones were removed from the walls of buildings to be used as raw material. The presence of a lime kiln at a site is therefore not a good sign, presaging less than optimal preservation of walls and structures.

During the summer 2011 excavation season in this area, we encountered late Second Temple (early Roman period) remains. A Jewish ritual bath cut into bedrock was found at the bottom of several steps, entirely coated in plaster. Next to it were grain silos measuring 1 m (3¼ ft) in diameter. These finds attest to a farmhouse at the highest part of the site during the Second Temple period.

Beneath the later remains, we uncovered the biblical period city at three different places in Area A. In the 2007 season we had already found the corner of a room, with pottery sherds and an oven on its floor. The walls that created this corner were unusually thick—three times the width of the wall surrounding the city. In the 2009 season we exposed a small part of a floor on which seven complete vessels were found. But only in the last two excavation seasons were ground-breaking results achieved here: as the excavated area was enlarged to the south, beyond the limits of the Byzantine fortified farmstead, we uncovered the remains of a large Iron Age building, including a wall 30 m (98 ft) long, together with its southeastern and southwestern corners. The wall is two to three times wider than those of the regular Iron Age houses uncovered in Areas B, C, and D, an indication of a structure some three stories high.

This building, located at the central, highest point of the site and three stories in height, would have been the dominant structure at the city. It must have housed the governor and administration that controlled the city and probably the entire region. When King David came from Jerusalem to supervise the western border area of his kingdom, he could have slept here overnight.

AREA B: FINE FORTIFICATIONS AND A FAMOUS OSTRACON

In this area on the western edge of the site we encountered two major periods of settlement. We first excavated late Persian–early Hellenistic-period remains, which, on the basis of coins found here and in other areas of the excavation, are dated to 350–270 BCE. But the main discovery was a portion of the biblical period city, constructed directly on bedrock. Here the fortifications of the city were uncovered in their full glory: a four-chamber city gate (two chambers on each side of the gate passageway) and the finely constructed casemate wall, which we excavated for a stretch of 30 m (98 ft) including four of the casemates and a small part of a fifth. Attached to the wall we found four houses, which incorporated the casemates as internal rooms at their rear. Such houses constructed against a city wall are a feature typical only for the Kingdom of Judah. In the second building north of the gate we found an inscription written in ink on a pottery sherd (an ostracon), the famous Qeiyafa Ostracon, which we shall discuss in detail in Chapter 5.

AREA C: WHO IS THE GOD OF KHIRBET QEIYAFA?

In Area C, in the southeastern corner of the site, we excavated 2,000 sq. m (21,528 sq. ft) and exposed two settlement strata. The uppermost stratum again dates to the late Persian–early Hellenistic period. Beneath this, we found the biblical period city, with a city gate entered from an open piazza and a 100-m (98-ft) long stretch of casemate wall. Sixteen casemates and six houses were uncovered. Here, as in Area B, town planning typical of the Kingdom of Judah is in evidence, with houses at the edges of the city built right up against the casemate wall and incorporating the casemate as their rear room. With the destruction of Khirbet Qeiyafa, the houses collapsed, leaving a striking picture that emerged as we excavated: the house floors were covered with hundreds of broken pottery vessels, stone implements, metal artifacts of bronze and iron, bone implements, beads, Egyptian scarabs, and stone seals. These will be discussed in detail in Chapter 4, which is devoted to the excavation's finds.

In the eastern part of Area C we excavated a room that contained a bench, a standing stone (*mazzebah*), a basalt altar, and a pottery libation vessel comprising two identical joined goblets. Such vessels were probably for pouring libations of water, wine, or other sacral liquid over the altar. In the western part of the excavation area two temple models were found in one room, one made of pottery, the other of stone. The significance of these finds is clear—the rooms undoubtedly served a cultic function. But who did the inhabitants of Khirbet Qeiyafa worship? Was it the God of Israel, or other gods? And if other gods, can we identify them? These are complex questions, and future analysis of the finds may provide more clues necessary to answer them.

AREA D: STANDING STONES AND LIBATION VESSELS

Area D is located south of the gate in Area B and was excavated from 2009 to 2011. Approximately 1,000 sq. m (10,750 sq. ft) were excavated here under the direction of Southern Adventist University, exposing two main strata, again dating to the late Persian–early Hellenistic period and the biblical period. The first of these, the upper stratum, yielded a large structure of some 700 sq. m (7,535 sq. ft) that included a press for olive oil. This building and its contents are discussed in the appendix. In the underlying biblical period stratum we again encountered the city wall, excavating a 50-m (165-ft) long stretch, as well as the continuation of the large gate piazza found in Area B, and one building extending along three of the wall's casemates. In this house more evidence of cultic activity was encountered, including two large, tall, standing stones erected on their narrow sides (ritual *mazzebot*; sing. *mazzebah*), a bench, and a libation vessel in the form of joined goblets similar to the one found in Area C. Taken together, Areas D and B constitute a 100-m (330-ft) long stretch of excavation and provide a clear picture of the area of the western entrance to the city, including the city gate, a gate piazza, dwellings, and a building in which cult activity took place.

AREA E: AN IMPRESSIVE CITY WALL

In the 2010 season we excavated 50 sq. m (538 sq.ft) in Area E, on the eastern side of the site and next to the city wall. It became clear that here, too, domestic dwellings were constructed up against the casemate wall. Preservation of the city wall is particularly impressive in this area, with the casemate still standing to a height of 3 m (10 ft). At the end our work here, we covered our excavations with earth in order to prevent visitors from falling into the deep pit we had dug.

AREA F: THE PUBLIC BUILDINGS AND MEETING POINT OF THE WALL

Part of the northern side of the site was excavated in Area F, where we uncovered *c.* 350 sq. m (3,770 sq. ft). We selected this area for excavation to obtain more information on the city wall casemates and the pattern of their openings. After excavating almost 50 m (165 ft) along the city wall at different places, we finally located a point where the openings of two casemates were found adjacent to one another, unlike the regular pattern. At exactly this spot we excavated a large building containing pillars, some of which were still in their original position. However, the building had been extensively reused in the late Persian–early Hellenistic era, and the original phase had been badly disturbed.

AREA W: INVESTIGATING THE SURROUNDING AREA OF THE SITE

During a survey conducted by Uri Davidovich in this area, some 100 m (300 ft) west of the fortified Iron Age city, a massive corner of a building was observed and in the last two seasons of our project (2012 and 2013) we excavated around 100 sq. m (1,075 sq. ft). This revealed an isolated square tower, probably used by local farmers. All the pottery found dated to the seventh century BCE, including jar handles with rosette impressions, typical of this period in Judah. A fragment of a clay female figurine of the type known as the "Judean pillar figurine" was also found.

דוד

i Mosaic floor representing King David playing his harp, from an ancient synagogue at Gaza, early 6th century CE.

ii Aerial view of Jerusalem, which King David founded as his capital. The extent and density of the modern city make excavations to trace David's city extremely difficult.

iii Lachish is a huge ancient tell made up of multiple layers of settlement. Only small areas have so far been excavated.

iv, v Aerial view of Khirbet Qeiyafa (left, looking north) and a reconstruction of the site in the time of King David. The city is enclosed by the ring of the fortification wall, with two gates and adjoining houses. In the center is a large administrative building.

vi The southern gate of the city in Area C opens to the south, and from it descends the track to the Elah Valley. The gate has four chambers, two on each side, with a biblical period drainage channel running along the right side of the passageway.

vii Aerial photograph of Area C. The four-chambered gate (right of center), casemate wall, and remains of the houses to either side are clearly visible.

viii Area C, with the houses incorporating the casemate of the wall at the rear. This style of construction is known only at sites in Judah, and not at Canaanite or Philistine settlements, or in the Kingdom of Israel.

ix Excavating the well-preserved and massive casemate wall. A casemate wall consists of two parallel walls which are divided by cross walls into long, narrow rooms.

x The outer side of the city wall next to the southern gate, where the wall is constructed of particularly large stones. The ground level naturally falls away from the gateway.

xi View over Khirbet Qeiyafa looking out to the fertile Elah Valley, where according to the Bible David fought and defeated the giant Philistine warrior Goliath.

It is interesting that in an excavation area of nearly 5,000 sq. m (54,000 sq. ft) of the fortified city from the time of King David of 400 years earlier, not a single female figurine had been uncovered.

To summarize the discoveries made in the excavation areas described above, we can say that three main settlement periods were revealed: Iron Age IIA, the late Persian–early Hellenistic period, and the Byzantine period. In addition to the settlement strata with associated construction remains, several tens of sherds of the late Chalcolithic period (5th millennium BCE), several hundred Middle Bronze Age sherds (c. 1700 BCE), a Jewish ritual bath, and a silo or storage pit from the end of the Second Temple period, as well as coins from a variety of periods, were found during the course of the excavation, as summarized in Table 3. The fact that several different periods are represented might create the

Stratum	Period	Nature of the finds	Type of settlement
I	Ottoman?	Two destroyed buildings, a path, a fence around the site enclosing 16 hectares (40 acres)	Farmstead
II	a. Early Islamic	Coins, pottery	Agricultural area
	b. Byzantine	A large structure at the highest part of the site	Khan or fortress
	c. Late Roman	Coins	Agricultural area
	d. Early Roman	Coins, pottery, silo, Jewish ritual bath	Farmhouse
	e. Hasmonean	Coins	Agricultural area
III	Late Persian– early Hellenistic	Peripheral wall, gate, dwellings, silos, coins, pottery	Administrative center?
IV	Iron Age IIA	Casemate wall, two gates, dwellings, destruction remains	Fortified city
V	Middle Bronze Age II	Pottery	Small village?
VI	Late Chalcolithic	Pottery, flint and basalt tools, mace-head	Small village?

Table 3: The chronological sequence at Khirbet Qeiyafa (the periods are presented from the most recent to the most ancient, as encountered in archaeological excavation).

impression that this is a multi-layered tell, the result of intensive human activity extending over a period of thousands of years. In fact, only very thin accumulations are present, consisting primarily of biblical period remains, and it is these that give the site its present form; subsequent periods of settlement were brief. Most of the archaeological remains are located around the periphery of the site, while in large areas in the center exposed bedrock is visible, with no building remains. Is it possible that this central area was also built up thousands of years ago and that the buildings collapsed and were swept away, leaving no trace? We tend to think not; rather, the center remained empty because any structures that existed here during the different periods lasted for brief periods of just a few decades, allowing no time for the development of a dense settlement pattern of the type seen at sites inhabited for hundreds of years.

THE CITY DURING THE TIME OF DAVID

What did the city of Khirbet Qeiyafa look like in King David's time? From the information we retrieved from the different excavation areas we can reconstruct its likely appearance (Pl. v). During the 10th century BCE, the city extended over an elliptical area of 2.3 hectares (5½ acres) and was surrounded by a massive wall formed of casemates, or compartments (Fig. 16). The city had two gates, one to the south and the other to the west. The dwellings of the city were built up against the wall's casemates, which served as the back rooms of the houses. This is typical Judahite city planning, well known from four other sites in Judah, namely Beth Shemesh, Tell Beit Mirsim, Tell en-Nasbeh, and Beersheba,[7] whereas city planning of this type is not known in the Kingdom of Israel, in Philistia or at Canaanite sites. Let us now take a "virtual tour" of the city's main features dating to the 10th century BCE.

CITY GATES

Ordinarily a city had only one gate, and those at most of the known First Temple period sites, such as Lachish, Megiddo, Beersheba, Tel Beit Mirsim, Gezer or Tell el-Far'ah North, were identified and excavated many years ago. For this reason, the opportunity to excavate a city gate is now rare. At Khirbet Qeiyafa we excavated not one but two city gates, the first in the 2008 season and the second in 2009, both similar in plan and with four chambers. The gates were positioned at points in the city

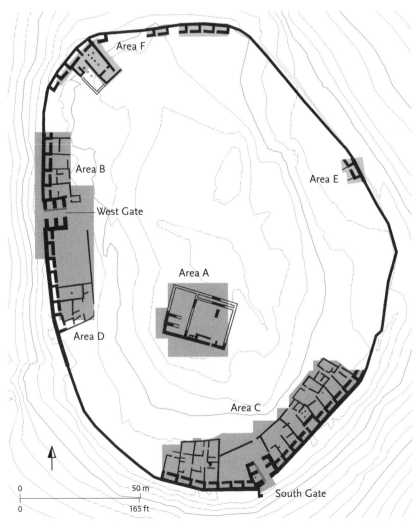

Fig. 16 Plan of the biblical period city at Khirbet Qeiyafa at the end of the project, showing excavation areas and the overall layout of the 10th-century BCE settlement, with the casemate wall and the dwellings adjacent to the wall which incorporate a casemate as their back room. A similar city plan is known at Beth Shemesh, Tell Beit Mirsim, Tell en-Nasbeh, and Beersheba, all sites in the territory of the Kingdom of Judah.

wall where the roads leading to the site approached. The southern gate, in Area C, opens to the road descending into the Elah Valley and from there leading eastward to the Judean Hills. The inhabitants would have used this gate when leaving the city to draw water in the Elah Valley. The road heading toward the coastal plain and connecting with the Elah Valley north of Azekah leads from the western gate, in Area B.

The site of Khirbet Qeiyafa covers a relatively large area, and has not been entirely excavated, so how did we know precisely where to find the gates? In fact, both were identified during reconnaissance at the site. At certain times of day, the angle of the sun and the shadows it casts reveal remains not visible at other times. We knew from an architectural survey of the site carried out prior to the excavation that the city wall consisted of a base of very large stones with a later wall constructed of small stones built on top of it. At two places in the wall we encountered something unusual: the small stones blocked an opening between the large stones. Simple measurement revealed that in both cases, the blocked opening was identical in size. What would have been blocked in a city wall if not a gate? Therefore, we began excavating at these points, and in a few days two large and impressive gateways were uncovered.

The first gate we excavated was that in Area B, on the west of the site (Fig. 17). Its façade is recessed slightly from the outer line of the wall, which would have made it easier to defend the wooden doors of the gate, the weakest point in the city's fortifications. Each side of the gate passage mirrors the one opposite, consisting of one long wall with three short ones perpendicular to it, forming the shape of the letter E. Two chambers are thus formed on each side of the passage. The walls of the gate are massive, 1.25 m (4 ft) wide, with especially large stones at the corners. On the southern side, the central wall was very well preserved so we could see that its lower part was built of fieldstones topped by three courses of trimmed stones. The original floor level seems to have been at the height of the base of the trimmed stones, covering the field-stones. The gate passage is 3.9 m (12¾ ft) wide and slopes, following the topography, from east to west, toward the gate's exit.

A single 3-m (10-ft) long stone formed the threshold of the gate, which we calculate weighs roughly 8 tonnes. A step carved into it would have held the panels of the gate in a straight line flush with the outer piers of the gate when closed. A thick beam or bolt placed against the door panels on the inside would have prevented them from being opened, as indicated in the biblical descriptions of fortified walled cities with double doors and bars (1 Samuel 23:7; Deuteronomy 3:5; 2 Chronicles 8:5). There

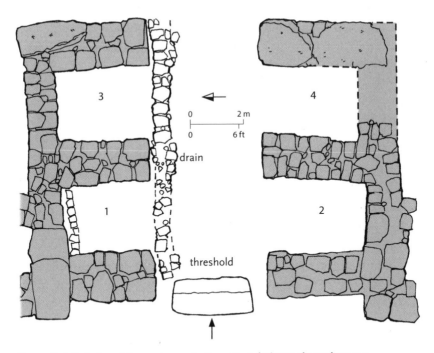

Fig. 17 Detailed plan of the western gate (Area B). A drainage channel passes along the left side of the passageway, as in the southern gate. The gate was partially damaged by late Persian–early Hellenistic period activity: its southeastern corner was destroyed.

must have been a ramp or outer gate here that was entirely dismantled during a later phase since there is now a difference of approximately 1 m (3 ft) between the level of bedrock outside the gate and that of the gate passage. The single huge threshold stone is unusual. At Lachish, for example, a threshold of similar width and also with a step adapted to the line of the outer piers of the gate consists of three separate and considerably thinner stones.

Running along the northern side of the gate passage at Khirbet Qeiyafa is a drainage channel covered with flat stone slabs that were found still in place. Drainage channels are known from city gates of the period of the kings of Judah and Israel at sites such as Megiddo, Lachish, Gezer, Beersheba, and Tell el-Far'ah North. Why this coincidence of city gates and drainage channels? The logic is simple: gates were generally situated in relatively low parts of cities so that anyone arriving there would not have to climb higher than necessary before entering. Such a location is also ideal for drainage since rainwater flows to the lowest point in the city.

From all the evidence uncovered, we can reconstruct the appearance of the city as it would have looked to people entering the city through the western gate during the biblical period. After emerging from the gateway passage, they would have seen on the left a row of houses built against the city wall, while to the right a large piazza opened out, with a cult room visible at its far end. From the gate the visitor ascended via a pathway across the central area of the site, an exposed area of bedrock. As the terrain is relatively steep here, steps carved in the rock made the ascent easier. At the highest part of the city visitors would have arrived at several large, tall houses.

When we closely examined the point where the casemate wall meets the gatehouse we discovered that the wall rests on the gate and abuts it on both sides— in archaeological parlance the wall is associated with the gate. While this small detail may seem insignificant to the casual observer, it demonstrates that the gate was constructed first, followed by the wall adjoining it. In this way, we are able to work out the consecutive phases in the construction of the city. Each of the casemate compartments forming the wall has an entrance from inside the city. These entrances are always on the side furthest from the gate, so in the casemates constructed north of the gate, the entrance is always at the northern corner, while in those constructed south of the gate, the entrance is always in the southern corner.

The second gate, similar in plan and dimensions to the first, is located in the south of the site, in Area C, where the road leading from the Elah Valley enters the city (Fig. 18). A significant part of the northern edges of the Elah Valley close to the site consists of steep white cliffs, limiting options for ascending from the valley to the hills above. The location of both the site and this gate pay close attention to the local topography, taking advantage of it for protection as well as mobility. At the point where the gate opens, the city wall curves sharply, which made it difficult for the builders to incorporate the gate into the wall. On the western side, therefore, the gate and the adjacent casemate are integrated, while on the eastern side the gate was completed first and only then was the casemate constructed joining it. The passageway through this gate also

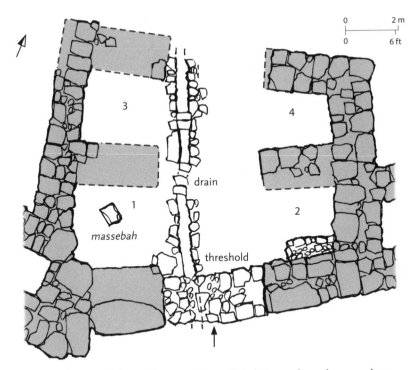

Fig. 18 Detailed plan of the southern gate (Area C). A drainage channel passes along the left side of the passageway, as in the western gate. It was partially damaged by late Persian–early Hellenistic period activity, including the side walls dividing the gate into four chambers.

features a drainage channel, partly cut into bedrock and partly dug into the earth and lined with stone slabs. The channel was covered with flat stone slabs, some of which were found in situ. We reconstructed the missing covering, and, to our surprise, the channel still functions today for draining rainwater, three thousand years after it was built.

At the start of our research at Khirbet Qeiyafa, some scholars doubted the identification of the southern gate. However, it is clear from the similarity of the dimensions and plan of the two gates, as well as other characteristics, that Khirbet Qeiyafa had both a western and a southern gate. Inside the city adjacent to each gate is a gate piazza, an open area almost surrounded on all sides by walls to create an enclosure. The entrances of the casemates also attest to the existence of two gates, as they are always located on the side of the casemate farthest from the gate, evidence of the fact that construction at Khirbet Qeiyafa followed a clear and systematic architectural plan.

One difference between the gates is that the façade of the southern gate is particularly imposing and incorporates two enormous stones, one on each side. In fact, it is the most monumental façade excavated to date at any city in the kingdoms of both Israel and Judah. For comparison, the façade of the western gate, of identical dimensions, was built of a number of medium-size stones. Clearly, the decision to use a single huge stone rather than three or four medium-sized ones arose from more than just practical engineering considerations of strength and stability. In times past, as today, buildings also served as a form of propaganda, conveying a message to both inhabitants of the kingdom and hostile neighbors that here is a political and economic entity capable of achieving impressive construction activity. The monumental stones at the sides of the southern gate at Khirbet Qeiyafa made the power and authority of its rulers immediately obvious to all entering the city. This would have been particularly important during the time when the city existed, the transition from Iron Age I (the period of the Judges) to Iron Age II (the period of the monarchy). A new political situation took shape, with a single, centralized kingdom ruling over an area that in the preceding Canaanite period had been controlled by a number of city-states; settlement composition changed accordingly. The location of Khirbet Qeiyafa at the top of a high hill in the Elah Valley gave it advantages in defense, but also placed it in a prominent place visible to all.

The monumental design of the southern gate, emphasizing and aggrandizing it over the western one, also shows that it was the main entryway into the city. From this we learn that the city's orientation was toward the southeast, the direction of the Kingdom of Judah. If it had been a Philistine site of the kingdom of Gath, the main gate would have faced west, toward the road leading to Philistia. A similar situation is found in the Old City of Jerusalem: the most splendid gate, the Damascus Gate, was constructed in the 16th century by the Ottomans at the entry of the main roads into the city during that period from the northwest. One, the road along the crest of the hill region arrives from Shechem; the second was the Beth Horon road, the route from the Coastal Plain.

Comparison of the two gate structures at Khirbet Qeiyafa reveals another interesting detail: while the southern gate has a monumental façade, no stone threshold was found at its entrance, unlike the western gate. There must have been a more modest threshold here—if it had been as massive as that of the western gate, it would have been nearly impossible to move—but it was dismantled at some point. Why would the western gate, of relatively modest construction, have had such an imposing threshold, while the main gate did not? The western gate, facing hostile Philistia, would have been regarded as a potential weak point and so an especially strong threshold was built here, making it more difficult for the enemy to break through the gate and penetrate the city.

At the center of the southwestern chamber of the southern gate, to the left on entering the city, stood an unhewn *mazzebah* (standing stone; pl. *mazzebot*), 1 m (3¼ ft) high. Standing stones are found in association with city gates at several sites: Tel Dan, Bethsaida, next to the Sea of Galilee, and Tell el-Far'ah North. Numerous studies have been written about this cultic phenomenon, which is apparently related to the biblical expression "high-places of the gate." The location of the *mazzebah*, on the left side of the entrance, recalls the biblical passage: "He broke down the shrines at the gates ... which is on the left of the city gate" (2 Kings 23:8). While that biblical passage refers to the time of Josiah, nearly 400 years later than Khirbet Qeiyafa, a parallel between our archaeological findings and the biblical description is apparent. The custom of placing the *mazzebot* on the left side of the city gate seems to have existed throughout the history of the Kingdom of Judah. The *mazzebot* at Khirbet Qeiyafa are discussed in detail in Chapter 6.

BUILDING A WALL

The city wall is around 600 m (1,968 ft) long in total, and we exposed it in five areas, over a combined length of 300 m (985 ft). It is constructed of two parallel walls, one outer and one inner, with short perpendicular walls dividing the space into rooms or casemates. Altogether 26 complete individual casemates and 16 segments were uncovered. The outer wall is the more massive, about 1.5 m (5 ft) wide, and built of large stones, sometimes 2–3 m (6½–10 ft) long and weighing up to 8 tonnes. The inner wall was smaller, about 1 m (3¼ ft) wide, and was mainly constructed from medium-sized stones weighing 100–200 kg (220–440 lb). The average length of a casemate is about 6.5 m (21 ft), so approximately 85 casemates would have been built around the city.

In several areas we excavated down to the base of the wall and discovered that it stands on bedrock. Building on bedrock provides greater stability in the event of earthquake, but there also appears to have been a further consideration here, linked to improving the city's defenses. One method of conquering a besieged city involves tunneling beneath its outer wall, either to gain entry into the interior or to undermine a section of the wall so that it collapses. If a wall is constructed directly on bedrock, it is virtually impossible to tunnel under it.

Houses built around the inner circumference of the wall incorporated the casemates at their rear, and since the city stands on a hill, these rooms were always the lowest part of the houses, and so the builders made staircases to provide access into them. The floors of the casemate rooms were generally less rich in finds than those of the other rooms, where we uncovered numerous signs of the destruction of the city. The explanation for this is apparently that the casemates were not intensively used on a daily basis and were usually kept empty. Large stone blocks in the casemates had clearly tumbled into them from the upper part of the city wall as it collapsed over the years.

As mentioned above, the entrances into the casemates are consistently positioned in the corner furthest away from the city gate (Figs 19, 20). Analysis suggests that four main teams of builders worked simultaneously on the construction of the city wall, with two starting from each gate and progressing in opposite directions. So from the gate in Area B, one team built the inner casemates toward the north and another toward the south, and likewise from the gate in Area C, one team built the inner casemates toward the west and another toward the east. We were able to identify a point where the teams met in Area F. Public construction in the Kingdom of Judah was clearly organized in an effective manner, with several units working simultaneously. The inscription found in the Siloam Tunnel in Jerusalem also documents the work of two teams tunneling toward each other.

"HER HUSBAND IS RESPECTED AT THE CITY GATE": THE GATE PIAZZAS

Next to each of the two city gates was an open area where the casemate wall was left freestanding, with no houses built against its interior (Figs 21, 22). Buildings visible next to the gates today date to the late Persian–early

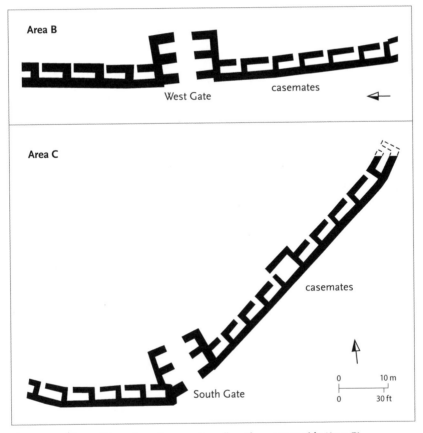

Figs 19, 20 Plans of the gate and casemate wall on the western side (Area B) and the southern side (Area C) of the city. The openings of the casemates are always on the farthest side away from the gate in both directions.

Hellenistic period (4th–3rd century BCE) and were not present during the First Temple period, some 700 years earlier.

These open areas undoubtedly served as gathering places, corresponding to the biblical term *rehov ha-sha'ar* (e.g., 2 Chronicles 32:6), usually translated as: "the square at the city gate," and perhaps the expression *ba-sha'ar*, which relates to the "king is sitting in the gateway" (2 Samuel 19:8). Ancient cities of the biblical period did not include public areas comparable to the central forum in Roman cities, the piazza in medieval European cities, or the shopping malls of modern cities. Instead, the gate area was the heart of the city, as everyone who entered or left

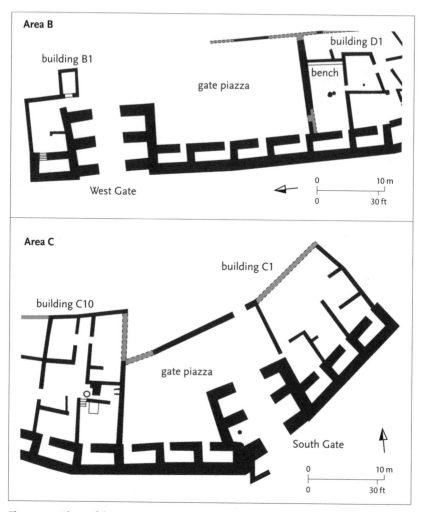

Figs 21, 22 Plans of the gate piazza on the western side (Area B) and on the southern side (Area C) of the city. In the south, the gate piazza is situated to the left of the entrance, while in the west it is situated to the right of the entrance. In each of the buildings bordering the gate piazza is a cultic room, situated next to the piazza. The biblical expression "the high-places of the gates" may refer to this phenomenon.

the city had to pass through it. On market days, when farmers from the vicinity brought their agricultural produce to the city, people would have gathered here and exchanged goods and news. Craftsmen from the city could also trade items they had made in their workshops, such as pottery, metal tools, jewelry, etc. The prophet Elisha states that "...a seah of the finest flour for a shekel and two seahs of barley for a shekel at the gate of Samaria" (2 Kings 7:1).

The city gate was where elders of the town sat and passed judgment on disputes brought before them. Thus, we hear of the woman of valor whose "husband is respected at the city gate, where he takes his seat among the elders of the land" (Proverbs 31:23). Ritual *bamot* (high places) were also established at city gates (2 Kings 23:8), and the prophets stood there and admonished the people (Amos 5:10; Jeremiah 17:19–20). The gate was also the place to demonstrate political strength: David sat there after the failure of Absalom's rebellion (2 Samuel 19:8–10) and Jehu placed the heads of Ahab's seventy sons on both sides of the gate at Jezreel (2 Kings 10:8). The two gate piazzas at Khirbet Qeiyafa indicate that by the end of the 11th century BCE city planners were already taking these functions into consideration, allocating significant open areas for social, economic, ritual, legal, and political activities. Such open areas are also found in the vicinity of the city gates at other sites including Beersheba, Tell Beit Mirsim, and Tell en-Nasbeh (see Fig. 32).

The gate piazzas of Khirbet Qeiyafa are noteworthy for an additional feature unknown at the other sites: adjacent to each is a cult room. In the ancient world, worshippers generally did not enter temples, but instead gathered outside them in an open area where a variety of cult activities could be carried out, such as the sacrifice of animals, prayer or dancing. The populations of nearby villages, or even from further away, would also make pilgrimages to the site on special days, and would assemble in these open places. Chapter 6 looks at the evidence for cult at the site in detail.

The piazza next to the southern gate is 20 m (66 ft) long and extends across three casemates. On the south side, the area is bounded by the casemate wall and the city gate; on the east and west by buildings; and on the north by a massive wall. A 2-m (6½-ft) wide opening in this wall provided the only access from the piazza into the city itself. Movement through this inner gate could have been controlled, so that possibly not everyone who was allowed into the piazza could then proceed further into the city. The 30-m (98-ft) long piazza next to the western gate extends along four casemates. This area is likewise enclosed on all four sides: on the west by the city wall and gate; on the north and south by buildings; and on the east by a long wall.

HOUSES AND STRUCTURES ATTACHED TO THE CITY WALL

In Area B we completely excavated four of the wall's casemates; each was incorporated as the back room of a dwelling which we believe were four separate houses (Fig. 23). The first of these, which we labeled building B1, is joined directly to the city gate and is divided into five rooms. An entrance corridor contained two installations: a *tabun* and a limestone basin that could have served for food preparation. *Tabun* is an Arabic term referring to round ovens used for baking, measuring around 0.5–1 m (1½–3¼ ft) in diameter and generally constructed of earth, though occasionally from a circle of rounded stones (Fig. 24). The sides of the *tabun* are made of a layer of clay, 1–2-cm (about ½ in.) thick; at Khirbet Qeiyafa it was customary to cover the outside of the *tabun* with large potsherds. The inside is hollow and was the combustion chamber where fuel consisting of twigs and branches was burned.

From the corridor, entrances opened into two rooms, one of which stood apart to the east and contained another *tabun*. The three other rooms in the house lie north and west of the corridor. In one room were two installations for food preparation: a mortar cut into bedrock and a large grinding slab of flint. The next room is long and narrow and contained a baking tray. A *mazzebah* was found incorporated upside-down in the partition wall separating the two rooms. The final room is the casemate, which served as the rear room of the house.

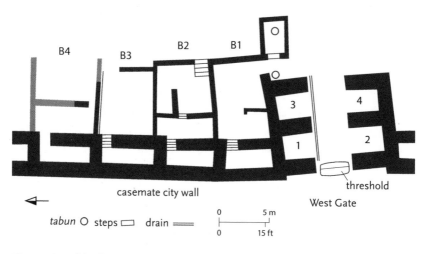

Fig. 23 Plan of the four biblical period buildings excavated in Area B.

Fig. 24 The inhabitants of the city's homes cooked in a circular oven, called a *tabun* today. Such ovens were constructed of clay and covered on the outside with layers of pottery sherds.

The second house north of the gate is labeled B2 and consists of four rooms. From the entrance, four large stone steps (a rare find in itself, as built stone steps are seldom uncovered in excavations) descended into the main room. It was in this structure that the famous Khirbet Qeiyafa ostracon, described in Chapter 5, was found. The third house north of the gate is labeled B3, and consists of a single large room and the casemate. There was probably a more complex internal division here, but builders during the late Persian–early Hellenistic period caused much damage by digging deep into the earlier remains, which prevented us from reconstructing the original structure. A drainage channel was found in the house, partly built and partly quarried into bedrock. In the east of the city we uncovered drainage channels in three different houses, so it seems the city's planners took careful consideration of the fact that the low-lying houses in the city might be flooded in rainy years and installed drainage systems. To the best of our knowledge, drainage channels have not been reported in ordinary dwellings in biblical period cities—only in the city gates—so this came as a surprise, and is further evidence of sophisticated planning at Khirbet Qeiyafa. The fourth house north of the city gate is building B4. It was even more severely damaged than B3 by building activity in later periods and it is difficult to determine its original plan. For this reason, we did not excavate further in Area B.

Until the 2011 excavation season, it appeared to us that the plan of the dwellings at the site was uniform: a long narrow building always constructed against the city wall and incorporating a casemate as the rear room. In the summer of 2011, with the expansion of excavation into

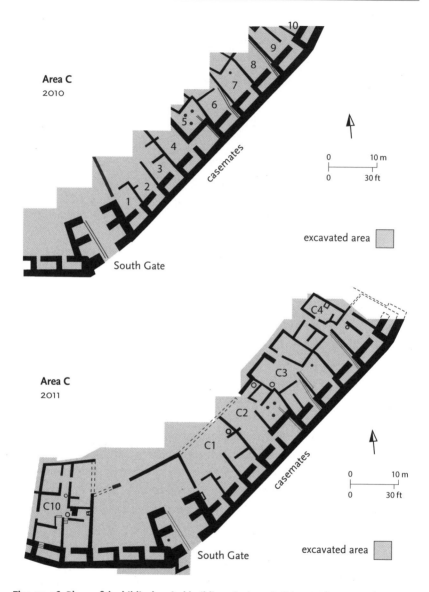

Figs 25, 26 Plans of the biblical period buildings in Area C. (Above) The excavation at the end of 2010: at this stage it seemed that there were nine buildings in this area, each of which utilized a different casemate. (Below) The plan of Area C on conclusion of the 2011 excavation season: with the continuation of the excavation, it became clear that there were only four buildings in the area, and that two, possibly three casemates, could belong to a single house. This demonstrates how the understanding of archaeological remains can change as an excavation progresses.

building C1   building C2   building C3

trough

standing stones

building C4

building C10

bath

building C11

== drain   ⌷ bench   • pillar   ○ tabun   ⊛ hearth

0   5 m
0   15 ft

Fig. 27 Plans of houses located east and west of the southern gate in Area C.

Area C to the east, however, it became clear that the houses here had a more complex pattern of construction, and that two or even three casemates were joined to create a single building (Figs 25–27). Instead of nine narrow buildings, as we had initially expected, there are four large, wide buildings divided into at least 35 different spaces including courtyards, corridors, rooms, and casemates. Two further buildings were uncovered in Area C west of the city gate. The first unit east of the southern city gate is building C1. Its southeastern section against the city wall is well preserved, unlike its northwestern part, which was constructed where bedrock is near the surface and was eroded and largely destroyed. The house contained at least eight spaces or rooms—some are casemates, some roofed rooms, and there appears to have been a large open courtyard to the north. The entrance to the house is immediately behind the gate, similar to the arrangement in the first house next to the gate in Area B. A bench stood next to the entrance—a feature found only in cultic rooms.

The second structure east of the gate, building C2, comprises eight distinct spaces including an open courtyard, roofed rooms, and a casemate. Where the fifth casemate northeast of the gate should have been, we found a chamber twice the width of a usual casemate and with thicker walls. The unusual thickness of the walls indicates that they had to support a greater weight than elsewhere and were probably also higher than those of the neighboring casemates. This appears to have been a watchtower, located at a strategic point from where the road ascending from the Elah Valley could be observed as it approached the city. Next to the tower in this house was a square structure containing three massive stone pilasters and a trough, which we interpreted as a stable. If the lookouts in the tower saw a need to move manpower or supplies in a hurry, they could use animals kept within. In order to determine if this structure could truly have functioned as a stable, we decided to test it with a donkey belonging to one of the Bedouin shepherds who graze flocks in the vicinity. On entering, the donkey stuck its head in the 3,000-year-old feeding trough as if it were completely familiar with it. There would have been room for four large animals, donkeys or even horses. A channel from the stable leading down toward the city wall would have drained the large quantities of urine produced by the animals. The watchtower and stable indicate that this was a building with a military function rather than an ordinary domestic dwelling.

Building C3, the third east of the gate, again contained eight spaces or rooms. An entrance leads via a narrow corridor to a large courtyard, where a *tabun* was found with animal bones next to it. Household cooking and perhaps also eating must have taken place here. Opening off the courtyard were the entrances to three rooms, two of them next to the city wall, and from these the casemates were accessed. One room (G) is unusual: it contained a bench, a stone basin, two *mazzebot*, a basalt altar, and a pottery libation vessel, all attesting to its use as a cultic room (see Chapter 6 for detailed discussion). A fourth building east of the gate, C4, was not fully uncovered, as its northern part lay beyond the excavation area, but 12 separate spaces/rooms were found in the excavated section.

Immediately west of the gate piazza is building C10 (Fig. 28). Its southern section abutting the city wall is well preserved, while its northern

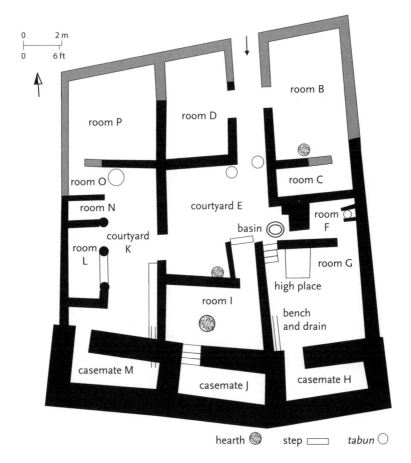

Fig. 28 Plan of building C10, located west of the southern gate Piazza.

edge was eroded and largely destroyed. It contained at least 16 spaces or rooms, arranged in two main wings—on the east, a corridor, a central courtyard, six rooms and two city wall casemates, and on the west a central courtyard, a corridor, three rooms and one city wall casemate. The southeast corner, comprising courtyard E and rooms F, G, and H functioned as the main shrine of the city.

The second structure west of the gate is building C11, consisting of only three spaces: a small entry room, a large area (either an open courtyard or a roofed room), and a city wall casemate. It is possible that this was a wing of a larger building located further west. The second Khirbet Qeiyafa inscription, "Eshbaal son of Beda," was found here (see Chapter 5).

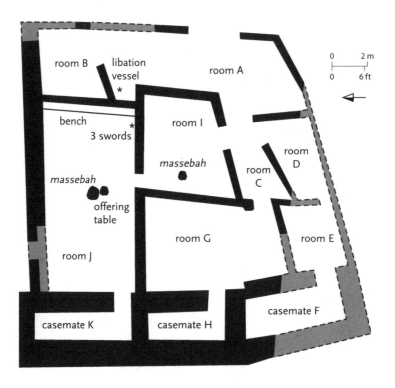

room B   libation
          vessel
            *
                    room A

bench   *   room I
  3 swords

massebah   room
                       D
                massebah   room
                                 C
massebah
                offering
                table
                         room G   room E

room J

                                        casemate F

casemate K   casemate H

0   2 m
0   6 ft

Fig. 29 Plan of building D1 located south of the West Gate piazza.

In Area D we uncovered the remains of a large and impressive biblical period structure (Fig. 29). An open piazza opens on the right of the
interior of the western city gate, extending for the length of four wall
casemates. Immediately after the piazza, building D1 incorporated the
next three casemates. The northern part of the building was severely
damaged by late Persian–early Hellenistic period construction activity,
in particular an olive press, but we can reconstruct eleven rooms.

The entrance to the building was from the east, into room A. Bedrock
is very close to the surface here, but we excavated a floor with numerous associated objects, including a libation vessel composed of two
matching goblets joined together (see Chapter 6). Room G, in the west of
the building, is the largest room we excavated, and differs from all the
others at Khirbet Qeiyafa in several details. A massive stone doorpost,
unlike any found in other buildings at the site, created an impressive

monumental entrance. The floor of the room had been carefully constructed of river pebbles arranged side by side in a bed of white plaster, something not encountered elsewhere at Khirbet Qeiyafa, where floors are usually of beaten earth or leveled bedrock. On the floor and resting against the northern wall were a number of broken vessels and fragments of a large cooking pot. This building probably functioned as a municipal storehouse, and the atypical entrance was designed to facilitate closing and locking it.

The northern wing of this house includes three rooms. Room I contained an upright *mazzebah*. In Room J was a carefully built stone bench against the eastern wall and, in the center of the room, the largest *mazzebah* found at the site. At its base, a large flat stone could have served as an offering table (see Chapter 6). Next to the bench, a remarkable discovery was made: in a destruction layer were three large iron swords.

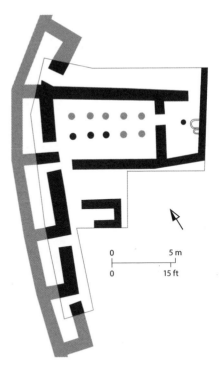

Fig. 30 Plan of the pillared building in Area F, located in the northern edge of the city.

CENTRAL STORAGE FACILITY

In Area F, in the northern part of the city, we excavated a large rectangular building, measuring 11 × 15 m (36 × 49 ft) (Fig. 30). Inside is an elogated hall, 12 m (39 ft) long, with pillars in the center, in addition to smaller rooms. This is clearly not a typical dwelling unit like those excavated in other areas, but a much more massive administrative building.

Pillared buildings are well known from the period of the kingdoms of Judah and Israel[8] and were used as public storehouses for the produce collected as tax from farmers. The existence of such a building at Khirbet Qeiyafa clearly indicates central authority and administration.

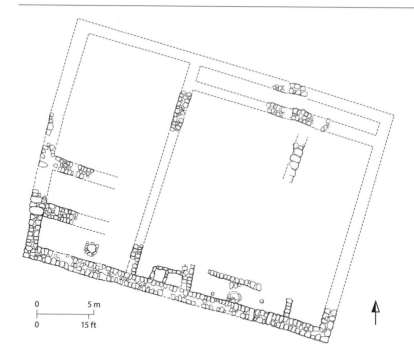

Fig. 31 Plan of the palace, a large administrative complex in the highest and central part of the city.

THE PALACE

The highest and most prominent part of the site is in the center, overlooking the entire city, and it was this location that was chosen for constructing a palace, a large building from which the city's administrative and military activities were conducted. In the Byzantine era, in the 4th century CE, a farm was built here, which destroyed much of the earlier structures, but we were able to recover remains of the biblical era palace, including a wide wall, 30 m (98 ft) long (Fig. 31). In addition to being much bigger than any other building in the city, the structure's walls are three times thicker than those of the houses, indicating that it stood several storeys tall. We know that in ancient times urgent messages were communicated over great distances by sending signals using fire or torches. Evidence of this practice in the Kingdom of Judah comes from an inscription on a pottery sherd from Lachish from the time when Nebuchadnezzar was besieging the city: "we are watching for the fire signals of Lachish according to all the signs which my lord

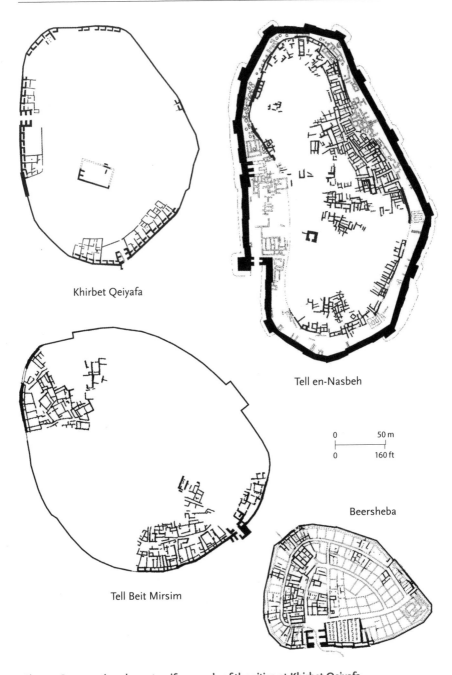

Fig. 32 Comparative plans at uniform scale of the cities at Khirbet Qeiyafa, Tell en-Nasbeh, Tell Beit Mirsim, and Beersheba.

has given".[9] The palace at Khirbet Qeiyafa would have been an ideal place for sending and receiving such torch-signals.

Based on all the information from our excavations, the architect Roy Albag was able to create an artistic reconstruction of the city by super-imposing on aerial photographs the reconstructions of the fortifications, the ring of houses, and the administrative building at the center (Plate v).

HOW WAS AN ANCIENT CITY CONSTRUCTED?

Yigal Shiloh, excavator of the City of David in Jerusalem, was one of the first to recognize a unique urban plan in the biblical period that consisted of houses constructed around and attached to the inner perimeter of the casemate wall, with the casemates incorporated as rear rooms. Until our excavations at Khirbet Qeiyafa, where this urban planning was revealed in all the areas we investigated along the city wall, it had been observed at only four sites: Beth Shemesh, Tell en-Nasbeh, Tell Beit Mirsim, and Beersheba (Fig. 32). All these sites are in the area of the Kingdom of Judah. No comparable examples are known from Canaanite or Philistine cities, and casemate walls found at sites in the Kingdom of Israel, including Hazor and Gezer, were free-standing, with no houses attached. At first glance this may appear insignificant, but in fact it reflects an important distinction: a city wall was a striking public statement, under the control and auspices of the municipal or royal administration; houses, on the other hand, were inhabited by ordinary citizens and represent private activity. When houses and casemate city wall are combined, the boundary between private and public in the urban space is not clearly defined.

A further characteristic of houses at sites in the Kingdom of Israel, for example at Hazor or Tell el-Far'ah North near Shechem, is that every house has its own outer wall, even when the buildings stand very close to one another. At Khirbet Qeiyafa, on the other hand, and at other sites in Judah, the houses are joined together, sharing walls in common. Thus, for example, the outer northern wall of building C3 also serves as the southern outer wall of building C4. In this way, the city planners saved on building material and also took better advantage of the limited settlement area available, even though a shared wall also compromises privacy, blurs ownership and responsibility for maintenance, and opens the way to disputes between neighbors.

This type of construction can also be seen as evidence of efficient construction methods applied to a predetermined plan that was worked out before the first stone was laid. Such planning and execution attest to a central responsible authority, and when the same plan is repeated at several sites, it is an indication that the kingdom purposely initiated the construction. It is probable that cities built according to a Judahite city plan, including Tell en-Nasbeh, Beth Shemesh, Khirbet Qeiyafa, Tell Beit Mirsim, and Beersheba, were primarily administrative and military centers.

In addition, this city planning may be a reflection of important aspects of the social structure of the southern Kingdom of Judah that clearly distinguish it from the northern Kingdom of Israel. According to the Bible, the northern kingdom, which controlled relatively extensive territory, was made up of a heterogeneous population belonging to ten different tribes. The Kingdom of Judah, which was limited in territory and mountainous, had a more homogenous population. The Bible describes it as dominated by the tribe of Judah (which had absorbed the tribe of Simeon), with the little tribe of Benjamin alongside it. In a small and unified tribal society there would be no opposition to combining the private and public realms in construction, with some walls shared by two buildings. Thus, the form of the city in Judah reflects a unified society that preserved tribal traditions.

During our work at Khirbet Qeiyafa we found no evidence in the built areas for repairs or renewal of floors, walls, or installations, as would naturally occur at sites inhabited for a considerable length of time. This indicates that the site existed for a short period only, apparently no more than a single generation. Another significant feature of the site is that in much of the area within the walls we encountered exposed bedrock, with no building remains. We think it unlikely that the center of the site was once built on and was then destroyed, since if that were the case, we would find scattered building remains and sherds. It seems therefore that the city was destroyed shortly after its construction and had no time to develop or expand.

Combining the evidence for a brief period of settlement at Khirbet Qeiyafa with the data available from other contemporary sites, we can identify three phases of development in cities in Judah in the biblical period (Fig. 33). In the first phase, the city wall and outer belt of buildings were constructed; it was at this phase that Khirbet Qeiyafa was frozen in

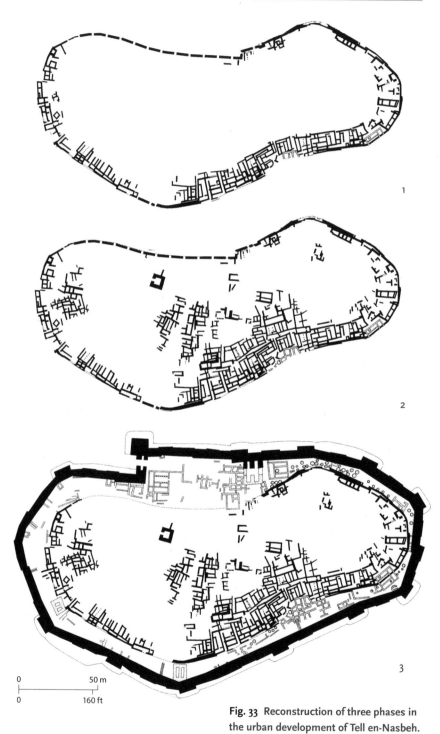

Fig. 33 Reconstruction of three phases in the urban development of Tell en-Nasbeh.

time. During the second phase, construction in the now fortified inner areas of the site took place. This is the situation found at Tell Beit Mirsim and Beersheba. During the third phase, with the growth of population and the need for more space, the built urban area extended beyond the casemate wall, and a new wall was constructed to expand the fortified area of the city. This development is clearly seen at Tell en-Nasbeh, where a solid wall with towers was built to encompass an expanded urban area outside the original casemate wall. Beth Shemesh appears to reflect a similar scenario: the early city of the 10th century BCE was surrounded by construction beyond the casemate wall at a later time. Ancient Jerusalem also developed gradually over the course of the First Temple period, expanding to the north and west, with the addition of new fortifications.

What is significant about Khirbet Qeiyafa is that it is the earliest example of urban planning in Israel involving a casemate wall with houses that incorporate the casemates as rooms. Thus it seems that this urban concept took shape in Judah in the initial phase of the kingdom's formation, in the time of King David, and Khirbet Qeiyafa was probably the first site constructed according to this plan. If so, then the cities of Beth Shemesh, Tell en-Nasbeh, Tel Beit Mirsim, and Beersheba, which were constructed in the 10th century and perhaps even in the 9th century BCE, were established according to a plan that originated at the end of the 11th century BCE. The biblical tradition emphasizes the military and political aspects of David's reign, and his building work in Jerusalem, the capital city (2 Samuel 5:9–11), but says nothing about construction of cities elsewhere in the kingdom. The excavations at Khirbet Qeiyafa thus reveal another important aspect of the historical figure of David, and show that not only did he build cities, but also that a new concept of urban planning emerged during his reign.

THE SECRET OF THE BUILDERS OF KHIRBET QEIYAFA

From the beginning of our excavation at Khirbet Qeiyafa it was clear to us that this was a model site whose builders had carefully considered and planned it before they began work.[10] Only a painstaking and thorough analysis of the architecture of the gates, the city wall, the casemate walls, and the walls of the private houses would enable us to decipher the system of the builders and determine the order in which the various elements were completed and how the city was constructed. Until now, no analysis of this type has been undertaken at any other site in Israel or, to the best of our knowledge, elsewhere in the ancient Near East.

The exposure of large areas at Khirbet Qeiyafa, an understanding of the building plan, and an analysis of the relation of the walls to one another indicate that the city was built in several major phases. In the first phase, the site was cleared of earlier settlement remains and bedrock was exposed around the future city. In the second phase, stones were quarried and brought up to the line of the city wall. No evidence of a single large quarry was found in the vicinity of the site, but remains of quarries were found within the city, where some large stones cut from bedrock remained. It appears that each quarry supplied stones for the section of the city wall nearest to it, generally at a distance of less than 10 m (33 ft) away. As construction of the wall progressed, the quarries were also moved, so that they were always next to the building site, eliminating the need to transport heavy stones over great distances. And since the city was built on a hill, the quarries were higher than the wall so that stones were moved downhill—a particular advantage when having to transport stones weighing several tons, such as found in the gates and city wall.

In the third phase, the builders began work on the gates and their chambers. The western side of the southern gate was built together with the adjacent casemate in the wall, probably because at this point the city wall curves, creating a protruding angle. Construction of the wall itself commenced in the fourth phase. The outer line of the wall was built first, and then the casemates. As mentioned, two groups of builders worked from each gate, one to the left and the other to the right, and the openings of the casemates are always located at the furthest point from the gate, showing the direction in which work progressed. We found a point where two teams of builders met in Area F (see Fig. 30). In the fifth and final phase, the private houses whose walls incorporate the casemates were constructed.

Examination of the sizes of stone at the site and their location tells us something about the identity of the builders and their level of professional skill. Stones weighing a tonne and more were found mainly in the gates and the outer city wall. Engineering knowledge is required to quarry, transport, and position stones of that size, and this work must have been carried out by master builders. Large stones weighing 100–200 kg

(220–440 lb) are found in the outer wall and in the inner walls of the casemates. Three or four strong men could move and lift such stones. Finally, small stones weighing an average of 20–30 kg (34–44 lb) are found in the walls of the private houses, which could have been constructed by the families who lived in them.

HOW DID WE DATE KHIRBET QEIYAFA?

During the summer 2008 excavation season it became clear that Khirbet Qeiyafa was unusual in terms of its date. Pottery found at the site was comparable to that from Stratum XII at Arad, Stratum VII at Beersheba, and Stratum IVb at Tel Batash. These are unwalled and unfortified sites, unlike Khirbet Qeiyafa. We later spread out the finds at the expedition laboratory at the Hebrew University of Jerusalem and invited fifty different scholars to examine them. That same day, various discussions were held concerning possible dates for the site. Scholars who accept the low chronology placed it in the 9th century BCE and those favoring the high chronology placed it in the 10th century BCE. At the end of the day everyone left happy and satisfied, each believing that the site supported her or his chronology. This was a good demonstration that the chronological dilemma cannot be resolved on the basis of pottery alone. Another method had to be sought to date the city at Khirbet Qeiyafa, and fortunately we now had material that could be used for scientific dating.

In the 2008 season we had discovered carbonized olive pits in the city wall and in rooms of the destroyed buildings in Area B. These would be of decisive importance in establishing the age of the city as they could be radiocarbon dated. This scientific method of dating is based on the radioactive isotope of carbon, carbon-14, the rate of decay of which is known. The olive pits were sent to the laboratory at Oxford University that specializes in dating organic materials using this technique. It is important to emphasize that we sent only olive pits for dating, as their age reflects with certainty the time when the site was in use, unlike, for instance, charcoal from wooden beams, which can be of considerably greater age than the building in which they are incorporated. We initially sent four olive pits that were collected from floor levels within one of the casemates as we wanted to date the fortification directly. Dating each sample using this method is very expensive, but we decided to devote some of our limited budget for this purpose, as we were aware that the results could be decisive in the debate over the chronology of the biblical period.

If the date of Khirbet Qeiyafa emerged as the 10th century BCE or the beginning of the 9th century BCE, it would prove the veracity of the low chronology (see Chapter 2). On the other hand, if Khirbet Qeiyafa was dated to the end of the 11th or beginning of the 10th century BCE, this would support the biblical tradition. Thus, the date of not only Khirbet Qeiyafa lay at stake, but also of King David himself. The enormous tension that accompanied sending the samples via express mail resulted in the credit card with which we paid for the shipment being mistakenly packed inside and sent to the laboratory at Oxford, along with the olive pits. Time passed very slowly as we impatiently awaited the results. If the dates obtained spanned the 10th century they would not be decisive in settling the chronological dispute. We hoped for a clear result, one way or the other.

The results of the first measurements were problematic. One date was 700 years earlier than the Iron Age, in the Middle Bronze Age, a period known at the site, but not the one that we wished to date. Another date was 700 years later than the Iron Age, in the Hellenistic period, also known at the site. In retrospect, we understood that there had been considerable mixing of the site's soil in the casemate wall where the samples were collected. Between the stones of the wall there are large gaps, through which soil spills out and into which animals dig burrows. This brought home the need to select olive pits from better-preserved living surfaces in other parts of the site. But the other two olive pits from the first sample did provide some hope. These fit the biblical period and even pointed to a date in the early 10th century BCE. This was the first indication that Khirbet Qeiyafa supports the high chronology. Since it was not possible to resolve the chronological debate based on these two samples alone, we immediately sent another group of four olive pits for analysis. More long weeks of impatient waiting passed to see if the new results would decisively resolve the chronological question.

It should be noted that the radiocarbon method does not provide absolute precision and cannot give a date within the range of a single year. Even when a group of seeds or olive pits found in the same container are dated, there will be differences of tens of years between the results, despite it being obvious that all were harvested in the same year. Thus, several samples are generally sent for dating, all collected in the same place, and an average of the dates obtained is then calculated.

A discovery made in our 2011 excavation season would provide a breakthrough in dating Khirbet Qeiyafa. A jar containing some 20 olive pits was found in the destroyed city. This was perfect: because olives are not kept for more than a few years, all these olives must have been harvested a year or two before the downfall of the city. We obtained 17 different radiometric dates from olive pits from this jar,[11] which clearly indicate that the city had been destroyed no later than 980 to 970 BCE. Today, the dating of the Iron Age city of Khirbet Qeiyafa is based on nearly 30 samples, probably the best radiometric dating we have so far for any level in a biblical city.

As already noted, determining the dates of the reigns of the kings of Israel and Judah is not a simple task, and the length of those of David and Solomon, exactly 40 years each, appears to be a literary device rather than reflecting historical reality. We therefore propose the round number of 1000 BCE as the date of David's accession to the throne, though this is merely an approximation. On the other hand, the radiocarbon method and the calibration of the dates using tree-ring dating have their own imprecisions, and leave open possible ranges in tens of years for dating Khirbet Qeiyafa. But it is clear from the radiocarbon determinations that Khirbet Qeiyafa can be dated to the time of David or Saul, but not to Solomon's reign, which is later than the results obtained. It will only be possible to decide conclusively if an inscription naming one king or another is found at Khirbet Qeiyafa. To be scientifically cautious, we accept the later date, to the reign of King David.

When the four initial dates for Khirbet Qeiyafa were received, criticism was expressed by scholars of the minimalist camp: we have 400 radiocarbon-dated samples of organic material from biblical tells that fix Iron Age IIA in the 9th century BCE,[12] so how can your four dates change the picture? The answer to this is very simple: every period has a beginning and an end. The examples from Khirbet Qeiyafa relate to the time when the period began, while the other examples are from its end. The criticism of minimalist scholars ignores the geographical aspect: the 400 samples cited were mainly collected at sites from the northern Kingdom of Israel: Dor, Megiddo, Tel Rehov, Tell el-Hama,

Tel Keisan, or Rosh Zayit, whereas the debate is about when the process of urbanization began in Judah. Each kingdom must be examined separately, and a distinction should be made between one geographical region and the other. Dating the main wave of urbanization in the northern Kingdom of Israel to the 9th century BCE comes as no surprise, as that is precisely the picture that emerges from the biblical narrative, which maintains that the southern Kingdom of Judah was established first, while the Kingdom of Israel arose later. Thus, according to the Bible, Samaria was built 120 years after Jerusalem. Paradoxically, the dating of sites in the Kingdom of Israel to the 9th century BCE, which minimalist scholars tend to emphasize, supports the Bible's narrative. The main problem that remains unresolved is the question of the United Monarchy. Did David and Solomon indeed head a united monarchy from Jerusalem? We cannot solve this problem on the basis of the excavations at Khirbet Qeiyafa, which is in Judah, and it would have to be addressed through the excavation of sites in the Kingdom of Israel.

Lili Singer-Avitz, Israel Finkelstein, and Eli Piasetzky, all from Tel Aviv University, propose that Khirbet Qeiyafa is earlier, and belongs to the final phase of Iron Age I rather than to the first phase of Iron Age II.[13] What underlies these technical labels, used by professional archaeologists? The term Iron Age I denotes the period of time that the Bible describes as the period of the Judges, when Judah was a rural society. Iron Age II is the term that covers the period the Bible describes as the monarchy, and Judah at that time was an urban society (see Table 1). According to the dating proposed by those scholars, King David and the fortified city of Khirbet Qeiyafa should be attributed to the period of the Judges, but this is an odd claim, since Iron Age I is characterized by hundreds of small and unfortified villages (settlement sites) that are entirely different from the large and fortified city at Khirbet Qeiyafa. Likewise, how is it possible to fit King David into a period when "there was no king in Israel; everyone did what was right in his own eyes" (Judges 17:6)?[14]

At Khirbet Qeiyafa we found evidence for the existence of a fortified city dated to the end of the 11th and beginning of the 10th century BCE in Judah. Even if modern research calls this period Iron Age I rather than Iron Age II, it is clear that in the time of King David a transition from a rural to an urban society took place and the Kingdom of Judah was established. It is no longer possible to maintain that this process began hundreds of years later.

PRESERVATION FOR FUTURE GENERATIONS

In addition to the excavation process, the documentation of architectural remains, the analysis of finds, and the publication of excavation reports, every archaeological expedition also has the responsibility of preserving the site for posterity. In the past, there was little awareness of this and many expeditions left their excavations littered with gaping holes and piles of debris. Over the years, exposed walls can collapse and everything becomes covered in weeds. Today it is agreed that excavation sites must be left in an orderly fashion, either by preserving the discoveries and turning them into sites that can accommodate visitors, or by backfilling the excavated areas. Our expedition at Khirbet Qeiyafa handles the site's preservation in several ways.

The first aspect of site maintenance involves the problem of accumulations of excavated debris. The "excavation dump" is the term commonly used by archaeologists in referring to the piles of earth and stones that they remove from the ground during excavation. When a site is excavated, it is common practice to deposit this debris in a single place on the site or at its edges. As a result, the slopes of many tells have become indistinguishable from the dumps that accumulated over the years of excavation. Khirbet Qeiyafa lies in a setting of outstanding beauty, which would be disfigured by covering the site with excavation dumps. Moreover, if the dumps were deposited on the slopes of the site, the city wall, which is clearly visible, would be obscured and disappear from view. For these reasons, we felt obliged to remove the excavation dumps to the foot of the site, some 200 m (650 ft) to the west.

This called for a special effort, since large-scale excavations produce large amounts of debris. During the first seasons, in 2008–09, a backhoe driver worked with us several days a week, removing the heaps of debris from the site to a lower valley below. During the 2010–11 seasons, when the expedition had 90–100 members, the rate of accumulation was far beyond the backhoe capacity. The solution was to hire a large wheel loader once a week, in addition to the backhoe. Sometimes the accumulation was too great even for it to handle and we hired a dump truck to carry the debris away from the site.

During excavation, walls, installations, and floors are exposed which have remained buried for thousands of years. While still under the ground, these remains are protected and preserved; after excavation, they begin steadily to deteriorate. Exposed to rain, wind, sun, and changes in temperature, the stones crack and crumble and walls collapse; rainwater collects in excavated pits, undermining the foundations of buildings and walls. Plants sprout between the blocks and tree roots loosen the soil and stones. Visitors walking on the walls and structures also harm them, speeding up the destruction of the ancient remains. Therefore, we requested that visitors to our site, as at every other archaeological site, walk around the excavation areas and not enter them. In addition small areas of the excavations were covered, such as Area E and parts of Area A.

In large excavation areas, where we exposed buildings in successive years, we left the walls uncovered so that aerial photographs could be taken of entire complexes. In order to prevent damage to the structures from one season to the next, specialist Orna Cohen supervised conservation work. She has worked on the preservation of archaeological sites and important finds all over Israel, including Hazor, the wooden boat found in the Sea of Galilee, and the Tower of David in Jerusalem. Protecting the buildings at Khirbet Qeiyafa involved strengthening the ancient walls by filling gaps between stones with the bonding material that was used in biblical times: plaster, mud, and small stones. In the 2011 season, three and a half weeks were devoted to conservation, with five volunteers assisting Orna Cohen. The plaster is made on the spot by combining earth, chopped straw, and water and its preparation requires training. The earth must be free of stones and was taken from the piles of sieved soil that accumulated next to the excavation areas. The chopped straw was purchased in large sacks from Palestinian farmers who still thresh wheat on a threshing floor using an ox or a donkey. When the plaster mixture is ready, it is spread using a plasterer's trowel, but mainly with bare hands. Mixing the water, mud, and straw, was grueling and left volunteers with sore muscles. But it was so different from the modern urban lifestyle that some volunteers particularly enjoyed it and repeatedly requested assignment to this job.

To prevent damage caused by puddles forming in low-lying places and undermining the foundations of nearby walls we found two solutions. First, these areas in houses, courtyards, or casemates already excavated were covered with special fabrics called geotextiles, which do not disintegrate when buried in the ground. We then put a 30–50-cm (12–20-in.) layer of earth on top, depending on the depth of the area being protected. If archaeologists return to the site in future and dig in places we filled in this way, they will know that our expedition excavated to that level. Second, as described above, there are ancient drainage channels in the gate areas that diverted winter rains. In the western gate, after the excavation and exposure of the late Persian–early Hellenistic period channel it was covered with stone slabs and once again drained rainwater, as in ancient times. In the southern gate, we covered the original biblical period channel with stone slabs along its entire length and it likewise serves today to drain rainwater.

Beyond the conservation activity aimed at strengthening existing remains, the expedition also undertook restoration of the two gates at the site, involving reconstruction of some of the missing walls. Both gates were partially damaged by people in the late Persian–early Hellenistic period, who reused the areas around them, dismantled portions of the

Fig. 34 Heavy machinery was used to move massive stones weighing several tonnes. Here, an experienced restoration staff of Druze from the Golan Heights is seen together with conservation expert Orna Cohen restoring the South Gate.

walls, and removed stones. Since the Iron Age gates were built of particularly enormous stones, the blocks were only moved a few meters away, where we discovered them. The question then arose of what to do with them. There were two options. One was to transport the stones to the dump at the foot of the site; the other was to use them to reconstruct and restore the damaged walls of the original gates. We chose the second option, as it was more logical to return the gate stones to their original positions than to discard them outside the site (Fig. 34).

Reconstruction of the gates would be tough physical labor, requiring great technical skill to move and position stones weighing hundreds of kilos. For this purpose Orna Cohen brought in an experienced staff of Druze from the Golan Heights who had already been involved in gate restoration at Hazor in the north of Israel. First, the western gate was restored thanks to a financial contribution by Foundation Stone. About a year later, the southern gate was restored at the initiative of Jeffrey Barrack of Philadelphia, who visited the excavation and was very impressed by the site. The restoration work was based on currently accepted principles according to which the conservators must always remain faithful to the remains and are limited to two activities: completing walls with missing sections or rebuilding them up. Such work must always be carried out in the original building materials used at the site; in other words, a stone wall must be restored using stone, while a mudbrick wall must be executed in mudbrick. At Khirbet Qeiyafa construction was entirely in stone, which lay around from the collapsed upper levels of buildings. Anyone looking at the gates today can clearly see a thin cement line bearing the words "restoration line," which distinguishes original from restored sections. The restoration offers visitors an outstanding visual dimension: they can walk where the inhabitants of the city walked in the time of David. It is particularly exciting to pass through the southern gate, which has a monumental outer façade with a single megalith on each side. This gate faces the Elah Valley and the road to Jerusalem; King David himself would probably have entered the city through this gate.

KHIRBET QEIYAFA IN A REGIONAL CONTEXT

The last excavation season at Khirbet Qeiyafa took place in the summer of 2013. In order to place the site and its finds in a regional context further excavations were then conducted at two other sites in the region of the Judean Shephelah: Lachish and Khirbet al-Ra'i, both located about a day's walk south of Khirbet Qeiyafa.

Lachish was the second largest city in the Kingdom of Judah and is a massive tell site (Pl. iii). Three earlier expeditions excavated here and uncovered impressive remains from the times of the kings of Judah, dating from the 10th to the early 6th centuries BCE, though the earlier levels, V and IV, are poorly known. An expedition headed by Yosef Garfinkel, Michael Hasel, and Martin Klingbeil worked at the site for five seasons, from 2013 to 2017,[15] focussing on investigating these levels. We uncovered large amounts of fresh data about fortifications, urban planning, and dwellings, as well as radiometric dating and fascinating finds. Having completed the fieldwork, this now needs to be analyzed and published.

Khirbet al-Ra'i is a small, little-known site, 3 km (almost 2 miles) west of Lachish. During a site survey conducted by Saar Ganor, pottery sherds of the types known from the early 10th century BCE at Khirbet Qeiyafa were found here. So far, four short excavation seasons have taken place, 2015 to 2018, with future ones planned.[16] These have uncovered a deep sequence of occupation at the site, with a thick accumulation of levels from the 12th and 11th centuries BCE. On top of these are impressive building activities from the early 10th century BCE, the time of King David. Further excavation seasons are needed to provide more information about the poorly known period of King David.

The location of Khirbet al-Ra'i is also interesting: it lies opposite the Philistine city of Ashkelon on the western edge of the Shephelah and on the border between Judah and Philistia, controlling the road running through the Lachish Valley. This geopolitical position is comparable to that of Khirbet Qeiyafa, which is opposite the Philistine city of Gath (Tell es-Safi) and controls the road running through the Elah Valley. The geography of both sites is of special interest in the context of the early 10th century BCE. David's lament over the death of Saul and Jonathan: "Tell it not in Gath, proclaim it not in the streets of Ashkelon" (2 Samuel 1:20) takes on new meaning when we appreciate that Khirbet Qeiyafa is located opposite Gath and Khirbet al-Ra'i is opposite Ashkelon. In 2007 it was possible to claim that nothing was known archaeologically about King David; ten years later the situation is very different, and archaeology can present two sites from his period in the Judean Shephelah.

4

A CITY FROZEN IN TIME: THE FINDS

Khirbet Qeiyafa has yielded an excellent quantity and quality of artifacts. In each of the excavation areas, the biblical period floors were associated with rich concentrations of finds, including hundreds of restorable pottery vessels and stone implements, many tens of iron and bronze artifacts, beads, and special and rare ritual and art objects. The site was clearly destroyed suddenly—its inhabitants did not have time to remove most of their possessions from their homes. At the end of each excavation season, the finds were taken to the expedition's research laboratory at the Hebrew University of Jerusalem. There, hundreds of crates of artifacts accumulated for sorting, analysis, drawing, photography, comparison with finds from other sites, and, finally, publication.

THE POTTERY VESSELS

The largest group of finds by far consists of pottery sherds. During the 2011 season alone, 70,000 broken pieces of pottery were recovered from the site, and since 2007, over 400,000 sherds have been found. Sherds collected from destruction layers were sent for restoration in the laboratories of the Israel Antiquities Authority in Jerusalem, where pottery restorer Adrienne Ganor spent many months piecing together complete vessels from the fragments.

Pottery uncovered during the first two seasons was published in detail in the first excavation report volume.[1] Additional rich finds were subsequently made, all of which underwent restoration and research.

Figs 35, 36 Iron daggers and swords, a bronze axe and bronze arrowheads found in different buildings (above) and storage jar handles with finger impressions (below).

Pottery vessels are classified into types on the basis of form, size, rim profile, handle design, base shape, decoration, etc. Such classification is of great importance as it enables archaeologists to determine the period when different vessel types were in use and thereby date the stratum in which they were found. We were able to establish the date of Khirbet Qeiyafa by the radiocarbon method, but such scientifically based dates are not available at other sites in Judah. If we compare our pottery vessels with ones found at other sites, we can work out which sites and settlement strata in the area are contemporary with Khirbet Qeiyafa, and which are later. By creating this reliable comparative anchor, the

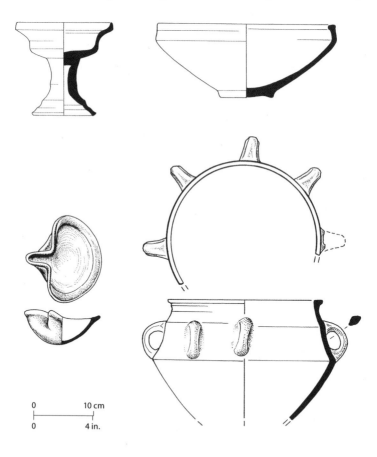

Fig. 37 Examples of Iron Age IIA open shape pottery vessels excavated at Khirbet Qeiyafa: a chalice (top left), bowl (top right), lamp (bottom left), and krater.

pottery from Khirbet Qeiyafa provides a chronological indicator for the 10th century BCE in southern Israel. This puts us in a position of great responsibility: we must examine the pottery, restore complete vessels, and draw and photograph as many examples as possible in order to create a large and wide-ranging database that can be used by scholars at other sites to compare their finds with ours.

The pottery vessels from the site include open and closed types (Figs 37–40). The open vessels are very varied, and include bowls with rounded sides and carinated bowls in several sizes. Some have bar handles, designed as a protruding strip on the vessel rim. Most are undecorated, but some were painted all over with a red slip, and occasionally rubbed or burnished with a pebble to create narrow, shiny stripes in no clear pattern on the vessel surface. Archaeologists use the term "red-slipped with irregular hand burnish" to describe this style of decoration, which was not common in Iron Age I and is a new feature appearing in the pottery of Iron Age II. A unique vessel from Khirbet Qeiyafa is the strainer bowl, a continuation in clay of a metal form characteristic of the Late Bronze Age. Large cooking pots with four or six handles were also found, and numerous chalices (ceremonial bowls on high bases—a kind of footed bowl) (Fig. 37 and Pl. xii). Most of the chalices are short and undecorated, though occasionally more elaborate examples were decorated with white slip and red and black stripes, as well as ones with red slip and white and black stripes belonging to the Ashdod Ware family (see below).

Cooking vessels include baking trays and cooking pots (Fig. 38 and Pl. xiv). The latter, both medium and large in size, are characterized by inverted rims. Baking trays take the form of shallow bowls of large diameter that were placed over a fire with the convex side uppermost, leaving signs of burning on the concave side. The outer surface features hundreds of tiny shallow holes that create a rough surface; when dough for pita bread or other baked food was placed on this side the holes prevented it from sticking. It is noteworthy that such baking trays are unknown in Philistia, so their appearance here indicates that the inhabitants of Khirbet Qeiyafa were not Philistines.

Closed vessels include small juglets and medium-sized jugs, both with a single handle, as well as special vessels for liquids referred to as pilgrim flasks. Among the range of juglets are small ones with a rounded

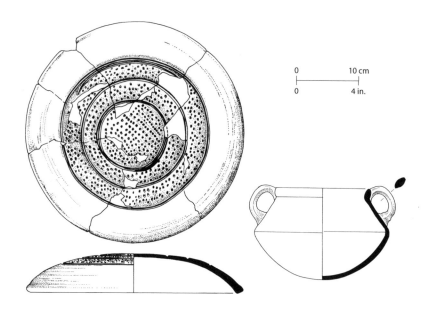

Fig. 38 Iron Age IIA pottery vessels for food preparation from Khirbet Qeiyafa: a baking tray with small holes on the upper surface (left) and a cooking pot (right).

body decorated with burnished black slip. This "Black Juglet" vessel type is known from Iron Age IIA onward. Petrographic examination of the clay fabric indicates that three of the four found were made in Jordan.[2] Two juglets belong to the type of Cypriot ware decorated with painted black parallel stripes or concentric circles executed with a fine brush on a white slip (Pl. xiii).[3] These vessels are evidence of the international trade that the people of Khirbet Qeiyafa were engaged in.

Among the pottery vessels are a large number of storage jars characterized by a short neck, horizontal or slightly sloping shoulder, and a body tapering toward the base, which is flat or rounded (Fig. 39 and Pl. xv). The walls of the majority are relatively thin, though in some examples are particularly thick. The base is also thick, with clearly visible round grooves that document the potter working on a wheel. Most of the storage jars have two large loop handles attached to the shoulder and the ancient potters often deliberately impressed the upper side of the handle with their fingers before the clay had dried (Fig. 36). Over the seven excavation seasons we found 693 of these finger-impressed handles.[4] Most impres-

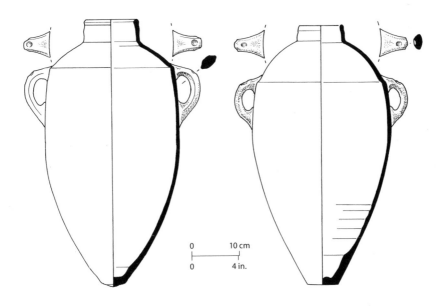

0   10 cm

0   4 in.

Fig. 39 Two Iron Age IIA storage jars from the Khirbet Qeiyafa excavations with finger impressions on the handles; one has a rounded base and the other a flat base.

sions consist of single fingerprint, but sometimes two finger impressions appear on the same handle, together or at its opposite ends, and there are also examples with three finger impressions. Such jar handles with finger impressions have been found at different sites dated to the end of Iron Age I and beginning of Iron Age II, but only in small quantities; Khirbet Qeiyafa is unusual for the large number of finger-impressed handles found. Analysis of the composition of the clay from which the jars were made shows the source was in the Elah Valley, near the site.

A limited number of small and medium-sized vessels decorated with red slip and black and white vertical stripes were recovered (Fig. 40 and Pl. xvii), as well as sherds of several similarly decorated chalices. First discovered in excavations at Ashdod in the 1960s, this style of decorated vessel became known as Ashdod Ware. Large quantities of such vessels are present at both Ashdod and Tell es-Safi (Gath), and they are consequently identified with Philistine culture. Their discovery at Khirbet Qeiyafa therefore immediately raised the question: were the inhabitants of Khirbet Qeiyafa Philistines? In order to answer this question, the vessels

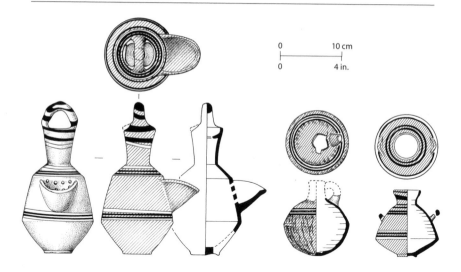

Fig. 40 Imported Iron Age Philistine vessels decorated with red slip and black and white stripes: a strainer-spouted jug (left), a juglet (center), and a pyxis (right). They appear to have been containers for transporting precious substances, such as perfumes or drugs.

were submitted for petrographic analysis to examine the composition of the clay from which they were made. The results indicated that the fabric contains sand and loess, in other words that they originate in a pottery workshop located in Philistia, to the southwest of Khirbet Qeiyafa.[5] If the population of Khirbet Qeiyafa were Philistine, the potters at the site could have manufactured similar vessels using local clay. Furthermore, these vessels constitute a minuscule proportion of the pottery assemblage found at the site. It is clear that they were not locally manufactured, but were luxury imports that probably contained precious substances such as drugs, perfume, or beverages. Just as two juglets imported from Cyprus found at the site do not attest to the inhabitants of Khirbet Qeiyafa being immigrants from Cyprus, so these imported vessels cannot be taken as evidence for identifying the inhabitants of the site as Philistines. They do, however, indicate that there were trade relations between the Philistine Coastal Plain and the population of the Shephelah.

The vessels belonging to the Ashdod Ware family at Khirbet Qeiyafa include a small, closed, boxlike vessel known by the Greek name pyxis and a so-called beer jug, a vessel with a strainer spout for pouring liquids. These continue the tradition of Philistine vessels of Iron Age I, while

Ashdod Ware vessels known from the end of the 9th century BCE at Tell
es-Safi are of different shapes.[6] Ashdod Ware vessels can therefore be
divided into two separate typological groups: early, as found at Khirbet
Qeiyafa, and late, as found at Tell es-Safi.

LIMESTONE, BASALT, AND ALABASTER: STONE ARTIFACTS

Prior to the invention of pottery and metal vessels, different types of
stone were used to make tools and containers. At Khirbet Qeiyafa, in
addition to the great quantity of pottery and some metal implements,
large numbers of stone objects with a variety of functions were found
on the floors of houses. These were studied by Haggai Cohen Klonymus,
who is preparing them for publication.[7]

A wide range of stones was used in the manufacture of stone implements: soft and hard limestone, chalk, basalt, flint that has undergone
a process of breakage and compression to form breccia, ordinary flint,
and sedimentary beachrock. Mortars and pestles were used for grinding,
with the hand-held pestle crushing food or other substances placed in
the mortar. Grains of wheat or other foodstuffs were also ground on large
stones of basalt or flint using a smaller hand-held stone. Limestone was
carved to make a variety of bowls and stone troughs used as mangers
for feeding animals. The inhabitants of the city also shaped flint pebbles
into ball-shaped objects, commonly referred to as hammerstones because
of the numerous signs of pounding visible, the result of the process of
shaping them. They could also have been used as slingstones in battle.
In building C4 we found a collection of 18 small polished pebbles,
apparently gaming pieces. Composite sickles for harvesting wheat or
barley were made by attaching several flint blades to a wooden handle.
Scattered individual flint sickle blades were found in each season, but in
2011 eight sickle blades were found as a group, apparently once forming
a sickle whose wooden handle had not survived.

One unusual discovery came in the form of fragments of two small
alabaster vessels, a material rarely found in Israel. Such a great variety
of different raw materials is not known at other sites of this period, and
both the basalt and alabaster are not local. They had to be transported
over great distances—the basalt from over 100 km (60 miles) away and
the alabaster from Egypt, over 500 km (300 miles) away—impressive
evidence for long-distance trade relations.

The greatest surprises among the stone artifacts were also the smallest: stone weights. These 12 small, well-formed and polished artifacts, with their upper part usually rounded and their base flat, were used for weighing small quantities of expensive commodities such as metals, jewels, or spices. They are of different weights, but all relate to the basic unit of 11.33 grams (0.4 ounces). Known in Judah in the 7th century BCE, this system of weights was apparently already in use at the city of Khirbet Qeiyafa several centuries earlier.[8]

DAGGERS, SWORDS, AND GOLD: METAL ARTIFACTS
Khirbet Qeiyafa is also rich in metal artifacts of different types. Nearly 100 bronze and iron objects were found, which have been studied by Alla Rabinovich for publication.[9] Usually when a site was abandoned, its inhabitants took any objects of value with them, or they were looted by conquering enemies. So it is surprising that these items remained in the ruined city for us to excavate. Even so, it is probable that there were originally greater quantities of metal artifacts present.

Weapons include 15 daggers, 10 arrowheads, 3 iron swords (Fig. 41) and a bronze axe preserved in its entirety (Pls. xviii and xix). Generally,

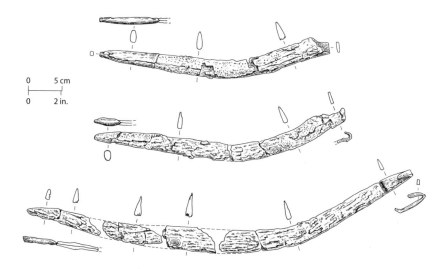

Fig. 41 These three iron swords were found together in a cult room in Area D. The curved end of the sword was inserted into a wooden handle that had decayed over the years and has not been preserved.

the daggers have iron nails for attachment to a wooden haft, but in one case the nails were of bronze. Other metal artifacts include a small bronze bowl, found hidden in a cave near the southern gate, and two pieces of thin gold leaf, just a few millimeters long, that were probably elements of a piece of jewelry or some other decorative object that has not survived. Evidence for the existence of bronze-production at the site came in the form of two small ceramic crucibles containing green slag. Metal would have been melted in the crucibles in a casting oven and the bronze was then poured into a mold.

Iron artifacts are rare finds at excavated sites of the 11th and 10th centuries BCE, and the quantity of iron objects at Khirbet Qeiyafa is unusual. In addition, the large number of metal weapons as well as the rounded flint stones mentioned above that served as hammers or possibly slingstones, make a most impressive arsenal, the likes of which has not been uncovered at any other site dated to the beginning of the Judahite monarchy. This, taken together with the site's important geopolitical position at the entrance to the Elah Valley, the impressive and massive fortifications, and the biblical tradition of border disputes in the Elah Valley during the period when the city existed, all attest to the military importance of Khirbet Qeiyafa.

The metal assemblage also has ethnic implications. As mentioned in Chapter 2, a comparative study of material from northern valley sites and the Beersheba Valley by archaeologist Yulia Gottlieb demonstrated that there are clear differences between metalworking in Iron Age I and Iron Age II in Israel.[10] In the early Iron Age the use of iron was common mainly in Judah, including Khirbet Qeiyafa, while in the north smiths continued to work in bronze.

EGYPTIAN SCARABS, LOCAL SEALS, AND BEADS

During the course of excavations we recovered 10 Egyptian amulets, either in the form of scarab beetles or square in shape, which were examined by Martin G. Klingbeil.[11] Some are typical of the Egyptian 19th Dynasty, around 1200 BCE, in other words the end of the Late Bronze Age (Pl. xvi). They were already 200 years old when they reached Khirbet Qeiyafa and were apparently heirlooms passed down from one generation to the next.

Three small stone seals were also found at the site, and were studied by Silvia Schroer (Fig. 42).[12] Conical in shape, their upper part is pierced,

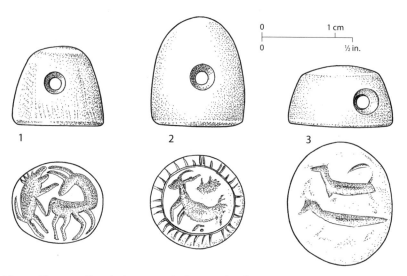

Fig. 42 Three small conical stone seals decorated with various animals.

apparently for attaching the seal to a string that was worn around the neck or on the wrist, as described in the Bible: "Place me like a seal over your heart, like a seal on your arm..." (Song of Songs 8:6). Seals are carved with a design or inscription so that when they are pressed into a soft substance they leave an impression in reverse of the image on the seal. One of the seals found portrays a horned animal, probably a gazelle, with its head turned back as another animal, standing on its hind legs with its tail above its back, springs on its prey, its open jaws touching the top of the victim's antlers (Fig. 42:1). The only animal of the cat family that waves its tail in this way in battle is the lion. The other seals portray various horned animals.

Since both scarabs and the seals are very small, ranging in size between just 1 cm and 2 cm (up to ¾ in.), they are generally recovered in the course of sieving earth from the excavation. The relatively large number of scarabs we recovered is a direct result of the systematic screening of earth from habitation layers at the site.

Even smaller objects were retrieved by this sifting of the excavated soil. Tiny white, red, and black stone beads, less than a few millimeters in size and with a hole in the center, would once have been strung together to form jewelry or decoration. One unusual bead carved from a semi-transparent pink-colored precious stone takes the shape of an Egyptian scarab, but its underside is plain.

ANIMAL BONES AND BONE ARTIFACTS

Over the course of the excavation seasons, many thousands of animal bones from sheep, goats, and cattle were found, the remains of food consumed by the inhabitants. The bones were studied by archaeozoologist Ron Kehati and are hugely informative since they show what animals were included in the diet, whether males or females were consumed, and at what age they were slaughtered. A significant feature already noted is that no pig bones were found at Khirbet Qeiyafa, whereas at two Philistine sites in the Shephelah, Ekron and Gath, pig bones were recovered in large quantities. Pig bones were also found at the Late Bronze Age Canaanite city of Lachish. Thus, some peoples in the Shephelah region ate pork, while the inhabitants of Khirbet Qeiyafa did not. Given the Bible's prohibition of pork consumption (Leviticus 11:7), this is an important consideration in establishing the identity of the site's population as Judahite rather than Canaanite or Philistine.

Animal bones also served as a raw material for producing a variety of artifacts. A number of long, narrow cylindrical objects with a hole at one end for suspension were found at the site. Perhaps pendants or earrings, they are decorated with various motifs, including concentric circles (Fig. 43). Similar artifacts are known from numerous Iron Age II sites in Judah and Israel; their occurrence at Khirbet Qeiyafa is evidence of their production by early Iron Age IIA.

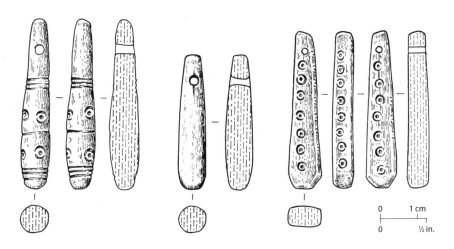

Fig. 43 Bone pendants decorated with parallel-line or concentric-circle designs.

5

GREETINGS FROM THE PAST:
THE KHIRBET QEIYAFA INSCRIPTIONS

On the morning of July 8, 2008, Oded Yair, a high school student who had volunteered to dig at the site for a few days, was working in the northwestern corner of a room in the second house north of the gate in Area B. A large sherd measuring around 16 × 15 cm (c. 6 × 6 in.) and of distinctive trapezoidal form attracted his attention. He examined the dusty sherd, which had earth stuck to it, but noticing nothing unusual he put it in the plastic bucket together with the other finds excavated there that day. In the afternoon, at the end of the workday, the bucket of finds was taken to the hostel where the expedition members were staying and was filled with water like all the other buckets brought from the field. It was then set aside until the time came to wash and clean the finds. About three hours later, when the supervisor of the square where the sherd was found, Sang-Yeup Chang, pulled that sherd from the water to wash it he noticed, to his surprise, signs of letters. The soaking had dissolved the dust and remains of earth that had encrusted the sherd, revealing an inscription written in ink and unseen for 3,000 years (Fig. 45 and Pl. xx). This modest sherd is perhaps the most important small find from Khirbet Qeiyafa.

In the ancient Near East there was no paper, and it was customary to write on a variety of different materials. Parchment, papyrus, and pottery sherds were used for this purpose, and particularly important inscriptions were engraved on stone. A potsherd with an inscription is known as an ostracon (pl. ostraca), with the letters either written in ink

Fig. 44 Aerial photograph of building B2, located north of the West Gate in Area B. The ostracon was found on the floor of a room here.

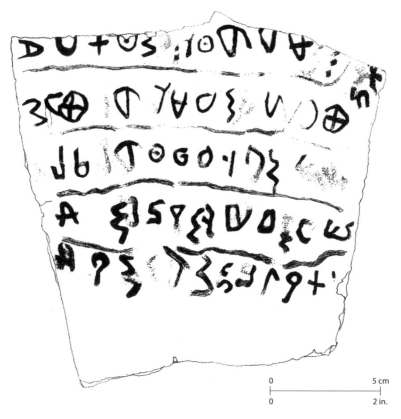

Fig. 45 Drawing of the Khirbet Qeiyafa inscription, written in ink on a pottery sherd (courtesy of Ada Yardeni).

or scratched into the sherd. In the Mediterranean climate zones of Israel, parchment and papyrus rot and disintegrate over the years, so two main types of inscriptions survive there: ostraca or engravings on stone.

The discovery of an inscription is hardly an everyday occurrence and causes enormous excitement among expedition members. After being photographed, the sherd was examined with great care. A large part of its surface was covered with a chalky coating that had accumulated over the ages—similar to the material deposited on the inside of a kettle in areas with hard water. Only a few letters were then visible, but even at this initial stage two things were already clear: the ostracon had rules dividing the lines of script; and the form of the letters was very ancient, recalling Canaanite writing of the Middle and Late Bronze Ages.

We debated how to deal with the wet sherd in order to prevent any damage to the writing and phoned the expedition conservator, Orna Cohen. She gave us simple instructions: place the sherd on absorbent paper indoors and allow it to dry slowly. At the end of the week, when the expedition returned to Jerusalem, the sherd was taken to the conservation laboratory, and for two weeks it underwent cleaning and conservation. The cleaned sherd was then photographed in the photographic laboratories of the Israel Antiquities Authority in Jerusalem by Clara Amit using both regular and infra-red lenses. Meanwhile, we approached epigrapher Haggai Misgav, proposing that he undertake the work of decipherment and publication of the inscription. The only condition was that publication should take place within a reasonable period of time: half a year, rather than the long periods (a decade or more is quite common) that many inscriptions languish prior to publication. He readily agreed.

Technically speaking, the preservation of the ink is not good in large parts of the inscription and it was therefore difficult to read the individual letters. Pnina Shor, then head of the Department for the Treatment and Conservation of Artifacts at the Israel Antiquities Authority, referred us to Greg Berman, an expert in photography and imaging techniques from the United States and who was in Israel at the time working on a project involving the Dead Sea Scrolls. Following consultation with him, it was decided to send the ostracon for a series of photographs at laboratories in the US. An immediate problem arose as the transport of antiquities from one country to another is governed by laws aimed at preventing the theft and smuggling of antiquities. However, the ostracon received an export permit from the Antiquities Authority of the State of Israel and was carried by hand in protective packaging. It was flown from Tel Aviv to Toronto, Boston, Los Angeles, and back to Tel Aviv. At every stop along the way, the strange object aroused surprise and questions from security officials.

We took advantage of the opportunity to present the ostracon at the annual scientific conference of the American Schools of Oriental Research, one of the most important in the world, which was being held in Boston that year. The convention had a special session devoted to Khirbet Qeiyafa, including four lectures on different aspects of the excavation. Hundreds were present in the lecture hall, with standing room only for many. The late Professor Frank Moore Cross of Harvard University, the greatest expert on the Canaanite script at the time, had the chance to examine the ostracon.

While the sherd was in the US, Greg Berman took it to two laboratories in the Boston area and two in the Los Angeles area for scanning and photographing by four different methods.[1] These laboratories have special devices that use the most advanced technologies available, including ones for photography in outer space. The resulting photographs made it much easier to read letters that had previously been unclear, and Haggai Misgav was able to propose a reasonable reading of the text. It was now clear that the inscription on the ostracon consisted of approximately seventy letters arranged in five lines, and that part of the ostracon was left empty. Between the rows of text, black guide lines had been drawn as an aid to keeping the writing straight. Today the Qeiyafa Ostracon is on public display in the Israel Museum in the writing exhibit in the archaeology section.

DECIPHERING THE "QEIYAFA CODE"

LETTER FORMS

Reading an ancient inscription that is poorly and partially preserved and written in a language that has to be identified is similar to deciphering a code. Of course, whoever created the inscription did so in a language and script that were intelligible to the writer and some of the writer's contemporaries. For us, examining it 3,000 years later, this is a secret system that requires considerable effort to understand and unlock. The letters and the direction of writing first have to be established, as do the words and language in which the text was written. Only then is it possible to attempt a suggested reading and interpretation.

Working from the photographs of the ostracon, two main fields of research were involved in studying and deciphering our "Qeiyafa code." One, known as palaeography, examines the forms of the letters; the other focuses on the language, and constructs words and sentences from the letters. Identifying the letters is the first phase in decipherment, and on the day of the inscription's discovery it was clear that the letters belonged to the Canaanite tradition; this conclusion has not changed following cleaning of the ostracon and examination of the photographs.

The Canaanite script (also known as Proto-Canaanite) seems to have been invented in the 18th century BCE by people from Canaan who were very familiar with Egyptian culture and Egyptian writing. This is apparent from the fact that the forms of the letters of the ancient alphabet were borrowed from the Egyptian hieroglyphic writing tradition. A complex pictographic system consisting of many hundreds of signs, it was cumbersome and difficult to use—only scribes who had studied for many years knew how to read and write. At some point someone, or a group of people, from Canaan familiar with Egyptian writing adopted 30 hieroglyphic signs and adapted them to create a simple and relatively easy-to-use phonetic alphabet. Instead of requiring many hundreds of signs, complex messages could be transmitted using just a small number of letters. This is one of the most important intellectual achievements of human civilization. Where and when did this transformation of Egyptian hieroglyphic writing into a simple alphabetic system that enables anyone to learn to read and write occur? According to Orly Goldwasser, Professor of Egyptology at the Hebrew University, it was the invention of a single individual of Canaanite origin named Khebeded, who was involved in activities at the turquoise mines of Serabit el-Khadim in southern Sinai in around the 19th century BCE, where he is depicted on a stela riding on a donkey.[2]

The Middle and Late Bronze Age Canaanite writing tradition based on the alphabet was not used at that time as the official writing system of royal and temple scribes, and thus a fixed direction of writing and letter positions did not emerge. It was only during the 10th century BCE, when this method was adopted by the Phoenicians and became the script of the port kingdom of Byblos in Lebanon, that writing became standardized and included 22 letters written in fixed positions, from right to left. This system was then taken up by the kings of Judah and Israel and by other peoples of the region: Arameans, Moabites, and Edomites. It appears that the script typical of the First Temple period, the Hebrew script that originated in Phoenicia, was still not in use at Khirbet Qeiyafa. Our ostracon is one of the latest examples of writing in the Canaanite tradition that had then been in existence for some 800 years.

Most of the letters of the alphabet occur in the Khirbet Qeiyafa inscription, including the relatively rare letter *tet*, which appears twice. The letter *aleph* appears five times, but the person who created the inscription did not write it uniformly—it is written in three distinct positions: on its side, standing upright, and upside-down.

THE DIRECTION OF WRITING AND FORMATION OF WORDS

After the decipherment of the letters, or at least a large number of them, the question then arose of how to read them—in other words, determining in which direction they were written. When we examine ancient inscriptions from periods when the practice of writing is known and widespread, it is always clear which is the first line and which the last. But this is not the case in inscriptions in the Canaanite tradition, because, as noted, the position of the letters and direction of writing had not yet been standardized. In those days texts could be written in three different directions: right to left, left to right, or "as the ox plows the field" (boustrophedon), with alternate lines written right to left and left to right. Which, then, is the first and which the last line of our inscription? Six different attempts were made at reading it: in three the ostracon was "read" with wide part uppermost and in three it was turned 180 degrees so that the wide part was at the bottom.

The simple criterion for determining the direction of the writing was obtaining meaningful words. Some words do not aid in this, such as those that can be read in either direction, for example, *shin-pe-tet* (judge) or *tet-pe-shin* (stupid). But certain combinations of letters, such as *'ayin-bet-dalet* (slave), produce a valid word in one direction only. After many months of work, eliminating possibilities that lacked sense and giving preference to ones with clear meanings, it was concluded that the ostracon should be read with the wider side at the top and the narrow side at the bottom. This is logical, since in this position the empty area of the ostracon is at the bottom of the sherd. Even today, when writing on a sheet of paper we begin at the top of the page and any blank space is left below. Likewise, it was decided to read the rows from left to right (as in English) rather than right to left (as in modern Semitic languages), the reason being that in doing so a relatively large number of words and combinations of words that had meaning were produced, such as "thou shalt not," "slave," "judged," "master," and "king."[3]

The combination that appears at the beginning of the inscription, *alep-lmed taw-ayin-shin* ("thou shalt not"), is of particular importance in determining the language of the Khirbet Qeiyafa ostracon. The verb "to do" in this form is known in Hebrew, and was not used in Canaanite and Phoenician. From this the epigrapher, Haggai Misgav, determined that the language is Hebrew, making this the most ancient known Hebrew inscription.

So clear words were identifiable, but understanding the text from beginning to end was still problematic.

BLAME, CHASTISEMENT, AND DESTRUCTION? PROPOSALS FOR IMPROVEMENTS IN READING THE TEXT

As we realized we had reached as far as we could in our reading of the ostracon, the time had come to present the results to scholars and the public at large. This was done on October 15, 2009. From the moment of its public presentation, the ostracon would become available for study and decipherment by scholars everywhere, and our exclusive analysis of it would end. Any error or misunderstanding on our part would be duly, and understandably, criticized, and we wished to avoid a situation where the reading that we proposed could be demonstrated as being fundamentally flawed. So to be certain that our conclusions so far were well-founded, some three months prior to the announcement we approached three experts on ancient inscriptions: Dr. Ada Yardeni, Professor Shmuel Ahituv, and Professor Aharon Demsky.

All three received a copy of Haggai Misgav's article summarizing his findings, a drawing of the ostracon, photographs, and free access to examine the original ostracon, which was kept in a safe at the Hebrew University. Each of the three wrote an article with notes and new insights into the inscription. All three, and all the other scholars who have written about the ostracon to date—around 20 in total—accepted the orientation and direction of reading proposed by Haggai Misgav. There were occasional alternative readings of one or more letters. Ada Yardeni, unlike Haggai Misgav, identified the word *shin-pe-tet* (judge) an additional time at the end of the second line of the ostracon.

The inscription fired the imaginations of many scholars, and each letter can contribute significantly to an understanding of what was written. Caution must be exercised, however, and readings must be supported by what can actually be read. Thus, for example, Gershon Galil of the University of Haifa, based on Haggai Misgav's and Ada Yardeni's interpretation, restored some letters, proposing to read the sentence

in line two and part of line three as: "Judge the slave and the widow /
Judge the orph[an] and the stranger."[4] This conveys a social message
related to the duty to defend and treat with justice the weaker elements
of society, the orphan and widow, which is similar to passages in the
Bible (compare Deuteronomy 10:18; Isaiah 1:17). While it is tempting to
accept this interpretation of line two, we must avoid circular arguments:
on the one hand, words like slave, widow, and orphan are restored on
the ostracon based on the Bible. On the other hand, it is only natural
that a text restored on the basis of the Bible would exhibit considerable
similarity to it.

In a similar spirit, through a significant restoration of letters and words,
Galil interpreted the next three lines on the ostracon as also emphasizing social justice. Moreover, following on from this reading, a second
level of interpretation was constructed, whereby the writing of parts of
the Bible may be dated to the beginning of the 10th century BCE based
on the evidence of the Khirbet Qeiyafa ostracon. However, attempts to
decipher the ostracon must take as a starting point the existing letters,
and any proposed reading should not rely on the restoration of a large
number of letters that can then entirely change the text.

Another interesting attempt at decipherment was made by Eythan
Levy and Frédéric Pluquet. Using computer software that they had
developed, they suggest that the inscription contains a list of personal
names.[5] Inscriptions consisting of a list of names are common in the
kingdom of Judah, and are evidence of the administrative organization
of manpower for public works, or for collecting tax.

We have a new proposal for understanding the second half of what
is written in the fourth line of the ostracon. According to Ada Yardeni
this reads *yod-bet-dalet* (unclear word?) *mem-lamed-kaf* (king), with
yod-bet-dalet being a scribal error that she corrects to read *bet-yod-dalet
mem-lamed-kaf* (a personal name: *bydmlk*).[6] In our view, it is possible
that what was really intended was *yod-(alef)-bet-dalet*, but the scribe
left out the letter *alef*. Such omission is known, for example, in the
Balaam Inscription, which was written on plaster at the site of Tell Deir
Alla on the other side of the Jordan Valley and apparently dates to the
8th century BCE. In this inscription, which describes a seer (or prophet)
named Balaam, son of Beor, a figure also known from the Bible associated
with the same geographical region, the letter *alef* is frequently dropped.[7]

According to this proposal, which does not require any changes or restoration, the text can be read as *yod-(alef)-bet-dalet mem-lamed-kaf*: "a king will be lost." A similar expression: *yod-alef-bet-dalet mem-lamed-kaf* appears in Hebrew in the Bible several times, in prophecies of punishment by various prophets: "Gaza will lose her king" (Zechariah 9:5) or "The king ... will lose heart" (Jeremiah 4:9).

In addition, one may add Shmuel Ahituv's proposal to complete the letter *shin* at the beginning of the line in question, giving the reading: *alef-shin-mem* (guilt) *nun-qof-mem* (revenge).[8] Combining these two proposals provides a continuous and clear reading of the fourth line of the Khirbet Qeiyafa ostracon as: "guilt, revenge, a king will be lost." If this reading is correct, then one clearly obtains an ominous text of a prophetic nature. We know of several inscriptions found in archaeological excavations that refer to prophecy from different periods: from the city of Mari on the Euphrates, dated to the 18th century BCE,[9] the Balaam, son of Beor inscription from Tell Deir Alla in Jordan referred to above, and a reference to a prophet in an inscription from Lachish from the end of the First Temple period.[10] A large number of the books of the Bible are prophetic texts, which is not surprising given that prophecy was regarded as the word of God and considerable effort was therefore made to document and preserve such texts from generation to generation.

Returning to the reading "guilt, revenge, a king will be lost" in the fourth line of the ostracon, various questions then arise. Who made this prophecy? Against which king? Could this be evidence for opposition to the rule of David? The Bible records various attempts to dethrone David, first by members of the house of Saul, his predecessor (2 Samuel 3:1); then by his own son Absalom (2 Samuel 15:10); and in the revolt led by Sheba, son of Bichri (2 Samuel 20:1).

It is to be hoped that new inscriptions will be found in the future, either at Khirbet Qeiyafa or at other sites dating from the same period, which will aid our interpretation of the Khirbet Qeiyafa ostracon. Today, despite our limited comprehension, this text is of enormous importance in understanding the development and diffusion of the alphabet, one of the most significant and far-reaching of the intellectual creations of humankind.

Fig. 46 Part of the inscription including the personal name Eshbaal, son of Beda, incised from right to left on the shoulder of a pottery storage jar by a skilled hand in Canaanite script.

THE ESHBAAL INSCRIPTION

A second inscription was uncovered at Khirbet Qeiyafa in the 2012 excavation season. This one had been incised in the clay of the shoulder of a pottery storage jar before firing. The letters—large and clear, similar in size and evenly spaced—were written from right to left by a skilled hand in Canaanite script, with a short straight vertical line (a word divider) between each pair of words. The inscription includes a personal name: Eshbaal, son of Beda (Figs 46, 47). The name Beda is unique, while the name Eshbaal is known from the Bible, but has never before appeared in an ancient inscription. All the occurrences of this name come from the 10th century BCE and are mostly connected with the reign of King David.[11]

The few first letters of the inscription are not fully preserved, but, judging by the upper or lower edges still visible, the first word seems to have consisted of four letters, the last one being *tav*, which here probably indicates the possessive. We tentatively propose the reading *hlqt* in Hebrew, that is, a plot of land. Interestingly, the Bible describes a plot of lentils in the Elah Valley, near Khirbet Qeiyafa, at the time of King

David, using the word *hlqt* (2 Samuel 23:11). In the context of an incised inscription on a large container, this would imply that the jar's contents came from the field or estate of Eshbaal, son of Beda.

The personal name Eshbaal is very interesting. As in any other aspect of human history, personal names change over time. If a particular name appears within a limited timeframe in both ancient inscriptions and the biblical tradition, it is an indication of authentic historical memories of that era. In the Bible, Eshbaal was the second king of Israel, the son of King Saul and a rival of David (1 Chronicles 8:33). The commonly accepted interpretation of this name is "man of Baal." Baal is the Canaanite storm god, and his name, translated as "lord" or "master," is also a noun meaning a deity.

Unlike Chronicles, the second book of Samuel uses the name Ishbosheth (2 Samuel 2:10), commonly interpreted as "man of shame,"

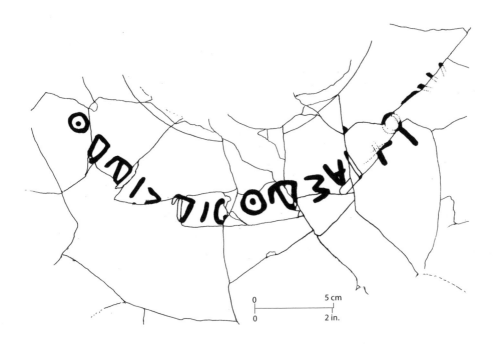

Fig. 47 Drawing of the Eshbaal, son of Beda inscription, incised in the soft clay of a storage jar before the vessel was fired in a kiln (courtesy of Ada Yardeni).

for this king. Reflecting a negative attitude to the Canaanite god Baal, the author or editor of Samuel censored the original name and replaced Baal with the word Bosheth ("shame"). Other examples of the replacement of Baal in biblical names can be found in versions of Gideon: Jerubbaal (Judges 6:32) and Jerubbesheth (2 Samuel 11:21); of Jonathan's son: Meribbaal (1 Chronicles 9:40) and Mephibosheth (2 Samuel 4:4); and of David's son: Beeliada ("Baal knows") (1 Chronicles 14:7) and Eliada ("God knows") (2 Samuel 5:16; 1 Chronicles 3:8). Moreover, it has been suggested that three other individuals bore the name Eshbaal, but that the Baal element was replaced and the final form became Jashobeam. These men all fought with David: one was one of his mighty warriors (1 Chronicles 11:11), another was the Korahite who joined David at Ziklag (1 Chronicles 12:6), and the third was the head of David's first division (1 Chronicles 27:2). All these names occur in the context of David's time or earlier.

So in the 10th century BCE the name Eshbaal was common, and is recorded for one biblical king and three other biblical individuals. In the following centuries, however, the personal name Eshbaal, or any other personal name including the element Baal, disappears from the biblical text, and the Bible contains no mention of it in Israel or Judah in later periods. Similarly, Eshbaal occurs in our inscription dated to the early 10th century BCE, the time of King David, but the name Eshbaal is not found in any of the hundreds of inscriptions or on over a thousand seals and seal impressions known from ancient Israel dating between the 9th and 6th century BCE and recording over 2,000 names. The correlation between the chronological distribution of personal names in the biblical tradition and in ancient inscriptions indicates that the biblical text preserves authentic traditions relating to the period of King David.

WRITING IN JUDAH DURING THE 10TH CENTURY BCE

For the 300-year period between the 12th and 9th century BCE we have very little written material from ancient Israel. Against the background of this paucity of finds, the Khirbet Qeiyafa ostracon and the Eshbaal jar are of outstanding importance. Two other inscriptions were then reported from the sites of Beth Shemesh and Jerusalem, also in ancient Judah.[12] The four inscriptions, all written in Canaanite script and discovered in the core area of the Kingdom of Judah, date from the end of the

11th and beginning of the 10th century BCE. The increased appearance of inscriptions in this region and at this time indicates a deep change in social and political organization. The inception of a kingdom would have required much greater exchange of information.

The inscriptions also of course bear witness to the fact that people of that period could record historical memories in writing, and thus preserve them from generation to generation, until the later codification of the biblical tradition. This contradicts the main claim of minimalist scholars that the editors of the Bible working in later periods had no historical information about the early period of the monarchy to call upon, and that they therefore invented tales with no historical foundation.

Fig. 48 The Ark of the Covenant in the Philistine temple of Dagon,
as depicted in an engraving of around 1540 by Battista Franco.

6

CULT IN JUDAH PRIOR TO THE CONSTRUCTION OF SOLOMON'S TEMPLE

The discoveries at Khirbet Qeiyafa make a major contribution to the investigation of ancient cult during the First Temple period in the region of Judah. According to the Bible, two unique religious concepts developed here and at this time: the belief in one God, that is, a monotheistic cult; and a cult that was aniconic, that is, one that rejects images in accordance with the commandment "Thou shalt not make unto thee any graven image" (Exodus 20:4). These two features set cultic practice in this region entirely apart from the worship of idols that was found in all the lands of the ancient Near East. However, while the biblical tradition describes these concepts as being adhered to by the people of Israel from early on, the same tradition also informs us that the reality was far more complex. Most of the population of the Kingdom of Israel, including the ruling elite, did not follow a monotheistic cult, but also worshipped Baal and Asherah "on every high hill and under every green tree" (1 Kings 14:23).

In Judah, too, we hear of conflicts between two different religious practices. Thus, for example, it is said that during the days of King Josiah, at the end of the 7th century BCE, the Asherah was removed from the temple in Jerusalem and burned in the Kidron Valley (2 Kings 23:6). From this we learn that at some point a statue or other representation of Asherah must have stood in the temple in Jerusalem. Elsewhere, we hear that King Hezekiah destroyed the copper snake that Moses had made in the desert (2 Kings 18:4). In other words, the image of a snake believed to belong to the days of Moses stood in Jerusalem and was attributed with medicinal and redemptive powers. Various prophets of biblical times repeatedly warned against the practice of the worship of idols that had spread among the people. Idol worship is also reflected in archaeological remains. In excavations conducted in Jerusalem over 1,000 clay figurines portraying a naked woman holding her breasts were found in strata dating to the end of the First Temple period.[1] Some identify these with the Asherah referred to in the Bible. Such figurines are also found at many sites in Judah and are particularly widespread at the end of the First Temple period.

To understand the significance of the discoveries at Khirbet Qeiyafa, we should first look at the information available for ancient cult in the preceding period, Iron Age I (12th–11th century BCE). Several cult places are known from this period. At Hazor a standing stone and a bronze figurine of a god were discovered by Yigael Yadin, and another cult area was excavated by Amnon Ben-Tor. In the Samaria region, Amihai Mazar excavated a site on a hilltop where a bronze figurine of a bull was found— the so-called "Bull Site." On Mount Ebal an accumulation of animal bones was examined by Adam Zertal, attesting to cult activity, and at Tel Qiri in the Jezreel Valley a cult room was excavated by Amnon Ben-Tor.[2] All of these are located in the area of the northern Kingdom of Israel.

We have no clear data relating to Iron Age I cult activity in the southern part of the country, the area of Judah. In the subsequent Iron Age IIA period (10th–9th century BCE), information on cult in Judah is still very limited and includes a single small room excavated by Yohanan Aharoni at Lachish which contained an assemblage of cultic objects including a limestone horned altar and several special pottery vessels.[3] More significant evidence of cult in the Kingdom of Judah comes from two other of Aharoni's excavations: the temple at Arad and at Beersheba a large four-horned altar. These, however, are dated to the 8th century BCE, 200 years or more later than the finds from Khirbet Qeiyafa.

In 2012 a temple with rich cult paraphernalia and dated to the 9th century BCE was uncovered at the site of Motza (Tel Moza), on the outskirts of Jerusalem.[4] This fascinating discovery indicates that temples were constructed not only in remote areas of the kingdom such as Arad, but also just one hour's walk from the kingdom's main temple in Jerusalem. Among the finds at Motza were two clay figurine heads, similar to one from Area A at Khirbet Qeiyafa described below.

The absence of archaeological finds on the one hand, and a critical reading of the Bible on the other, led to scholarly approaches that cast doubt on the claim that the belief in one God and an aniconic cult appeared in the Kingdom of Judah at the beginning of the Iron Age.

Various scholars proposed instead that they were much later developments, and suggested various dates for them: either at the end of the Iron
Age, or in the Persian or the Hellenistic period.[5] According to this view,
later editors of the Bible moved these cult practices back in time, attribut-
ing them to periods during which they did not exist. Since no evidence
regarding the cult of the 12th–10th centuries BCE had been excavated in
Judah, there were no relevant data to settle these questions. However,
our excavations at Khirbet Qeiyafa have now uncovered considerable
and varied evidence for cult in the early Kingdom of Judah, including
mazzebot, cult rooms, temple models, basalt altars, libation vessels, and
even a clay figurine.

THE ANCIENT CULT OF STONES: THE *MAZZEBOT*
Several cultic *mazzebot* (standing stones; singular *mazzebah*) were found
in different locations at Khirbet Qeiyafa. One large example was discovered in the first gate chamber on the left of the city's South Gate (Fig. 49).
This recalls the Bible's statement that King Josiah of Judah abolished the
bamot (high places; singular *bamah*) that stood to the left of the entrance
to the city gate (2 Kings 23:8). The fact that it was felt necessary to abolish
them indicates that they were apparently common in the gates of cities in
the Kingdom of Judah. The *mazzebah* in the gateway at Khirbet Qeiyafa
is evidence that the practice had already begun in the initial phase of
the foundation of the kingdom.

On the left side of the West Gate, in building B1, we discovered a
large *mazzebah* of hard limestone that had been incorporated into
a wall, upside-down and completely concealed—a clear indication that
it had been taken out of cult use and intentionally hidden from view.
Furthermore, its upside-down position suggests that whoever hid it in
the wall sought to denigrate or negate its power. It may once have stood
in a public place, perhaps within the city gate, but for some reason the
decision was taken to remove it from sight and build it into the wall.

In building C3 we excavated a room identified as cultic which contained two standing *mazzebot* as well as other objects (described in
more detail below). One of the *mazzebot* stands to a height of 80 cm
(30 in.), while the second is much smaller, measuring just 20 cm (8 in.)
(Fig. 50). At the base of the taller *mazzebah* was a large flat stone.
This is reminiscent of a similar find at Hazor consisting of a large group

of tens of standing stone *mazzebot* of the Middle Bronze Age (earlier than the biblical settlement at Khirbet Qeiyafa). Flat stones are frequently found at the base of *mazzebot* and it appears they were used as tables where worshipers could leave their various offerings of food, water, or other items.[6]

Two tall, narrow stones were also found in Area D, in separate rooms of a single structure, D1. The location, in the vicinity of the western gate of the city in the first southern house after the gate piazza, is again significant. Two other unusual finds in this house—libation vessels and a long bench built along one of the walls of the room, discussed in the following section—occur only in cultic contexts. Both *mazzebot* are naturally occurring long, narrow stones, with virtually no signs of stonecutting. One of them is the largest *mazzebah* found at Khirbet Qeiyafa, 1.5 m (5 ft) high, and again with a flat stone at its base. Unfortunately an olive

---

MAZZEBOT

Mazzebot are well known both from biblical tradition and from a large and varied number of examples found throughout the ancient Near East from the Neolithic period onward. Tall, narrow stones, *mazzebot* were generally left in their natural form, and as such are distinct from pillars that were hewn into a defined geometrical shape.

We learn about *mazzebot* in the biblical period from the story of Jacob at Bethel. In the evening Jacob rested his head on a stone and fell asleep. As he slept he dreamt of a ladder reaching up to the heavens, with the angels of the Lord ascending and descending upon it. In the morning, when he awoke, he took the stone that had served as his pillow, erected it on its narrow side and anointed it with oil, and it thus became a *mazzebah* (Genesis 28:11–18). This story indicates that *mazzebot* did not have to be carved, and it was common practice to erect stones in their natural state.

When the Bible describes the reorganization of cult, we hear of the breaking of *mazzebot* and the cutting down and burning of the *asherah* (2 Kings 18:4; 2 Kings 23:14), which reveals that the *mazzebot* were made of stone while the *asherah* was made of wood.

Figs 49, 50 Examples of *mazzebot* (standing stones) found at Khirbet Qeiyafa: (left) from the South Gate chamber, on the left side on entering the city and (right) two standing stones found in the cult room in building C3.

press constructed during the late Persian–early Hellenistic period had destroyed large parts of this structure.

A total of seven *mazzebot* have been discovered at Khirbet Qeiyafa, five of which were in the vicinity of the city gates, a phenomenon known to scholars and one which has been discussed in several articles and books.[7] All of the *mazzebot* at Khirbet Qeiyafa preserve the natural form of the stone, with only rare signs of limited stonecutting; none have decorations of any type, nor are anthropomorphic or zoomorphic figurines found associated with them.

How can we explain the connection between the cult of *mazzebot* and the city gate? The gate is the passage between the protected and civilized city and the wild and hostile world outside. According to the noted anthropologist and scholar of religious studies Victor Turner, this can be defined as a "liminal" situation, a threshold of passage between one state and another. In order to maintain social order and security, rites of passage are created to protect the individuals crossing this threshold. For those entering the city, the *mazzebah* in the gate signals their safe arrival at their desired destination, while for those leaving the city and setting out for regions that may be full of dangers it is a place of prayer and supplication for a successful journey. It is not surprising, therefore, that we find considerable evidence for cultic activity at city gates, including *mazzebot* of various types, as known also at Tel Dan and Tell el-Far'ah North.

THE "HIGH-PLACES OF THE GATES"? CULT ROOMS AT KHIRBET QEIYAFA

We have identified three rooms as cultic at Khirbet Qeiyafa. But what are cult rooms, and how do they differ from temples? A temple is a structure that generally stands apart, while a cult room is a single room devoted to religious activity within a domestic dwelling. It is quite probable that when no cult activity was taking place, the room functioned like others in the house. Also, a temple is usually elaborately constructed and follows a fixed, symmetrical plan with a clear division of space, while cult rooms are simply built and each is different in size and form, according to its location. Unlike temples, which remained in continuous use for hundreds of years, cult rooms were in use for only short periods of time. While temples are entirely devoted to cult and are generally regarded as the earthly dwelling of the deity, a cult room can simply serve as a gathering place for believers for religious ceremonies. We can also speculate that unlike temples, where a specialized priestly role was passed down from father to son, cult rooms were created independently by charismatic individuals, perhaps similar to shamans in tribal societies. The building and maintenance of temples requires developed social and economic organization, such as existed in the Canaanite city-states, in Philistine cities, and in the kingdoms of Judah and Israel. However, the rural society of Iron Age I and early Iron Age IIA had not developed a complex religious system and its cult was improvised and spontaneous. According to the Bible, there was no temple in Jerusalem in David's time, and it was only built later, by Solomon, at a more developed stage of the monarchic period.

One of the cult rooms at Khirbet Qeiyafa is in building C3, which is located about 30 m (98 ft) east of the southern gate and is divided into eight rooms. The room we labeled G measures 6 × 5 m (20 × 16½ ft) and is constructed on bedrock sloping to the east, making its western half higher than the eastern by about half a meter (1½ ft) (Fig. 51). The entrance to the casemate next to the eastern side of the room is blocked by a stone wall, apparently in order to create a closed and intimate space. Room G differs from all the others we excavated at the site in terms of the installations and finds it contained. A stone bench ran along the

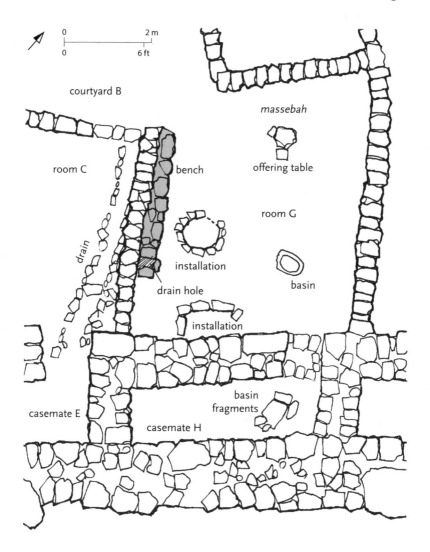

Fig. 51 Plan of the cult room discovered in building C3 during the 2010 season.

southern wall, and in the floor of the room were two installations, one round and one rectangular; nearby an arrangement for draining liquids connected this room to a drain in the next room (C). The bench, made of flat stone slabs, could have been used as a seat for those participating in the ritual or to receive offerings. In addition to the two stone *mazzebot* described above, the room also contained a basalt altar, a large limestone basin, a pottery libation vessel, a seal, and a scarab. At the base of the taller of the room's two *mazzebot* was a large flat stone that may have served as a place to make offerings. In the eastern half of the room the large limestone basin was found upside down and broken. Another stone basin had been tossed into the adjacent casemate and had once probably been in use in the cult activities, but was discarded at some point.

The rectangular basalt altar stands on three legs and is relatively low. It is carved with what seems to be an architectural motif on the shorter sides and the image of a date palm on the longer ones (Fig. 52 and Pl. xxi). For comparison, we looked at a clay altar found in the excavations of Amihai

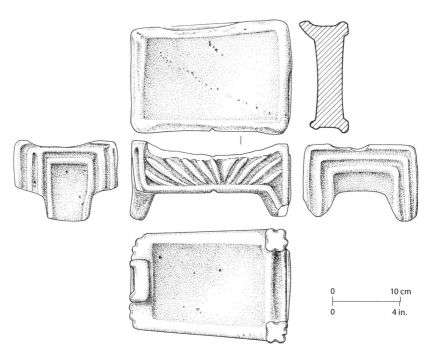

0   10 cm

0   4 in.

Fig. 52 A small altar with three legs carved from basalt discovered in the cult room in C3.

Fig. 53 A clay altar excavated at Tel Rehov, dated to the beginning of the 9th century BCE. It features architectural and date palm motifs, comparable to those on the basalt altar found at Khirbet Qeiyafa. However, the two nude females (fertility goddesses?) are not present on the Khirbet Qeiyafa altar.

Mazar at Tel Rehov in the Jordan Valley, dated to the beginning of the 9th century BCE (Fig. 53), which is decorated with the images of two nude female figures (goddesses?). Female figurines were also found at the site. In contrast, no human figures are shown on the Khirbet Qeiyafa altar and no figurines were found in this room.

Next to the stone basin in room G lay a broken clay vessel that even in its fragmentary state appeared different from the pottery generally encountered at the site. It takes the form of two joined goblets on a single high base (Fig. 54, 1), and is similar to a vessel found in Area D (see below). Other such vessels have also been discovered by Amnon Ben-Tor in a cult room at Tel Qiri (Fig. 54, 2), dated to the 11th century BCE, and in the temple at Khirbat al-Mudayna in Jordan (Fig. 54, 3), excavated by Michèle Daviau and Margreet Steiner, dated to the 8th century BCE; one was also found at Tell Deir Alla in Jordan. All these five vessels were found in cult contexts and were probably used in rituals involving libation offerings. The cult room in building C3 where the libation vessel was found also contained a stone basin and a drainage channel, suggesting that an important part of cult activity here involved liquids such as water, oil, or wine. In addition, a total of 101 pottery vessels of different types were found here, some complete but most represented only by rim sherds, a surprising quantity for a single room, even in comparison to other areas at a site rich in finds.

Most of the cult objects in this room had been broken. One half of the basalt altar was discovered at the western end of the room, next to the bench, while the other half was on the eastern side. The limestone basin had been turned upside down and broken. The pottery libation

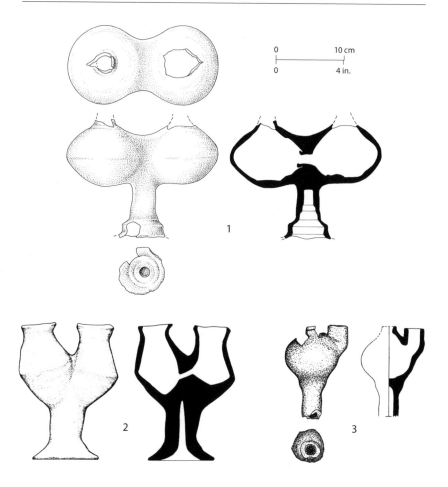

Fig. 54 Drawings of three libation vessels consisting of two goblets: 1. from the cult room in building C3 at Khirbet Qeiyafa; 2. from a cult room at Tel Qiri in the Jezreel Valley; 3. from a temple near the city gate at Khirbat al-Mudayna in Jordan.

vessel was also smashed. The same phenomenon was observed in the cult area in building C10 (Fig. 55).

A standing joke among archaeologists is that the most important find of an excavation is always found on the last day of the season, moments before closing the operations and departing. Our experience in excavating building C10 certainly confirmed this. The uniqueness of this structure became clear at the last moment of the last day of the 2011 season, when an American volunteer discovered a fragment of a

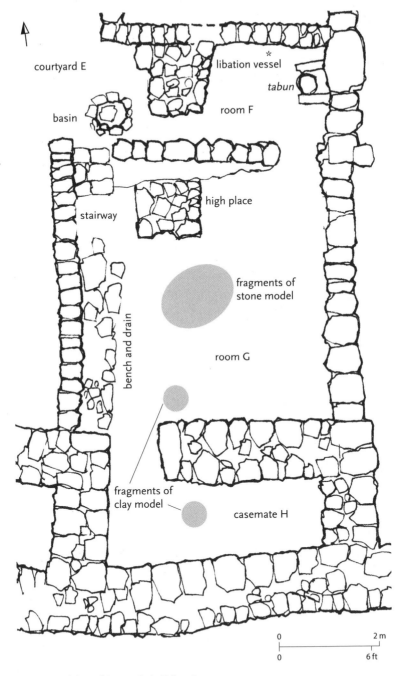

Fig. 55 Plan of the cultic area in building C10.

small, decorated clay temple model with several protrusions that at first appeared to be representations of animal heads, but after cleaning proved to be birds (the decoration will be described in detail below). The object was found on the floor of the fourth casemate to the west of the Area C gate. The following day, which was intended to be devoted to cleaning, photographing, and dismantling the excavation, started out as an ordinary workday. We continued to excavate the casemate, and more pieces were found, including two columns and two images of lions. Suddenly, it occurred to us that perhaps we had encountered other parts of the model in the days prior to its identification. That afternoon, we opened the bags containing the sherds collected in the casemate and in the adjacent room over the previous days. Additional fragments of the model's walls and roof were recognized. These simple fragments, with no decoration, had not been initially identified as belonging to this unusual object. During restoration, all the sherds successfully joined to produce a nearly complete object, though unfortunately the bottom of the building was not found (see Fig. 59 and Pl. xxii).

Several days earlier, fragments of a stone object had also been discovered in this room. These fragments were carved in an unusual manner, which we had not encountered in previous seasons. The object was made from particularly soft stone that is easily damaged, and some of the pieces retained traces of red paint. For that reason, we carefully packed the pieces, without washing them, and sent them to the conservator, Orna Cohen. A week or so after the end of the excavation, she informed us that the fragments were from a temple model (see Fig. 60 and Pl. xxiii). There is a saying that the most important find of an excavation is always made on the very last day—but here, as fate would have it, the object was identified in the laboratory a week after the end of fieldwork.

If these finds had been made earlier in the season, we would have devoted greater effort at the time to uncovering in its entirety this unusual building, which lay at the edge of the excavation. But the importance of the finds forced a decision to extend the excavation season by a week. The work was carried out by students of the Hebrew University's Institute of Archaeology and other volunteers. As the official organization of the dig had been wound down, we had to improvise: we rented two vehicles, and every morning, before sunrise, picked up the ten diggers from their homes in Jerusalem, excavated at the site until the afternoon, and at the end of the day returned the staff to their homes. The finds from the excavation accumulated and by the end of the week there were some 80 plastic buckets full of sherds that we did not have time to wash. So the next week we invited all the participants in the excavation to a "pottery washing party."

During this week of extended excavation we were able to clarify the nature of the cult activity in building C10, and in the course of the 2012 excavation season the entire building was finally uncovered. The cultic area includes courtyard E, cult room G with adjacent casemate H and a small room, F. Courtyard E is located in the center of the building and measures around 6 × 5.5 m (20 × 18 ft). Three cooking installations were found on the floor around its edge: a *tabun* in the northeast corner, with another nearby, and a hearth adjacent to the southern wall. Three more cooking installations were uncovered in this building, whereas only one or two are usual in a normal house at the site. This remarkable concentration probably indicates that elaborate ceremonies took place here involving feasting. The floor and the debris above it were rich in finds, including a large amount of restorable pottery vessels, fragments of a perforated stand, two seals, and a broken basalt altar, similar in size and shape to the one uncovered in the cult room in building C3, though undecorated.

A rounded basin lined with stone slabs was sunk into the floor in the southeastern corner of the courtyard, exactly in front of the entrances to rooms F and G, so that anyone entering these rooms would have had to pass by it. A drain ran from under it to the south into room G, clearly indicating some activity related to liquids. The basin probably served for washing, perhaps as a purification ceremony before entering the inner sacred area.

Room G together with adjacent room F, in the southeastern corner of the house and next to the gate piazza, stand out from all of the other rooms excavated at Khirbet Qeiyafa. In addition to the basin in front of them, each opens to courtyard E and also has an inner doorway connecting them. Room G is square, measuring 5 × 5 m (16½ × 16½ ft) internally. Against its northern wall is an installation, measuring 1.2 × 1.2 m, (4 × 4 ft), only a single course of which survives. No similar feature has been found in any other building at the site, and we assume it is the base of a *bamah* ("high place") that was originally taller, and on which would have stood the two unique temple models whose fragments we found here. Room F is rectangular, measuring 2.5 × 1.8 m (8¼ × 6 ft). A small, even miniature, oven was built against its eastern wall. A thick layer of ash next to it indicates that cooking or baking activity took place here, though given the dimensions of the oven it must have been on a relatively limited scale, insufficient for an ordinary household. Special food was perhaps prepared here, such as sacred bread for rituals, a custom we read about in the time of David in 1 Samuel 21:6: "So the priest gave him the consecrated bread, since there was no bread there except the bread of the Presence that had been removed from before the Lord and replaced by hot bread on the day it was taken away."

Fragments of a special double pottery vessel were found in this room, consisting of a larger, bowl-shaped vessel with a cup-shaped vessel inside, which were joined before firing. This type of composite vessel is popularly referred to as a "cup and saucer," and is known from the Middle and Late Bronze Age Canaanite culture and also occurs at Iron Age sites. The example from Khirbet Qeiyafa differs from most other vessels of this kind in its large size and multiple handles. There is only one vessel of comparable form and size, but it comes from the antiquities market and is of unknown provenance.[8] The function of such vessels remains disputed: some see them as oil lamps while others regard them as libation vessels for pouring liquid during religious ceremonies. Given the number of handles and the fact that it does not have a soot-covered spout typical of oil lamps, we interpret the example from Khirbet Qeiyafa as a libation vessel.

To summarize: architecturally, this cultic zone in Area C has features unknown in any other room at the site, in particular the basin and the *bamah*. The temple models (discussed in the next section) are extremely rare finds, and the presence of two in the same room indicates that this is a particularly important cult center. Its location is also noteworthy as it is in the first building immediately adjacent to the piazza of the southern and more important of the city's two gates. The presence of cult activity in this particular place appears to have public and administrative significance.

The third cult room discovered at Khirbet Qeiyafa is in building D1, immediately adjacent to the piazza of the western gate, in the first building to the south (Fig. 56). A major problem in attempting to understand the nature of the activity that took place here, however, is that the area

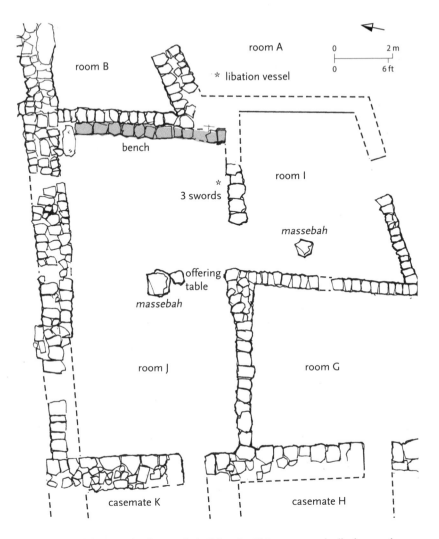

Fig. 56 Plan of the central cult room in building D1. This room was badly damaged when an olive oil press was built here in the late Persian–early Hellenistic era.

was severely damaged during the late Persian–early Hellenistic period, when an olive oil press was constructed here. The few surviving remains from the biblical phase, the 10th century BCE, include a bench, a libation vessel consisting of twin goblets, similar to the one in building C3, and two large *mazzebot* (described above), the larger of which has a flat stone at its foot for offerings. Three large iron swords were found as a group next to the bench. We know that weapons were often deposited in temples in the ancient Near East, and the Bible also refers to this custom, as, for example, when the sword of Goliath the Philistine, taken as booty by David, was kept in a cult place (1 Samuel 21:9). Later the armor of King Saul was placed by the Philistines in the temple of Ashtoreth, again a cultic context (1 Samuel 31:10).

The concentration of all these cult elements in the first buildings next to the gate piazzas is surely not coincidental, but is evidence that this area was the focus of religious activity. Perhaps the biblical expression "high-places of the gate," which we discussed above in connection with the *mazzebot* found next to the city gate, actually relates to these cult rooms, and not just to a *mazzebah* in the gate chamber itself. The rooms in buildings C10 and D1 appear to be associated with the city's administration and reflect public activity. On the other hand, the room in building C3, an inner space of a building in a row of houses, appears to represent a private cult of an individual or a family. There is a hierarchy of cultic activity here, indicated by the location of the cult rooms, their architecture, and the finds discovered in them.

Also of interest is the precise location of the cult room within the two buildings next to the city gates—both are adjacent to the gate piazza. This repeated pattern is again not coincidental and appears to reflect a deeper concept. During cult ceremonies, most of the worshipers would have stood in the gate piazza immediately outside the building. In this way they could be near the cult place without actually being inside. There may possibly have been a window in the outer wall through which worshipers could see into the room. On important holidays, the masses of celebrants who made a pilgrimage to the city could have congregated in the piazza, where various cult activities would have been performed, such as the sacrifice of animals, dances, and prayers. The priest might have stood on the roof of the room to bless or address the believers in the piazza below.

The discovery of these cult rooms at Khirbet Qeiyafa made us wonder whether this phenomenon was unique to our site or was widespread at this period. We examined excavation reports of other sites in Israel and found that such cult rooms in private houses are known from the 11th and 10th centuries BCE at a number of sites (Fig. 57). In Amnon Ben-Tor's excavations at Tel Qiri, in the Jezreel Valley, an ordinary dwelling in Stratum VIII, dated to the 11th century BCE, contained a stone *mazzebah*, a stone basin, a libation vessel with double cups, other special pottery vessels, and a group of animal bones consisting exclusively of the right legs of sheep and goats;[9] similar cult objects were found at Khirbet Qeiyafa. At Megiddo, the Chicago Oriental Institute excavations uncovered in Stratum Va–IVb, dated to the second half of the 10th century BCE or the beginning of the 9th century BCE, an elaborate building with several rooms, Building 2081. In the corner of one room was a collection of cultic artifacts including two limestone horned altars, a *mazzebah*, pottery stands, a basalt three-legged bowl, a bowl

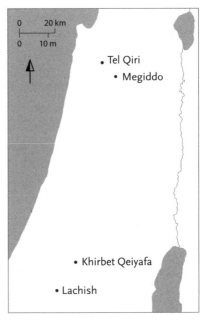

Fig. 57 Map showing sites where cultic rooms dated to the 11th–10th centuries BCE have been found.

filled with astragali (the talus bone in the heel of ovicaprids), and two seals.[10] And at Lachish, Yohanan Aharoni excavated Building 49 in Level V, dated to the end of the 10th or beginning of the 9th century BCE, which contained a concentration of cultic artifacts including a three-horned altar carved from limestone, pottery cult stands, and pottery chalices.[11]

In the biblical tradition relating to this period we find at least four cases of cult activity in private houses. One story tells of Micah on Mount Ephraim preparing a statue, ephod (priestly garment), and teraphim (possibly small idols), and taking a Levite youth to serve as a priest in his house (Judges 17). Another tradition relates how the Ark of the Lord was returned from its captivity in the Philistine cities and placed at Kiriath-jearim in the house of Abinadav. Eleazar, his son, is entrusted with the protection of the Ark (1 Samuel 7:1). A third episode describes King Saul asking the advice of a sorceress in her house at En-Dor, who calls up the prophet Samuel from the land of the dead (1 Samuel 28:7–8). Finally, when the Ark was brought to Jerusalem by David, it was placed initially in the private house of Obed-edom the Gittite (2 Samuel 6:10–12). In addition, it is interesting to note how the biblical tradition of the end of the period of the Judges describes life in the cult center at Shiloh. Where did Samuel, the prophet who crowned both Saul and David, live in his youth? The Bible states that "Samuel was lying down in the Temple of the Lord, where the Ark of the Lord was" (1 Samuel 3:3). In other words, ordinary everyday activity took place in the holy of holies, something that could never occur in the temple in Jerusalem.

Thus, the evidence for cult rooms excavated at various sites (Tel Qiri, Megiddo, Khirbet Qeiyafa, and Lachish) and references to them in the biblical tradition complement each other. Khirbet Qeiyafa, dating from the beginning of the 10th century BCE, prior to the construction of Solomon's Temple, provides the most ancient archaeological evidence we have for cult in the early Kingdom of Judah, showing that it was practiced in cult rooms rather than in temples.

FROM "SNAKE HOUSES" TO TEMPLE MODELS

At Bronze and Iron Age sites in the Levant archaeologists occasionally encounter objects in the form of buildings, either round or rectangular, which can measure up to half a meter (1½ ft) high. They are usually made of clay, but one, from our excavations at Khirbet Qeiyafa, was carved from stone. In the past, the function of these objects was not certain and they were commonly referred to as "snake houses," based on the erroneous assumption that snakes were kept in them. Over the years, their intended use has become clearer, particularly thanks to the excavations at Ashkelon, where one was found with a bronze calf figurine inside. Today, it is accepted that they were temple models, with figurines of gods, or gods in the form of animals, placed inside. Today they are often called "portable shrines."[12]

Four such models have been excavated at Khirbet Qeiyafa. The first, found in the courtyard of building C4, is a simple one made of clay (Fig. 58) with a single opening on one side, which could be closed with a separate clay door. A small lug handle on each side of the opening and one on the door would have been used to secure the door. It was found nearly complete, missing only a small applied relief of an unknown motif above the entrance, and was also empty, with no figurine found near it.

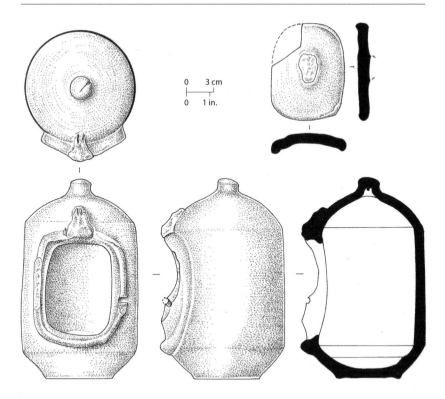

0   3 cm

0   1 in.

Fig. 58 A simple clay temple model, found in building C4. It imitates a building with a door opening on one side and is not elaborately decorated.

As described above, at the very last moment of the 2011 season, a fragment of a pottery temple model was found in Area C, additional parts of which were recovered later. Unlike the previously described model, this one had shattered into numerous small pieces when the site was destroyed—some were thrown into the casemate, some into a room to the north adjacent to the casemate, and others have not been found. What is special about this model is its elaborately decorated opening, which is very precisely executed with various elements arranged symmetrically. Fortunately, most of the decorated parts were recovered, except for a small section of the right side (Fig. 59 and Pl. xxii). On either side of the entrance at the bottom stands a lion; the one on the left is preserved in its entirety and is portrayed in a crouching position. Statues of lions are known from city gates or buildings of the Late Bronze Age in the Near East and Mediterranean regions, for instance at Hattusha,

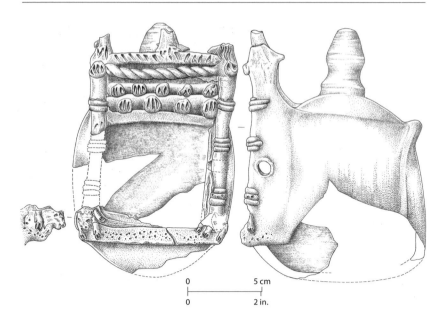

0   5 cm

0   2 in.

Fig. 59 The elaborate clay temple model found in building C10, with a decorated entrance including two lions and two upright columns. Circles above the entrance appear to indicate the ends of roofing beams, and three birds perch on the roof.

the Hittite capital, and at Mycenae in Greece. A closer parallel, both geographically and conceptually, comes from the Late Bronze Age temple at Hazor, where next to the entrance a 2-m (6½-ft) long statue of a lion was found buried in a pit.

On each side of the model's entrance is a tall column. Temple entrances flanked by columns have been found archaeologically in the Near East, for instance at the Hazor temple mentioned above, and in temple models from Israel and neighboring countries. The Bible famously tells of two columns, named Jachin and Boaz, which stood one on each side of the entrance to Solomon's Temple. On the Khirbet Qeiyafa model, the columns have ropes tied horizontally around them, a detail not seen on other examples found to date. This rope motif occurs three times on the column on the right side of the opening, which is completely preserved, wound three times around the column at the bottom and in the middle, and twice at the top. Above the opening of the entrance are five horizontal bands of clay placed one above the other, some of which seem to represent roof beams. Beams are generally shown on such models as a single band, or two, and it is rare for the roof to be emphasized in this manner. The fourth band is a twisted coil of clay. What might this represent? Perhaps the craftsman intended it to portray a rolled up curtain. If so, this would be a portrayal of the *parochet*, a curtain that was hung above an entrance and which could be rolled up to leave the doorway clear. The *parochet* appears in descriptions of the temple in Jerusalem, where it separated the Holy of Holies from other parts of the building. The fifth and highest beam on the model represents the roof of the building and is decorated with diagonal incisions.

Another intriguing element of the decoration are the applied clay circles, incised with straight parallel lines, four on the first beam, five on the second, and one above the top of each column. No comparable decoration has been noted on other temple models from Israel, but at several sites in Syria similar circles are found on clay models, always applied to the upper part, above the entrance and near the roof.[13] This motif probably reflects an element of construction, but what specifically? The question confounded us until we made another discovery at Khirbet Qeiyafa that enabled us to propose a solution, discussed below.

On the uppermost part of the roof are three birds, now lacking their heads and parts of the wings. Several examples of similar representations of birds on the roofs of buildings are known from elsewhere in the ancient Near East, including Israel and Jordan. They may be more than purely decorative, perhaps alluding to the practice of conducting bird sacrifices under specific circumstances (for example: Leviticus 5:7; 12:6; 14:4–7, 22; Numbers 6:10).

Especially notable in this context is the 2002 discovery near Tel Yavneh of a repository pit (one in which sacred remains are placed in an ordered way) containing nearly 100 clay temple models dating to the 9th century BCE and attributed to the Philistine culture.[14] All of the models are rectangular house-shaped boxes, unlike ours at Khirbet Qeiyafa which is essentially a round, closed pottery vessel. A variety of motifs are found as decoration on the Tel Yavneh models including columns, lions, roof beams with diagonal lines, human figures, and applied bulls' heads. While the models from the two sites share elements, comparison of the composition of the motifs, the order of their appearance, and the artistic style create the impression of separate traditions drawing on a shared world of visual concepts and employing them in different ways.

In 2011 fragments of a third temple model were found at Khirbet Qeiyafa and were restored by Orna Cohen. This is a unique find, unparalleled at any other excavation. It is carved from stone, whereas temple models are generally made of clay, and consists of a large rectangular box, 35 cm (14 in.) high with a flat roof that slopes down from the entrance. And while other examples of temple models are generally schematic, this one is highly detailed, with special features carefully executed and emphasized, and it was also entirely painted red. But most impressive are the architectural elements it portrays (Fig. 60 and Pl. xxiii).

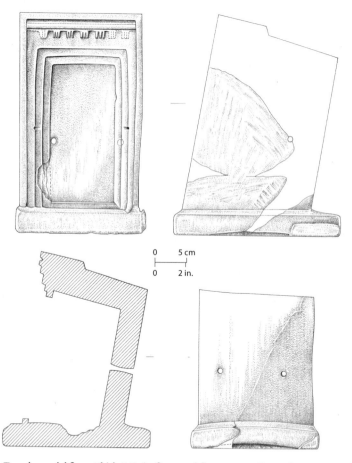

Fig. 60 Temple model from Khirbet Qeiyafa carved from stone. Above the entrance the ends of roofing beams are visible and the entrance itself is emphasized by three receding door frames. Remains of red paint were preserved over the entire model.

Three sides of the stone box are simply executed, having smooth walls with no carved decoration. The front façade has a high, narrow opening, 20 × 10 cm (8 × 4 in.), which is very carefully fashioned. These same proportions, twice as high as wide, appear in various descriptions of the dimensions of the entrances to the Second Temple, as preserved in the Mishnah. All the openings were 20 amah high and 10 amah wide (Tractate Middot 2,3), while the main opening of the temple was 40 amah high and 20 amah wide (Tractate Middot 4,1).

The model is carved with three parallel rows of doorposts on each side of the entrance and three parallel lintels above, an arrangement that creates a triple rectangular doorframe, with each frame set back from the one in front. The uppermost lintel is separate from the two lower doorframes and reaches the roof, precisely the way in which the doorways of the First Temple and the Second Temple were organized (see Chapter 8, and Tractate Middot 3,7). About a thousand years separate the Khirbet Qeiyafa temple model and the Second Temple, yet both reflect a similar aesthetic concept relating to two aspects of the entrance: the ratio of height to width and the design of the recessed doorframes.

Two small holes were drilled in the façade of the model at the sides of the entrance, apparently for fastening a door. This may have been of wood and hence has not survived, but when closed it would have concealed any image or symbol of the god kept inside. A parallel from precisely this period is known from a Philistine temple at Tell Qasile, where, in the holy of holies, at the foot of the altar, a clay temple model was found containing two naked goddesses.[15] The Tell Qasile model has two door hinges, one on each side, so the goddesses could have been hidden from view.

Just below the roof of the Khirbet Qeiyafa temple model was a row of seven protruding rectangles; four were preserved in their entirety and three scars attest to missing ones. These rectangles, grooved with lines to create three small protrusions, clearly represent the ends of wooden beams that supported the building's roof. As soon as we understood that, we realized we had the key to the riddle of the grooved circles on the roof of the clay temple model: these, too, apparently represent wooden beams that extended the length of the structure, their narrow ends protruding from the façade.

Such decoration of grooved rectangles beneath the roof is well known in Classical Greek temple architecture, where they are referred to as "triglyphs." The temple model from Khirbet Qeiyafa indicates that these architectural features were known in the Middle East by the beginning of the 10th century BCE, some 400 years earlier. This revolutionizes our understanding of the development of public architecture, as it is evidence that architectural elements in the East influenced Classical Greek architecture.

This design of an opening with recessed frames is known from a number of biblical period ivories that feature representations of architecture (Fig. 61 and Pl. xxiv), for instance from Samaria, capital of the Kingdom of Israel, and three other capital cities in Mesopotamia—Arslan Tash, Khorsabad, and Nineveh. They take the form of the well-known motif, dated to the 9th–8th centuries BCE, of a woman looking out of a window, which is reflected in the Bible in descriptions of Sisera's mother and of Queen Jezebel, wife of Ahab, peering from a window (Judges 5:28; 2 Kings 9:30). Since these artifacts are made from a precious raw material (ivory) and were found in palaces in capital cities, the women depicted would have been royalty or, according to other suggestions, a goddess peering from the window of a temple.[16] Archaeologists have discussed these ivories extensively, in particular the window balustrade, which consists of columns in the form of a palm tree, as an actual balustrade of this form has been found at Ramat Rachel, near Jerusalem, in excavations conducted by Yohanan Aharoni. From our point of view, it is the window itself—generally ignored in these discussions—that is of greatest interest as it consists of an opening with multiple recessed window frames. A similar window is portrayed on a limestone stela found near

Fig. 61 Carved ivory found in excavations of a palace at the Aramean city of Arslan Tash (Hadātu) in northern Mesopotamia, dated to the 9th century BCE. The carving portrays a woman looking through a square window decorated with three lines of frames receding inward toward the opening. Similar ivories have been discovered at the palaces of kings of Israel at Samaria, and in the palaces of Assyrian kings.

Figs 62, 63 Carved stone stela from the vicinity of Kourion in Cyprus (left). The window, with a balustrade, is surrounded by with three sets of frames receding inward. The entrance to the burial chamber of an Iron Age Phoenician tomb at Tamassos in Cyprus (right; shown at similar scale for comparison) is also decorated with three rows of doorframes set back from each other. Beneath the roof were protruding rectangles, representing the ends of the wooden roof beams.

the site of Kourion in Cyprus, carved with an inscription and dated to the 8th century BCE.[17] Unfortunately, the inscription is largely obliterated and so cannot help in understanding this artifact. The closest parallel to the model from Khirbet Qeiyafa is the entrance to a burial chamber of an elaborate Phoenician tomb at Tamassos, also in Cyprus, dating to the 7th century BCE. It also consists of three recessed frames and has rectangles representing wooden beams below the roof, though at Tamassos these were not grooved.[18] Such entrances—one in a temple— were also found at Tell Tayinat in southern Turkey, in a level dated to the 8th century BCE.[19]

The model from Khirbet Qeiyafa thus fits squarely within the pattern of luxury architecture of the biblical period in the Levant and has parallels in the façades of temples, palaces, and tombs. In-depth research undertaken together with Madeleine Mumcuoglu has gathered numerous other examples, some earlier than the biblical period and some later. To date, we know that these entrances appear in temples of the Middle Bronze Age in the 18th–17th centuries BCE at Mari on the Euphrates River in Mesopotamia and at Alalakh in southeastern Turkey.[20] Entrances to buildings with recessed doorframes can be identified from Mesopotamia in even more ancient periods, from the end of the prehistoric period onward.

In the floor of our temple model, opposite the entrance and near its rear wall, is a small rectangular depression. It would have been possible to insert a base with something attached to it here, perhaps a statue or a symbol of a divinity. On the exterior rear side of the model, roughly at mid-height, are two holes, which could have served to fasten the model to a wooden cabinet or a wall, or to secure an object placed inside.

As noted, stone temple models are exceedingly rare; only two examples are known from the Middle Bronze Age (18th–17th centuries BCE), from excavations at Byblos in Lebanon. These were found in temples and were intended to contain statues of gods. The stone artifact is thus not merely a model of a temple, it would have served as an actual house for the god and was the "holy of holies" of the cult in building C10 west of the southern gate of Khirbet Qeiyafa.

A final item connected with temple models at Khirbet Qeiyafa is a pottery fragment found in the upper surface layer in Area C, above the South Gate. Unlike the other three temple models, which were closed boxes, this belongs to a different category of objects, usually referred to as stands. The fragment is thick and flat and decorated with engraving and appliqué (Fig. 64) consisting of three lengthwise strips. On the lowest one is a row of three engraved rectangles, and to the right of them is the upper portion of a schematic palm tree, or perhaps a column with a palm-shaped capital. Large rectangular pottery stands dating to the

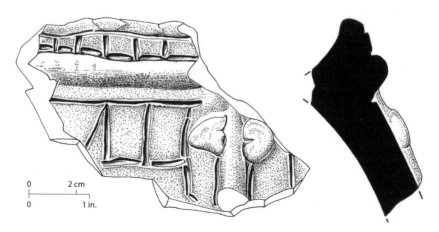

0   2 cm

0   1 in.

Fig. 64 Fragment of a pottery stand decorated with the image of a building and a date palm.

10th century BCE in the form of temples are known in Israel, for instance from Taanach in the Jezreel Valley. Our fragment seems to be from such a stand since it is particularly thick and therefore cannot be a pottery vessel, and it is also straight rather than rounded like most pottery vessels. As the top is not broken, we can surmise that the three decorated strips represent elements of the roof: the engraved rectangles are the narrow end of the wooden beams, similar to the triglyphs carved on the stone model, and the middle band appears to be the lintel, projecting slightly above the opening. The column capital in the form of a palm tree is therefore also in a logical position to support the roof. Columns of similar design appear on a temple model from Tell el-Far'ah North, on one from Jordan of unknown provenance, and on several from the repository pit at Tel Yavneh.[21]

In summary, three of the four temple models at Khirbet Qeiyafa were found near the southern gate, two on the original floor of a cult room and the third, the stand fragment, a surface find. The two temple models found together offer an interesting contrast. One is of clay with decorations reflecting Canaanite temple architecture of the Late Bronze Age, while the second is carved from stone with decoration reflecting the luxury architecture of the Iron Age. This neatly encapsulates the nature of Khirbet Qeiyafa as a site preserving elements of an earlier period alongside ones that become typical in the next.

These two models also raise many questions about their function. One possible explanation is that they were study kits for priests in training; another is that they stood permanently in the cult room and housed a statue or symbol of a god, similar to the ark in synagogues in which the Bible is kept. We know that temple models housed statues of gods from the clay example found at Ashkelon, which contained a bronze figurine of a calf covered with silver.[22] In that case, they were not mere models, but sacred objects that housed gods. A third possibility is that they were portable shrines that could be moved from place to place as required, for instance carried in a religious procession and displayed to an audience or even taken onto the battlefield in time of conflict. It is quite probable that this is the type of object that the Bible refers to as the "Ark of the Lord," which was carried into battle on several occasions. This possibility is particularly interesting since it allows us to connect the objects with a key biblical tradition.

ARKS OF GODS (BY Y. GARFINKEL AND S. GANOR)

The Bible uses the terms ark in various contexts: "Ark of the Testimony," "Ark of the Covenant of the Lord," "Ark of the Covenant," "Ark of the Lord," and "Ark of the God of Israel." The term "Ark of the Testimony" appears in stories relating to the wanderings of the Children of Israel in the desert following the exodus from Egypt (for example, Exodus 25:10; Numbers 4:5). This is a portable box described as being made of boards of acacia wood covered with gold, in which were placed the Tablets of the Covenant that Moses brought down from Mount Sinai after remaining there 40 days and 40 nights without eating or drinking. On these stone tablets the finger of God had engraved the Ten Commandments. The term "Ark of the Covenant of the Lord" appears in a parallel tradition in the Bible concerning the giving of the law at Mount Sinai (Deuteronomy 10:8). The written evidence indicates that the book of Exodus uses the term "Ark of the Testimony", while Deuteronomy uses the term "Ark of the Covenant of the Lord." The tradition that the two Tablets of the Covenant were kept inside the ark recurs in the book of Kings, which describes the ark in Solomon's Temple: "There was nothing in the ark but the two stone tablets that Moses placed there" (1 Kings 8:9). None of the other numerous references to the ark mention the Tablets of the Covenant.

The book of Joshua, which recounts the entry of Israel into the Promised Land, uses the term "Ark of the Covenant of the Lord" or a shortened version, "Ark of the Lord" (Joshua 3:1–8), and places it in various cities. In David's day, the ark is brought to Jerusalem and moved from place to place until, with the construction of Solomon's Temple, it was installed in the Holy of Holies there. From this point on, for the hundreds of years that the Kingdom of Judah and the First Temple stood, the Bible does not mention the ark, except for a prophecy of Jeremiah referring to the "Ark of the Covenant of the Lord" (Jeremiah 3:16).

The ark appears in various contexts of war: in the conquest of Jericho it is carried by the priests who circumambulate the city once each day for the first six days and seven times on the seventh day, until the walls of the city miraculously collapse (Joshua 6:4–11); it features in the story of the concubine at Gibeah and the war against the tribe of Benjamin (Judges 20:27); in the battle of Ebenezer, the ark was taken as booty by the Philistines (1 Samuel 4:5); it is also present in King Saul's battle against the Philistines (1 Samuel 14:18) and during Absalom's rebellion when David left Jerusalem (2 Samuel 15:24–25). Not only does the ark accompany the people in time of war, it also acts against Dagon, the god of Ashdod, decapitating and amputating the hands of the statue and leaving them upon the threshold of the temple (1 Samuel 5:4).

The tradition of the ark is characterized by supernatural events. In the time of Joshua, when the priests carrying the ark stood in the waters of the Jordan River, the stream was stopped and the people miraculously entered the Land of Israel. The walls of Jericho collapsed after the ark was carried around them for seven days. Taken as booty by the Philistines, the ark was moved among their cities: Ashdod, Gath, and Ekron, causing serious damage to each. After it was finally returned to Beth Shemesh, in the Sorek Valley, the ark caused death (1 Samuel 6:19) and was therefore sent to Kiriath-jearim. When David brought the Ark of the Lord to Jerusalem, it slipped from the cart carrying it. The man who caught it momentarily to prevent it from falling was killed on the spot by God (2 Samuel 6:6–7). The emphasis on the miraculous aspect of the ark is indicative of the nature of the traditions that surrounded it—more so than for any other cult object mentioned in the Bible.

Among these traditions, three characteristics are shared. The first is that it is an object that appears in public situations of paramount importance, and is featured in connection with the leaders Moses, Joshua, Eli and his sons the priests, Samuel, Saul, David, and Solomon. The ark thus differs from other cult objects mentioned in the Bible called "teraphim." Although we do not know exactly what these were, they occur mainly in the context of home and family, and are mentioned in relation to women, for example, Rachel, the wife of Jacob, and Michal, the daughter of King Saul (Genesis 31:19–35; 1 Samuel 19:13–16).

The second characteristic is that the ark is a portable cult object. Nearly every reference in the Bible describes it being moved from one place to another. Once installed in a permanent building in its final location in the Temple, it disappears from history. The third characteristic of the traditions surrounding the ark is that it appears in connection with warfare. Moreover, the Bible preserves an ancient prayer connected to it in war: "Whenever the ark set out, Moses said: Rise up, Lord! May your enemies be scattered; may your foes flee before you. Whenever it came to rest, he said, Return, Lord, to the countless thousands of Israel." (Numbers 10:35–36).

As noted earlier, modern research cannot ignore traditions of a legendary nature merely because they contain supernatural elements. Instead it must seek to uncover the historical kernel in these traditions and examine the extent to which they coincide with the findings of archaeological research. Such analysis of the traditions connected with the ark lead us to conclude that it cannot have been too large and heavy, otherwise it would not have been possible to carry it from place to place. On the other hand, it was clearly a key cult object, involved in public contexts at pan-tribal and royal cultic centers, and so cannot have been a small, insignificant object, but must have been prominent through its special form and perhaps color. The stone model from Khirbet Qeiyafa can be seen to fulfill these characteristics. Relatively large, at 35 cm (14 in.) high, it was carefully carved in stone, with receding doorframes and triglyphs, and painted red for emphasis, which would have made it stand out from its surroundings. It was found in a cult room at the entrance to which was a stone basin, suggesting careful washing and purification prior to entry.

It seems to us that the stone temple model from Khirbet Qeiyafa is a concrete archaeological example of the phenomenon known from the Bible as an ark. This is, of course, not the biblical Ark itself, but another type of object that existed during the same period, consisting of a closed box in which the symbol of the god was placed. The socket in the stone model from Khirbet Qeiyafa indicates that a statue or symbol of a god stood inside it. It is portable; it has a particularly thick base, which is wider than the rest of the model, giving it great stability. On the back and one of the sides are holes that could have been used to fasten the object for transport. In terms of chronology, the model from Khirbet Qeiyafa fits the periods during which such objects appear frequently in the biblical narrative: the days of Saul and David, in the second half of the 11th century and beginning of the 10th century BCE. Contrary to earlier biblical episodes involving the ark—the time of the wanderings in the desert, the period of Joshua, and the campaign in Philistia—which are characterized by numerous miracles and active involvement of the ark in political events, the later traditions lack such legendary aspects, with one exception: the punishment of individuals who touch the ark without authorization.

The stone model found at Khirbet Qeiyafa is thus an "ark," a small portable temple which was kept in a central cult place and which could be moved to the battlefield in time of need. Perhaps the presence of this object at Khirbet Qeiyafa, on the border with Philistia, is no coincidence; it could have been taken down to the Elah Valley during battle to encourage the warriors and strengthen their resolve.

A CLAY FIGURINE: TOY, VOODOO DOLL, OR LOCAL GOD?

The head of a male figurine made of clay (Fig. 65) was found in Area A, the highest part of the site, in earth layers associated with biblical period buildings in an area severely disturbed by Second Temple and Byzantine period construction. Does this artifact relate to the 10th century BCE city? Until proven otherwise, it would appear to be the case. It is relatively large, 5 cm (2 in.) high, very carefully made and well executed. The head itself is not broken, and seems originally to have been attached to a body or to a cultic stand, which has not been preserved. The upper part of the head is flat and straight, with a series of small incisions surrounding it, and the ears are perforated for earrings. It is interesting that a bust with a row of incisions on its upper part and ending in a straight line was found in excavations at Tel Kinneret, though the facial details are otherwise entirely different from those on our example.[23]

On the day the Khirbet Qeiyafa figurine head was found, two important scholars were working with us: Silvia Schroer of the University of Bern, who specializes in the iconography of the ancient Near East, and David Ben-Shlomo, who a few years ago wrote a comprehensive book on Philistine iconography. Both noted that the artifact is unusual in form and not reminiscent of other figurines then known in the biblical period.

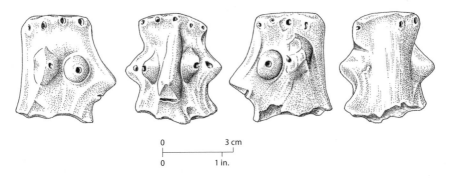

0   3 cm

0   1 in.

Fig. 65 Head of a clay male figurine discovered in Area A in fills dated to Iron Age IIA.

The figurine could be taken as evidence of a cult of idols in Judah during the period of the monarchy, but other interpretations are also possible. Archaeologist Peter Ucko, who examined the use of figurines in traditional cultures, noted that they served a variety of purposes in antiquity: some represented divine images while others were children's toys, objects for magical practices, or educational or instructional items.[24] Thus, not every figurine found in an excavation can be regarded as evidence for cult activity. On the other hand, one cannot rule out that at least part of the population practiced a cult of idols at the site, particularly if slaves and servants of Canaanite or Philistine origin lived there. If so, the head may represent a divine image of some sort. Such objects could reach the city by way of traders or travelers. For our purposes, however, it is significant that in the three cult rooms excavated at Khirbet Qeiyafa, no human or animal images were found, setting them apart from cult buildings of the Philistines and Canaanites. A petrographic examination of this figurine will be carried out to determine the source of the clay from which it was made, which will indicate whether it was created by a local potter or was imported from another part of the country.

Then in 2012 two similar pottery heads were uncovered at the Judean temple of Motza (Tel Moza), dated to about a century later than the fortified city of Khirbet Qeiyafa.[25] All three heads have similar iconographic characteristics: they are large, solid, well made, are flat at the top, and have detailed facial features. The eyes were made in two stages: first a rounded pellet of clay was applied to the head, and this was then pierced to represent the iris.

KHIRBET QEIYAFA AND CULT

The abundant information relating to cult at Khirbet Qeiyafa was gathered from different parts of the site, in both public and private contexts, and includes a range of objects made of various raw materials: pottery, limestone, and basalt. Cult activity at the site was not carried out in special buildings separated from the other parts of the city, as is the case with Canaanite and Philistine temples, but within buildings that apparently served everyday functions of living or administration. Nonetheless, it is possible to divide the cult activity at the site into two main spheres: the two cult rooms next to the gates adjacent to the gate piazzas represent public cult, while the room in building C3 reflects domestic cult. Of the two cult rooms next to the gates, the one near the southern gate stands out. Here, installations not known from the other rooms were present: a basin at the entrance, a *bamah*, and an adjacent storage room. The room also contained unique objects including two temple models, which are among the most beautiful and fascinating examples encountered to date in Israel.

It is important to note the absence of anthropomorphic or zoomorphic figurines in the cult rooms where public cult activity was practiced, and that no figurines were found in the areas where large public gatherings took place. Two temple models and the basalt altar were not decorated with human images, though we do not know if figurines or symbols of gods were kept inside them. In any event, the discoveries in the cult rooms at Khirbet Qeiyafa are significant for the absence of human images, which are present at Canaanite and Philistine sites. Furthermore, as mentioned above, at Tel Rehov in the northern Kingdom of Israel, several clay figurines were found and images of naked goddesses appeared on a temple model.

The finds from Khirbet Qeiyafa provide a window to understanding the development of religion in the Kingdom of Judah. Over the course of time this became a cult that was both monotheistic and one that did not employ images; in these two respects it was entirely different from the polytheistic world of the ancient Near East, where multiple gods were revered whose images were represented in works of art. It is an extremely complex topic and researchers have proposed various theories to explain this development. However, information was lacking from the phase of the establishment of the Kingdom of Judah, and there was therefore no solid basis for the different proposals. Now, for the first time, Khirbet Qeiyafa provides a starting point for research to reach an understanding of the processes involved.

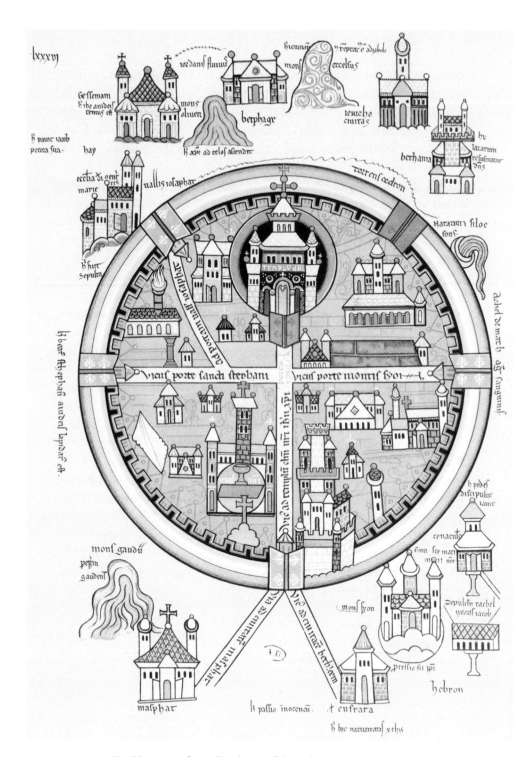

Fig. 66 A copy of a medieval map of the Holy Land, with the city of Jerusalem and the Temple of Solomon at the center.

7

DAVID'S KINGDOM

KHIRBET QEIYAFA AND BIBLICAL SHAARIM

Having guided the reader through the features of the site and presented details of the various discoveries, the time has come to assemble the body of data and create a clear picture of the overall significance of the results of the excavation. The first aspect of the city that we shall set out to clarify is its identification. Khirbet Qeiyafa is an Arabic place name that means "the ruin of Qeiyafa," but we propose that the biblical name of this city was Shaaraim.[1] In doing so, we enter an area of research known as historical geography, a field that attempts to identify place names appearing in ancient sources with archaeological sites.

Shaaraim is mentioned three times in the Bible. The first time is in the list of cities of the Tribe of Judah. For the Shephelah region the list includes the following cities: Jarmouth, Adulam, Socoh, Azekah, Shaaraim, Adithaim, Gederah, and Gederothaim (Joshua 15:35–36). As Shaaraim comes after Socoh and Azekah, it seems reasonable to infer that it is a city located in vicinity of the Elah Valley. The Bible attributes this list to the days of Joshua, in other words the 12th-century BCE transition between the Late Bronze Age and the Iron Age. However, based on archaeological findings and the description of the period in the book of Judges, the settlement pattern in Judah at that time comprised tens of small, scattered villages, so dating this list to Iron Age I is not compatible with modern research. The list itself contains no information that would allow us to date it, but in general it appears to reflect the settlement map of Iron Age II.

The name Shaaraim occurs a second time in the Bible in the story of the fight between David and Goliath. This took place in the Elah Valley, between Socoh and Azekah, and after David had killed Goliath, the

Philistines fled along the road to Shaaraim (1 Samuel 17:52). Shaaraim is thus clearly connected with memories of David, dating to the end of the 11th and the early 10th century BCE, and, as in Joshua, this tradition again places biblical Shaaraim near Socoh and Azekah. Shaaraim should thus be sought near the Elah Valley.

The third reference to Shaaraim appears in the list of the Tribe of Simeon in the Negev (1 Chronicles 4:31–32), which might lead us to think that there were two cities called Shaaraim, one in the vicinity of the Elah Valley and the other in the Negev. But in fact the interpretation of this list is quite complex. There are three different versions of the lists of cities in the territory of the Tribe of Simeon, one in Joshua 15 (within the list of cities of the Tribe of Judah), another in Joshua 18 (where two separate lists were combined), and the third in 1 Chronicles 4 (where again two separate lists were combined). Each list differs slightly or significantly from the others. The longest version is in Joshua 15 and includes 36 place names, but the total at the end of the list indicates only 29 cities. The lack of correspondence between the number of names in the list and the total number given, as well as the recurrence of a city called Hazor several times, attests to copyists' errors over the generations. The list in Joshua 18 refers to 14 cities by name, but at the end of the list the total is given as 13. In 1 Chronicles a short list of 13 cities is presented, but instead of the numerical total at the end as in the other two lists, a peculiar notation appears: "these were their cities up to the reign of David."

The name Shaaraim in the list in Chronicles is replaced by Shilhim in Joshua 15 and by Sharuhen in Joshua 19. So which city should appear in the list of the Tribe of Simeon: Shaaraim, Shilhim, or Sharuhen? Numerous scholars have examined this problem. The phrase "these were their cities up to the reign of David," occurs after the name Shaaraim only in the list of 1 Chronicles; five other cities then follow. The two parallel lists have numerical totals instead. What does this mean? It seems to us that the name of the city of Shaaraim and the following phrase "these were their cities up to the reign of David" belong together, and perhaps both were erroneously copied here from another source that has not been preserved. Only Shaaraim in the list of the Tribe of Simeon relates to David, not Sharuhen or Shilhim mentioned in the other lists.

Shaaraim is mentioned in the Bible twice in the vicinity of the Elah Valley; Khirbet Qeiyafa is on a ridge of hills overlooking the Elah Valley from the north. Various proposals placing Shaaraim near Tell es-Safi or in other locations far from the Elah Valley ignore these two traditions positioning it near Socoh and Azekah. The Bible also includes two references to Shaaraim in connection with the young David, before he became king; Khirbet Qeiyafa is dated by radiocarbon to the end of the 11th century BCE, the time of King David. Proposals to locate Shaaraim at other sites suffer from the problem that research has not yet demonstrated that they were settled during the relevant period. Shaaraim does not occur in the traditions connected with the time of other kings such as Hezekiah or Josiah. Finally, Shaaraim means "two gates," and, indeed, at Khirbet Qeiyafa two gates were discovered, one in the west of the city and a second in the south. So both information from our excavations at Khirbet Qeiyafa and biblical traditions led us to identify Khirbet Qeiyafa as biblical Shaaraim.

This view was accepted by the late Anson Rainey, one of the foremost experts in the field of historical geography, who dealt extensively with problems related to the identification of the biblical sites. In reponse to our proposal, Nadav Na'aman of Tel Aviv University claimed that the appearance of two gates at Khirbet Qeiyafa is not necessarily conclusive in identifying it as the city of Shaaraim.[2] The element in the name Shaaraim that indicates something that is dual (so, "two gates) is common in place names in the Bible that do not necessarily convey the sense of a pair. According to this view, a city with a single gate could also be called Shaaraim. However, our identification rests on two other important considerations: the location of the site and the period of its existence, which are consistent with the data concerning Shaaraim in the Bible. So our interpretation does not rely solely on the name of the site referring to two gates. In addition, in the opinion of Edith Doron of the Department of Linguistics of the Hebrew University of Jerusalem, a distinction should be made between names in which the dual ending does not reflect a clear linguistic doubling, such as Yerushalayim (Jerusalem's name in Hebrew), Adorayim, or Ephraim, and names where it is meaningful. Names of places such as Beerotaim ("two wells"), Shaaraim ("two gates"), or Machanaim ("two camps") certainly stem from descriptions of features associated with those particular sites.[3] In any case, even if a city with a single gate might be called Shaaraim, how much more appropriate would it be for one with two gates?

Turning now to our excavations and the site of Khirbet Qeiyafa itself, we will summarize our findings and present the implications for our understanding of the historical kingdom of David and for our perception of King David as a historical figure.

WHAT HAVE WE LEARNT AT KHIRBET QEIYAFA?

Khirbet Qeiyafa is located at the western edge of the upper Shephelah and controls the entrance to the Elah Valley, the main route from the coastal plain to the hill country and the cities of Jerusalem and Hebron. The city was founded on bedrock rather than being a multi-layered tell with underlying remains of a Canaanite city of the Late Bronze Age. This raises the question of why this location suddenly became important at the end of the 11th and beginning of the 10th century BCE, the date of the site established by radiocarbon dating of olive pits found there.

A very impressive casemate wall surrounds the city, which incorporates megaliths weighing up to 8 tonnes and is pierced by two gates, one in the west and the other in the south. The gates are of identical proportions and have four chambers each. This is the only known example in First Temple period Israel or Judah of a settlement with two gates. The houses at Khirbet Qeiyafa adjoin the city wall and are incorporated into it, with the wall's casemate chambers forming the back rooms of the buildings. Such distinctive urban planning is known at four additional sites: Beth Shemesh, Tell en-Nasbeh, Tell Beit Mirsim, and Beersheba, all sites dated to Iron Age II and located in the southern part of modern-day Israel, in the Kingdom of Judah. In terms of date, Khirbet Qeiyafa is the oldest of these, indicating that this planning concept took shape at the end of the 11th century BCE. Casemate walls are also known at northern sites, such as Hazor and Gezer, however there they are freestanding and the dwellings do not attach to them.

The range of locally produced pottery vessels at Khirbet Qeiyafa is limited, with a small number of vessel types, including shallow bowls and cooking pots, deep cooking pots, simple juglets and jugs, strainer jugs, baking trays, and storage jars. The last generally have finger impressions on one or more of the handles—in total 693 such handles were found.[4] Petrographic examination of the clay indicates that these jars were produced in the vicinity of the site. Most of the vessels found at the site are undecorated; rarely, bowls or jugs are red slipped, and occasionally the red slip is randomly hand burnished. Thousands of animal bones were found, indicating the diet of the inhabitants, including goat, sheep, and cattle; no pig bones were found. Nearly every house contained a baking tray, a shallow bowl that was placed over an open fire with the dough baked on its rough outer side.

Objects that had to be imported from various distances include Ashdod Ware from Philistia, basalt vessels from the eastern Galilee or the Golan Heights, copper from the Aravah, tin for bronze production possibly from Turkey, gold, alabaster vessels and scarab seals from Egypt, and juglets of Cypriot ware. Such a range of commercial contacts all converging at Khirbet Qeiyafa is evidence of the city having been a central place with a developed economy.

The inscription on the ostracon found at the site with five lines comprising 70 letters is, in the view of epigrapher Haggai Misgav, written in Hebrew, an opinion accepted by numerous scholars. This is the longest inscription known from the 12th–9th centuries BCE in Israel, and the oldest known Hebrew inscription.

Cult rooms were uncovered in three buildings at Khirbet Qeiyafa, in which were found various items of equipment, but no human or animal figurines. Other cult rooms in dwellings are known from the 11th–10th centuries BCE at Tel Qiri, Megiddo, and Lachish, where no human or animal figurines were found either.

The city was destroyed suddenly, as demonstrated by the hundreds of artifacts found scattered upon the floors and in the collapse of the buildings—pottery, stone and metal implements, scarabs, and seals. The question arises: who destroyed the site? Following this destruction, the site was abandoned and was not resettled until the end of the Persian period. Why did the inhabitants not re-establish the site, and why did it not it become a multi-layered tell?

WHY IS THE SITE OF KHIRBET QEIYAFA SO SPECIAL?
How can we interpret these various features at Khirbet Qeiyafa? To put the site in context, we shall briefly compare Khirbet Qeiyafa to Canaanite sites of the Late Bronze Age, Philistine sites of Iron Age I, and Iron Age I sites in the hill country (generally referred to as "Israelite settlement sites").

One obvious difference between Khirbet Qeiyafa and Canaanite cities of the Late Bronze Age, particularly those also in the Shephelah such as Gezer and Lachish, is that the latter existed for hundreds of years and stood on the accumulated remains of earlier cities of the Early and Middle Bronze Ages. These were city-states, with palaces and temples as well as domestic dwellings. The large and elaborate temples such as the two found at Lachish are outstanding for the richness of their artifacts. The Late Bronze Age cities show no clear urban planning; they took shape organically over hundreds of years of development. Khirbet Qeiyafa, on the other hand, displays an entirely new urban concept as outlined above, not known at any Canaanite city. Moreover, storage jars in Canaanite cities were not systematically marked with identifying finger impressions on their handles, as was the case at Khirbet Qeiyafa.

There are also significant differences between Khirbet Qeiyafa and Philistine settlements of the 12th–10th centuries BCE, such as Ashdod, Ashkelon, Ekron, Gath, or Tell Qasile. In Philistia pork was commonly consumed, while baking trays were not used—the opposite of the situation at Khirbet Qeiyafa. Unique iconography including anthropomorphic and animal images is in evidence at Philistine cult sites such as Tell Qasile and Nahal Patish near Gilat in the northern Negev. At Khirbet Qeiyafa, on the other hand, the cult rooms did not contain human or animal images. And in Philistia it was not common to mark jar handles with identifying impressions. Diet and food preparation, on the one hand, and the nature of cult practice on the other, clearly indicate that the inhabitants of Khirbet Qeiyafa were not Philistines.

Comparison with Israelite settlement sites also emphasizes the uniqueness of Khirbet Qeiyafa. Hundreds of such settlement sites are known in the hill country dated to the 12th and 11th centuries BCE. Archaeological excavations have been conducted at some, including Gilo and Izbet Sartah. Relatively small sites, generally 3–5 dunams (1 dunam = 1,000 square meters) in area, they are rural in nature, without a surrounding wall and gates. Khirbet Qeiyafa, with an area of 23 dunams and massive fortifications, is very different from a site of this type.

From this brief survey it is clear that the site of Khirbet Qeiyafa marks a new development. Its closest parallels in terms of fortifications, urban planning, size, and impressed storage jar handles appear only later, in the 9th and 8th centuries BCE, in the Kingdom of Judah, at cities such as Beth Shemesh, Tell en-Nasbeh, Tell Beit Mirsim, and Beersheba. It would seem, therefore, that Khirbet Qeiyafa also belongs to the Kingdom of

Judah. The radiocarbon dates of the site fall in the first third of the 10th century BCE, placing it at the beginning of the period of the monarchy in Judah, the time of King David.

Despite archaeological excavations at many sites in Judah over several decades, very little is known about these early phases in the 10th–9th centuries BCE. Since the pottery from Khirbet Qeiyafa is associated with the first phase of the establishment of the Kingdom of Judah, the question then is, at which other sites and in which settlement layers have similar vessels been found?

Sherds resembling those from Khirbet Qeiyafa were also found at Khirbet ed-Dawwara, 12 km (7½ miles) northeast of Jerusalem. Israel Finkelstein excavated at the site for two seasons in 1985–86, and a single settlement phase dated to the 11th and 10th centuries BCE was uncovered.[5] The significance of the site was not recognized, and in the *New Encyclopedia of Archaeological Excavations in the Holy Land*, it was summarized as follows: "The historical circumstances that motivated the foundation of a settlement of this particular shape at this unusual location or those that provoked its abandonment one century later, have not been clarified by the excavations; neither has any progress been made in identifying the site."[6] While the preservation at Khirbet ed-Dawwara is not good since bedrock is very close to the surface and large parts of the site are missing, remains of a casemate wall consisting of two parallel walls can be seen, with a thicker outer wall and a thinner inner one, with houses attached to it. This is the same urban planning concept as known from Khirbet Qeiyafa, Beth Shemesh, Tell en-Nasbeh, Tell Beit Mirsim, and Beersheba. The appearance of similar pottery at the two sites indicates that they are contemporary, and it is noteworthy that both were constructed on bedrock rather than on the remains of preceding Canaanite cities. The location of the two sites is also interesting: Khirbet ed-Dawwara is half a day's walk from Jerusalem to the northeast, while Khirbet Qeiyafa is about a day's walk to the southwest. Is this a coincidence? Could these two sites represent the urban core of the emerging Kingdom of Judah?

Based on a comparison of pottery, it is clear that at the time when Khirbet Qeiyafa and Khirbet ed-Dawwara were already fortified, the village settlements in the Shephelah of Judah and in the Negev remained unfortified—for example, Stratum 4 at Tell Beth Shemesh, Stratum IV at

Tel Batash, Stratum XII at Arad, or Stratum VII at Beersheba. Analysis of the pottery likewise shows that during this phase many sites, such as Lachish or Tell Beit Mirsim, were not settled. It appears, therefore, that Khirbet Qeiyafa represents the southwestern border of the urban core of the Kingdom of Judah during this period. This urban core was initially a relatively limited area in the hill region and a small portion of the Shephelah, and should be viewed as the ancient historical nucleus of the kingdom. Gradually, in later phases, at the end of the 10th and during the 9th and 8th centuries BCE, fortified cities were established at more southerly sites such as Lachish, Tell Beit Mirsim, Beersheba, Arad, and Tel Ira. Clearly, the Kingdom of Judah developed by degrees, over hundreds of years, and an urban society did not suddenly emerge and extend from Jerusalem to the Negev.[7] The great challenge for archaeological research is to establish precisely when the first fortified settlements were established at Lachish, Tell Beit Mirsim, Beersheba, and Arad. Only in this way will it be possible to reconstruct the settlement, demographic, and economic history of the kingdom with any degree of certainty.

CENTRAL PLACE THEORY AND THE EARLY KINGDOM OF JUDAH

In discussing the settlement pattern of the Kingdom of Judah, particularly during the phase of its establishment, it should first be determined when the pattern made up of hundreds of small villages typical of Iron Age I begins to give way to one that includes fortified sites, urban planning, and public administration which is typical of Iron Age II. In order to speak of a kingdom, the existence of a number of basic features of social organization must be demonstrated, including territorial continuity, fortified centers of control, a hierarchy of settlements, and a road network.

Settlement analysis uses tools from the field of settlement geography, and the two most important characteristics for study are the size of settlements and their locations relative to one another. A simple analytical model suited to the analysis of ancient settlement patterns is Central Place Theory, proposed by the German geographer Walter Christaller in 1933.[8] One of the foundations of this theory is that the basic limitation on any spatial organization is mobility. Before the invention of motor transport, movement was by foot or using pack animals. The distance that can be comfortably covered in a day is not more than 30 km (18½ miles), and this dictates the nature of settlement distribution. If we take an example from another period, khans were established along the road between Cairo and Damascus during the Mamluk period on the basis of this constraint. A further limitation is related to the nature of a society's economic organization, which, prior to the industrial age, was predominantly agricultural. In order to be near the fields being cultivated, a settlement pattern would naturally develop consisting of a large number of small villages with a small number of urban centers between. Each urban center had its agrarian hinterland, and mutual relations developed between the two. The hinterland could provide the city with food and manpower, while the urban center could provide villagers around it with its specialist products such as metal tools, pottery, religious and legal services, etc. Two urban centers could not coexist too closely to one another as they would be in competition.

The settlement pattern of the five Philistine cities during the biblical period illustrates this principle well. Three Philistine centers, Ashdod, Ashkelon, and Gaza, were located on the Mediterranean coast 30 km (18½ miles) apart, and maintained settlement stability through the Iron Age. On the other hand, the two other Philistine cities, Gath and Ekron in the Shephelah of Judah, are only 10 km (6 miles) apart, a proximity that did not allow both to develop into large urban centers simultaneously. Thus, as outlined in Chapter 2, when Ekron was the important center in the 12th and 11th centuries BCE, Gath was relatively small. In the 10th and 9th centuries, however, Gath was the major urban center, while it was Ekron that was a relatively small settlement. In the 8th and 7th centuries BCE, following the destruction of Gath, Ekron developed into a large city once more.[9] The two cities competed for the same agricultural hinterland and so, at any given time only one of them was able to develop into a large urban center.[10] Christaller's model neatly explains that the settlement history of the different Philistine centers is a function of their location in relation to one another. Another example is the settlement pattern in Judah at the end of the 8th century BCE, which consisted of six main administrative centers located a day's walk apart: Jerusalem, Beth Shemesh, Lachish, Hebron, Beersheba, and Arad.[11]

Settlement processes generally take place over the course of hundreds of years, and it is possible to propose such gradual development in the case of the Kingdom of Judah. We should look at all possible sources of data at our disposal and not dismiss one or another in advance. If there is geographical logic in the biblical tradition concerning settlement in a given period, such as territorial continuity, fortified centers of control, and a network of roads, this should be accepted as reflecting historical memory. Bearing in mind all these considerations, four phases may be defined in the development of settlement in the early Kingdom of Judah (Fig. 67).

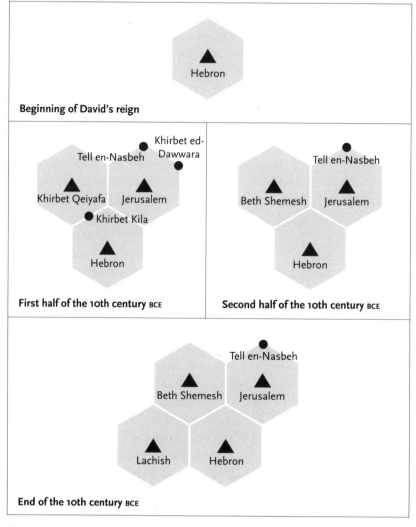

Fig. 67 Pattern of settlement and main sites in the ancient Kingdom of Judah, from its founding until the end of the 10th century BCE.

THE FIRST PHASE: DAVID IN HEBRON
(END OF THE 11TH CENTURY BCE)

According to the Bible, David was crowned in Hebron, and only in the seventh year of his reign did he move to Jerusalem. Hebron should therefore be seen as the core from which the Kingdom of Judah developed. Unfortunately, only limited excavation has taken place at Tell Rumeidah, identified as biblical Hebron, and the results have not been published in detail. The presence of the modern city makes survey and excavation difficult, so archaeological research cannot contribute greatly to our understanding of the period of David in the city. In terms of geographical logic, Hebron, situated in the center of Judah, is the ideal location for the capital of the kingdom. It is referred to as a central place in various cultic and political contexts: the Patriarchs (Abraham, Isaac, Jacob, and their wives) are buried here; David sent the elders of Hebron offerings before becoming king; Absalom crowned himself in Hebron; and Abner, the son of Ner, was murdered here. In chronological terms, all of these traditions relate to the period preceding Solomon. It should be noted that Hebron is not mentioned in the Books of Kings, and it appears to have lost its importance with the establishment of Jerusalem as the capital of the kingdom and the construction of the temple there. The only evidence for Hebron's administrative importance in the 8th century BCE is the appearance of its name on *lmlk* jar handles (see box, p. 174). Future excavations may clarify the history of Hebron during the Iron Age.

THE SECOND PHASE: THE BEGINNING OF THE 10TH CENTURY BCE

Toward the beginning of the 10th century BCE, a city was constructed at Khirbet Qeiyafa. From a comparison of the pottery assemblages, it appears that other sites in the Shephelah of Judah were still unwalled villages, such as Stratum 4 at Beth Shemesh, or had not yet been settled, including Lachish. The Bible describes David's conquest of Jerusalem at this time, making it the capital of his kingdom. From this information we can reconstruct a settlement pattern in Judah consisting of three urban centers: Jerusalem, Hebron, and Shaaraim (Khirbet Qeiyafa).

The location of Khirbet Qeiyafa has few advantages, which explains why it did not develop into a multi-layered tell over time, like Lachish or Azekah; instead it was settled for only brief periods. The question then arises why a fortified city was suddenly built at this location and why it

ADMINISTRATION IN THE
KINGDOM OF JUDAH: *LMLK* JARS

In the earliest excavations in the region at the end of the
19th century, a particular type of storage jar was found at several
sites—dark brown in color, with a capacity of approximately
50 liters (around 12 gallons), and four handles. On the handles
were a variety of seal impressions made before firing and
containing the word *lmlk* ("to the king")—hence these are
known as *lmlk* jars. The first letter (a Hebrew *lamed*) is used as a
preposition before the Hebrew word for king, indicating possession
and demonstrating that these jars belonged to the king. More
than 2,000 such handles have been found over the years at many
sites in the Kingdom of Judah, evidence of a developed royal
administration active during the 8th century BCE. In the 7th century
BCE, large storage jars with handles impressed with a rosette are
known. During the Persian period in the 6th–4th centuries BCE,
various types of stamp seals appear on storage jars, referred to
as lion seal impressions, *mẓh* seal impressions, and *yhd* seal
impressions. In the Hellenistic period, in the 3rd–2nd centuries BCE,
a seal impression in the form of a five-pointed star and the word
yršlm (Jerusalem) occur.

As coinage did not exist during the biblical period, taxes in the
kingdom were collected, transported, stored, and redistributed in
the form of agricultural products such as oil, wine, wheat, lentils,
and other crops. Empty vessels were apparently distributed to the
agricultural population and collected when filled, then transferred to
the royal administration. These foodstuffs were later redistributed as
salaries to officials and military personnel.

At Khirbet Qeiyafa in the seven seasons of excavation we found
693 storage jar handles bearing impressions. This phenomenon
recalls the *lmlk*, rosette and other seal impressions on the handles
of storage jars of the biblical, Persian, and Hellenistic periods.
Such systematic marking of storage jars is not coincidental and
is testimony to the development of an administrative mechanism
for collecting taxes in the initial phase of the establishment of a
kingdom in Judah, a custom that then continued over a period of
800 years. This tradition is not found in Canaanite sites, Philistia
or the Kingdom of Israel.

was not resettled following its destruction? One explanation is that the advantages of the site should be looked at in relation to other sites: first, Khirbet Qeiyafa is situated about one day's walk from Jerusalem and one day's walk from Hebron, the two main centers of the Davidic Kingdom in the hill region. Secondly, Khirbet Qeiyafa lies on the main road from the coastal plain to the hill country, to Hebron and to Jerusalem. Thirdly, it marks the western border of the kingdom and is opposite Tell es-Safi, Gath of the Philistines. Indeed, the Bible locates the battle between David and Goliath in the Elah Valley, at the foot of the site.

In order to better understand the significance of the distance between Jerusalem and Khirbet Qeiyafa and the possibilities for movement between the two cities prior to modern transportation, we tested this at first-hand. In mid-December 2010 eight people gathered at 6:30 in the morning at the City of David in Jerusalem and set out on foot for Khirbet Qeiyafa with food and water. We had an accompanying vehicle that would be available should any problems arise. At first, we climbed from the City of David to the old Ottoman railway station and then walked along the train tracks in the Rephaim and Sorek valleys. Near the village of Batir, we had to cross the range of hills to the south to reach the drainage basin that leads to the Elah Valley. Here, security was uncertain and we continued several more kilometers along the Sorek Valley. To compensate for walking the extra distance, we rode in the vehicle for a similar number of kilometers. We also took a 45-minute rest break at Khirbet Hanut, where, incidentally, Christian tradition places the tomb of Goliath. From here we continued to walk without stopping. In the vicinity of Beit Natif, we strayed slightly from our course and descended into the Elah Valley, following it until we could see Khirbet Qeiyafa on its hilltop in the northern part of the valley. At 3:30 in the afternoon, we were on a comfortable course and arrived, tired but satisfied, at the southern gate of Khirbet Qeiyafa.

In geographical terms, when primary centers are located a day's walk from each other, secondary centers develop around them at a distance of half a day's walk. Establishing the capital of the kingdom at Jerusalem resulted in settlements flourishing in the north of the kingdom. Half a day's walk from Jerusalem to the northwest lies Gibeon, and the same to the northeast is Khirbet ed-Dawwara, discussed above. Gibeon is mentioned in the Bible in relation to the time of David and Solomon

(2 Samuel 2:13; 2 Samuel 20:8; 1 Kings 3:5), and in the inscription of the Egyptian king Shoshenq or Shishak describing his military campaign to Israel around 920 BCE.

Half a day's walk from both Khirbet Qeiyafa and Hebron is Khirbet Kila, identified with biblical Keilah. Keilah is referred to as an important site in the time of David and could, like Khirbet ed-Dawwara or Gibeon, function as a secondary site in the kingdom. Excavation of the site would obtain information about the settlement, its nature ,and size during the 10th century BCE. Likewise, there was probably an important site midway between Jerusalem and Khirbet Qeiyafa at the same date. Perhaps this was Kiriath-jearim, referred to in David's time in connection with the Ark (1 Samuel 7) and apparently also in the Shishak inscription. In 10th-century BCE Judah there were certainly small villages and farmsteads that have not been identified or correctly dated by archaeological surveys. The reason for this is that formerly the pottery types characteristic of the beginning of the 10th century BCE were not known. Now that there is the Khirbet Qeiyafa pottery assemblage and it is clear what is typical of the 10th century BCE in Judah, it will be possible to identify these sites.

On the basis of the above, we propose that there was a hierarchy of settlements in the Kingdom of Judah as early as the first half of the 10th century BCE, comprising three types. The first consists of the royal centers. Historical sources and archaeological excavations attest to three central sites: Jerusalem, Hebron, and Shaaraim/Khirbet Qeiyafa. We do not know the size of Jerusalem or Hebron in this period, but it is likely that they were not greater than 25–30 dunams, as the cities of the beginning of the Iron Age II were particularly small—Khirbet Qeiyafa was 23 dunams and Khirbet ed-Dawwara was only 5 dunams. The early sites in the Kingdom of Israel were of similar size: Stratum X at Hazor covered only a limited area of the upper tell, no larger than about 25 dunams, while at Gezer the casemate wall surrounded a small part of the site.[12] Only in later phases were large settlements built, such as Level IV at Lachish with an area of 75 dunams. We wonder whether there might be a small city of some 40 dunams fortified with a massive wall at Tel Lachish in Level V, beneath Level IV?

At each of the three primary centers there is evidence for cultic activity, either as indicated by the biblical tradition or by archaeological finds.

xii (left) A clay chalice on a high foot, one of the numerous simple pottery vessels found at Khirbet Qeiyafa.

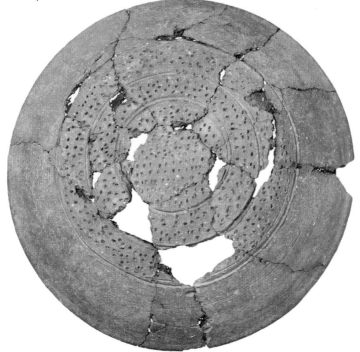

xiii (right) This small pottery jug decorated with white slip and circular black painted stripes is a Cypriot import that may have been used to transport perfume or drugs.

xiv A typical baking tray from Khirbet Qeiyafa: the convex upper surface was pitted to prevent dough or other foodstuffs sticking during cooking over an open fire.

xv Hundreds of storage jars were found at Khirbet Qeiyafa. Their handles are frequently marked with round finger-impressions made by the potter before firing.

xvi a, b Two views of an Egyptian scarab seal, dating to around 1200 BCE and therefore already 200 years old when it reached Khirbet Qeiyafa.

xvii Some of the pottery vessels from the site were decorated with a red slip and added black or white stripes. Similar vessels were first discovered at Tel Ashdod and are known as "Ashdod Ware."

xviii, xix An iron dagger (left) and a bronze axe head (above), two of the numerous metal weapons and tools found in different buildings at Khirbet Qeiyafa. The large number of iron implements is unusual for this period and is evidence of the special importance of the site and its military role.

xx The Khirbet Qeiyafa ostracon—the inscription was written in black ink on a large sherd of pottery, with four straight lines dividing five rows of script. The writing is not clear, and large parts of the inscription still await decipherment.

xxi A basalt altar found in the cult room in building C3; it had been broken in half and the two parts were tossed to different sides of the room (see also Fig. 52).

xxii An ornate clay temple model from Area C found smashed into tens of fragments. The entrance is decorated with two crouching lions, pillars with ropes tied round them, roof beams, and a rolled up curtain; three birds perch on top (see also Fig. 59).

xxiii A carved limestone temple model, 35 cm (14 in.) high, after restoration. The rectangular opening is surrounded by three recessed doorframes, with the representation of the ends of wooden beams above (see also Fig. 60).

xxiv A carved ivory depicting a woman looking out from a window with recessed frames; this example, around 5 cm (2 in.) high, is from Nimrud in Iraq and dates from the 9th–8th century BCE.

xxv, xxvi Two reconstructions of a gate piazza at Khirbet Qeiyafa, with a standing cultic stone (above), and a view looking north to the central administrative building with tall tower (below).

Hebron is the site of the tomb of the Patriarchs; Jerusalem was the location of the Ark of the Covenant (and later the temple); and at Shaaraim there were cultic rooms next to the city gate and in private dwellings.

The second type of site in the hierarchy of settlements comprises regional centers. Khirbet ed-Dawwara fits this category, and we can assume that Gibeon, Keilah, or Kiriath-jearim might also. The third type includes small unwalled villages and farmsteads. While until now no sites of this type have been excavated or located, if a site like Khirbet Qeiyafa was missed by surveys, one can hardly expect that small sites from this period would be identified.

THE THIRD PHASE: THE SECOND HALF OF THE 10TH CENTURY BCE
Khirbet Qeiyafa was suddenly destroyed, as shown by the hundreds of pottery vessels, dozens of metal artifacts, and other finds on the floors of its buildings. If it had been abandoned in an orderly fashion, the inhabitants would have taken their belongings with them, particularly bronze and iron tools and weapons as these were costly items in that period. The question of course arises: who destroyed Khirbet Qeiyafa? It appears to us that the "prime suspect" is Philistine Gath, located just 12 km (7½ miles) west of Khirbet Qeiyafa. The Bible describes numerous border disputes in the vicinity of the Elah Valley, precisely at this time, the end of the 11th and the beginning of 10th century BCE. It is no coincidence that Khirbet Qeiyafa, located on the border opposite Gath, was destroyed a short time after its establishment.

Following the destruction of Khirbet Qeiyafa in the first half of the 10th century BCE, how was the defense of the settlements in Judah then organized? In our view, the answer lies at Beth Shemesh. Yigal Shiloh of the Hebrew University demonstrated that there was a fortified city here, with a casemate wall with houses incorporating the casemates as back rooms. New excavations conducted at the site by Shlomo Bunimovitz and Zvi Lederman of Tel Aviv University have made it clear that Stratum 3 should be dated to the second half of the 10th century BCE.[13] Thus it appears that Beth Shemesh replaced Khirbet Qeiyafa as the main site in the northern Shephelah, one day's walk from Jerusalem. The meticulous urban planning found there, in exactly the same arrangement as at Khirbet Qeiyafa, attests to a Judahite central government.

THE FOURTH PHASE: THE END OF THE 10TH CENTURY BCE

At the end of the 10th century BCE the Kingdom of Judah expanded to the southern Shephelah and reached as far as the sites of Lachish and Tel Zayit. Settlement layers at these sites contained pottery vessels more advanced than those found at Khirbet Qeiyafa. A large number are red slipped with random burnishing, and occasionally burnishing in geometric patterns. Cypriot imports of the black-on-red family are also found at these sites. A stone bowl at Tel Zayit was inscribed on its base with the letters of the alphabet in Phoenician-Hebrew script (as opposed to the Canaanite script of the Khirbet Qeiyafa ostracon). Geographically, the expansion to Lachish corresponds with the list of cities constructed by King Rehoboam in Judah (2 Chronicles 11:5–10), and it seems the list does indeed preserve a historical memory of the 10th century BCE. This could be examined at one of the other sites mentioned in the list of Rehoboam's fortifications, perhaps Socoh in the Elah Valley, southeast of Khirbet Qeiyafa, which itself had been destroyed by this time.

HAVE YOU PAID AND BROUGHT YOUR DUES? THE ROYAL ADMINISTRATION OF ANCIENT JUDAH

A centralized administration in the ancient world generally operated through placing economic obligations upon the population in two main forms: collection of a certain percentage of the agricultural production, and conscription of manpower for public works. Evidence for both of these can be seen at Khirbet Qeiyafa. Nearly 700 storage jars with finger impressions on their handles have been found at the site.[14] An examination of the clay they were made from indicates that they were centrally produced. The jars were apparently delivered empty to the rural population and returned by them filled with agricultural produce. A similar tax collection system continued in Judah for hundreds of years, as mentioned above. Marking the jars allowed control of their contents and distribution, and prevented corruption.

The second form of taxation, conscription of manpower for public works, is reflected in the scale of construction at Khirbet Qeiyafa. The city's fortifications, with the two gates and a casemate wall, surpass the modest building activity of Iron Age I villages and would have been beyond the capabilities of the local population, which we estimate to have been about 100 families. Particularly large stones weighing 2–8 tonnes were found only in the gates and the line of the outer wall, while the rest of the stones in the wall and casemates were of medium size. Quarrying and transporting such large stones requires professional specialists with engineering knowledge and working to an architect's plan. Strong men without specific skills would have sufficed for transporting and handling the medium-size stones, the main element in the city's fortifications. We suggest that men were recruited from around the kingdom to work in construction at Khirbet Qeiyafa for several weeks before being replaced by a new group.

The appearance of writing is, of course, important evidence for the existence of administration. The ostracon from Khirbet Qeiyafa does not provide direct information in this regard, unlike the administrative ostraca of the First Temple period found in excavations at Samaria, Arad, and Lachish. Those ostraca speak of shipments of oil and wine, the provision of food to mercenaries, or lists of manpower.[15] Nonetheless, the ostracon from Khirbet Qeiyafa does indicate that there were individuals who knew how to read and write at a site on the edge of the kingdom, and not only in the capital city of Jerusalem. By way of comparison, at most sites of the Kingdom of Israel such as Megiddo, Hazor, Tel Dan, Tell el-Far'ah North, Beth Shean, or Tel Rehov, no significant evidence for literacy was found for the 9th–8th centuries BCE. The few inscriptions known are at most engravings of personal names on clay vessels.

BARLEY AND LENTILS IN THE ELAH VALLEY: ECONOMY

What did the inhabitants of biblical Khirbet Qeiyafa do for a living? They probably engaged in a range of occupations including agriculture, crafts, trade, and administration. These should not be viewed in modern economic terms—in the societies of 3,000 years ago most households raised their own food, and there were no means of payment such as coins, so a large part of commercial activity was in the form of barter. Working the land involved cultivation of the typical Mediterranean crops that the Bible refers to as the "seven species." Field crops included mainly grains (wheat and barley) and also pulses (lentils, chickpeas, peas, and broad beans). Fruits included grapes, figs, pomegranates, and olives. Large numbers of olive pits were found at Khirbet Qeiyafa, but no large storage pits for keeping crops, nor olive or wine presses for producing oil and wine. Agricultural activities appear to have been conducted on a relatively limited scale, mainly for private consumption and not for export to other sites. The crops could have been raised in fields in the fertile Elah Valley, and orchards could have been planted on the slopes of the hills surrounding the valley to the north. The Bible mentions plots of barley and lentils in this location (2 Samuel 23:11; 1 Chronicles 11:13), and no doubt the productive fields of the Elah Valley were a decisive economic factor in the conflict between Judah and Philistia here.

Each of the families at the site probably kept a small flock of goats and sheep, and possibly a few cows, which would have been grazed in the hills and perhaps along the banks of the valley. These flocks were the main source of protein and fats, consumed as dairy products or meat.

The inhabitants of Khirbet Qeiyafa also engaged in various crafts, especially pottery and metalwork. The large quantity of bronze and iron artifacts and two crucibles containing copper slag are evidence of a significant metal industry. It is probable that in every household the women were engaged in spinning wool and weaving cloth and rugs for clothing and household furnishings, though the small number of loom weights found do not represent intensive activity.

Trade at the site was on a regional, national, and international level. Merchants brought imports of decorated pottery of the Ashdod Ware family to Khirbet Qeiyafa from the area of Philistia, a distance of 10–20 km (around 6–12 miles) away. Relatively small vessels with a capacity of up to 2 liters (½ gallon), they apparently contained special products such as perfumes, medications, or beverages. At a national level, basalt implements were transported from a distance of 100–150 km (60–90 miles). These include simple objects such as grinding stones, but also a carefully made and polished bowl and a decorated altar. Copper used to manufacture bronze objects found at the site could have come from mines at Faynan or Timna in the Aravah, near the Dead Sea. Connections with Transjordan are represented by small pottery vessels known as "Black Juglets." Evidence for international trade comes in the form of finds of bronze, gold leaf, alabaster vessels, and pottery from Cyprus. The nearest tin mines are in Anatolia in Turkey; gold and alabaster would have been brought from Egypt.

The extent of commercial activity is impressive when one considers its geographical range, though quantitatively it is represented by a small number of objects. There was probably no regular passage of caravans of traders, instead commerce would have involved individuals who had connections beyond the city and undertook this trade in addition to their agricultural and administrative activities. In terms of the products themselves, on the whole they were objects necessary for daily activities and not luxury items, which were relatively few and include the Ashdod Ware from Philistia. The goods that came from greater distances, from Cyprus and Egypt, are very rare and probably arrived at the site as a result of its position on a main road between the coast and Jerusalem, so that luxury goods destined for the capital passed through.

The military importance of the site is evident from its geopolitical location, on the border opposite Gath and on the main road from the Coastal Plain to Jerusalem, its massive fortification, and the large number of weapons found there. Many of the site's inhabitants would have been soldiers and commanders who were positioned in the border region in a state of preparedness against invasions from Philistia. Was the site a border post whose occupants were all soldiers? If so, they would all have been men, whose only purpose was to defend the border and they would not have been engaged in food production. While it may be assumed that the men at the site were organized as a military unit for rapid deployment when necessary, this does not seem to have been their sole function and they were probably engaged in part-time agricultural activities for food supply. The urban planning, combining domestic dwellings with the city wall, indicates that there was no clear division between public and private, and between civilian and military.

Several of the storage jars with finger impressions on their handles were found in every house, and one possibility is that the inhabitants, as soldiers, would have received regular food rations from the kingdom in the form of jars filled with wheat, lentils, oil, wine, or other agricultural produce collected from the rural population and brought to Khirbet Qeiyafa. An entirely different explanation, already mentioned, is that the empty jars were given to the inhabitants, who had to return them filled at the end of the agricultural season as a form of tax collection. A third possibility is that the jars were not connected to royal administration and that every family purchased jars according to its needs from the local pottery workshop. This, however, does not explain why the jar handles were marked. It is a fascinating question that requires further research and the excavation of additional sites from this period in the

Shephelah. Such a comprehensive regional picture will also allow us to better understand administrative activity in the early Kingdom of Judah.

EXTENDED FAMILY VS. INDIVIDUALISM: SOCIAL ORGANIZATION

The dwellings at Khirbet Qeiyafa are arranged around the periphery of the settlement adjoining one another—all except those next to the gates would have shared two external walls. This type of construction has certain advantages, especially as it avoids having to build two external walls for adjacent houses, allowing maximal land use while also saving on construction materials. The internal division of the houses at Khirbet Qeiyafa is indicative of a social structure consisting of several nuclear families living together around a shared open courtyard. Every building reflects such an extended family, and the uniformity in the size of the buildings points to a lack of major class differences between families. It seems that in the initial phase of its existence, clear economic classes had not yet emerged in Judah, and there is no evidence for the accumulation of wealth in the hands of a minority of the population, in contrast to the situation at the end of the First Temple period. The urban structure that consolidated at Khirbet Qeiyafa is testimony to an underlying social organization: there is a density and connectedness here, physical but also social, that is unique to the Kingdom of Judah. This is different from city plans of the northern Kingdom of Israel during the 9th–8th centuries BCE, such as at Hazor and Tell el-Far'ah North, where houses stood entirely separate, with no shared walls. A more materialistic and individualistic society would appear to have developed in the northern kingdom.

The same form of urban settlement as found at Khirbet Qeiyafa appears also in cities of the Kingdom of Judah in the 9th and 8th centuries BCE, for instance at Beth Shemesh, Tell en-Nasbeh, Tell Beit Mirsim, and Beersheba, and it seems that a collective social organization continued. No elaborate tombs with burials accompanied by lavish grave goods are known in Judah at this period. When Shebna "who is in charge of the palace" quarried an impressive tomb for himself in Jerusalem in the days of the prophet Isaiah at the end of the 8th century BCE, he was strongly criticized: "What are you doing here and who gave you permission to cut out a grave for yourself here, hewing your grave on the height and chiseling your resting place in the rock?" (Isaiah 22:16).

For most of its existence, some 300 of the 400 years, social organization in the Kingdom of Judah was relatively egalitarian and no dramatic class distinctions emerged. In the second half of the 8th century BCE this began to change. Jerusalem grew into a metropolis of some 800 dunams or more, with over 10,000 inhabitants. Signs that clear economic classes developed take the form of the magnificent tombs and rich grave goods of the 7th century BCE found in several places in the city.[16] The egalitarian society of the 10th–8th centuries BCE disappeared over several generations. At the Judahite city at Tel Ira in the Beersheba Valley dated to the end of the 8th century BCE, the houses were not high density and did not share walls.

Society appears to have remained essentially tribal, despite the processes of urbanization and a move toward centralized government. Against this background we must attempt to understand the stability of the House of David, a single dynasty that lasted some 400 years and came to an end at the hands of an external enemy, Nebuchadnezzar of Babylon, who destroyed the kingdom, rather than as a result of internal upheaval. By comparison, the northern Kingdom of Israel, which existed for only 200 years, was ruled by eight different dynasties, with kings assassinated and replaced with great frequency. It seems the House of David was regarded as a legitimate dynasty. What rebellions there were, such as Absalom's, and those of Sheba, son of Bichri, and of Jeroboam, are all dated to the 10th century BCE. Even when a king was murdered in Judah, as in the cases of Joash (2 Kings 12:21–22) and Amaziah (2 Kings 14:19–21), the son immediately took the throne.

In Judah it appears therefore that no serious alienation developed between the throne and the population. As long as the ruler and those close to him did not exploit their power to accumulate excessive wealth and oppress the people, their legitimacy was not challenged. And the temptation to seize power was not strong, since that power did not produce any particularly great advantage. This perhaps helps to explain the Bible's unique moral perspective, so different from that in other parts of the Near East, which incorporated concepts such as aid for the poor, the freeing of the Hebrew slave after seven years, and the release of land during the Jubilee Year rather than it being sold in perpetuity, to name but a few. Such a socioeconomic perspective could not develop in a competitive urban society.

Templum Deo, fibiq̃ regiam ædificat. ·4·

Fig. 68 Solomon overseeing the building of the Temple in Jerusalem,
an engraving after Maarten van Heemskerck, 1554.

8

SOLOMON'S PALACE AND THE FIRST TEMPLE

By the time of our 2008 season, it was clear that our excavation at Khirbet Qeiyafa had contributed to the understanding of the period of King David, but we did not imagine that the finds we were uncovering could also offer insight into royal construction in Jerusalem and the Solomonic temple itself. A major surprise awaited us a week after the conclusion of the 2011 excavation season, when we saw the reconstructed stone model discussed in Chapter 6 for the first time. Initially, we noted a connection between the elements on the façade of the stone model and the biblical description of Solomon's palace. Later, particularly thanks to research by Madeleine Mumcuoglu, we noted the correspondence between the design of the entrance on the stone model and the biblical description of the entrance to the First Temple, which, according to tradition, was also built by King Solomon.[1]

SOLOMON'S PALACE

In the Bible in 1 Kings 7 is a description of the palace of King Solomon, with its entrance wing known as the "House of the Forest of Lebanon" (Fig. 69). Several aspects of the biblical text are unclear, and it includes technical terms that generations of Bible commentators have found difficult to interpret. Here we will focus on particular aspects that the stone model from Khirbet Qeiyafa can help shed some light on. The model depicts a building façade with triglyphs supporting the roof and a profiled entrance consisting of three receding doorframes (see Fig. 60 and Pl. xxiii), both elements which aid our understanding of two obscure technical terms in the Bible's description. First, we shall read what the Bible says about the building from the beginning, as it appears in 1 Kings 7:1–6 (Table 4).

Table 4: The Hebrew text and various translations of 1 Kings 7:1–6.

	Hebrew Massoretic Text	King James Version (1611)	Revised Standard Version (1901)	
1	וְאֶת בֵּיתוֹ בָּנָה שְׁלֹמֹה שְׁלֹשׁ עֶשְׂרֵה שָׁנָה וַיְכַל אֶת כָּל בֵּיתוֹ	But Solomon was building his own house thirteen years, and he finished all his house.	Solomon was building his own house thirteen years, and he finished his entire house.	
2	וַיִּבֶן אֶת בֵּית יַעַר הַלְּבָנוֹן מֵאָה אַמָּה אָרְכּוֹ, וַחֲמִשִּׁים אַמָּה רָחְבּוֹ, וּשְׁלֹשִׁים אַמָּה קוֹמָתוֹ, עַל אַרְבָּעָה טוּרֵי עַמּוּדֵי אֲרָזִים, וּכְרֻתוֹת אֲרָזִים עַל הָעַמּוּדִים	He built also the house of the forest of Lebanon; the length thereof was an hundred cubits, and the breadth thereof fifty cubits, and the height thereof thirty cubits, upon four rows of cedar pillars, with cedar beams upon the pillars.	He built the House of the Forest of Lebanon; its length was a hundred cubits, and its breadth fifty cubits, and its height thirty cubits, and it was built upon three [sic] rows of cedar pillars, with cedar beams upon the pillars.	
3	וְסָפֻן בָּאֶרֶז מִמַּעַל עַל הַצְּלָעוֹת אֲשֶׁר עַל הָעַמּוּדִים, אַרְבָּעִים וַחֲמִשָּׁה, חֲמִשָּׁה עָשָׂר הַטּוּר	And it was covered with cedar above upon the beams, that lay on forty five pillars, fifteen in a row.	And it was covered with cedar above the chambers that pillars were upon the forty-five, fifteen in each row.	
4	וּשְׁקֻפִים שְׁלֹשָׁה טוּרִים וּמֶחֱזָה אֶל מֶחֱזָה שָׁלֹשׁ פְּעָמִים	And there were windows in three rows, and light was against light in three ranks.	There were window frames in three rows, and window opposite window in three tiers.	
5	וְכָל הַפְּתָחִים וְהַמְּזוּזוֹת רְבֻעִים שָׁקֶף וּמוּל מֶחֱזָה אֶל מֶחֱזָה שָׁלֹשׁ פְּעָמִים	And all the doors and posts were square, with the windows: and light was against light in three ranks.	All the doorways and windows had square frames, and window was opposite window in three tiers.	
6	וְאֵת אוּלָם הָעַמּוּדִים עָשָׂה חֲמִשִּׁים אַמָּה אָרְכּוֹ וּשְׁלֹשִׁים אַמָּה רָחְבּוֹ וְאוּלָם עַל פְּנֵיהֶם וְעַמֻּדִים וְעָב עַל פְּנֵיהֶם.	And he made a porch of pillars; the length thereof was fifty cubits, and the breadth thereof thirty cubits: and the porch was before them: and the other pillars and the thick beam were before them.	And he made the Hall of Pillars; its length was fifty cubits, and its breadth thirty cubits; there was a porch in front with pillars, and a canopy before them.	

The Jerusalem Bible (Jones 1966)	Anchor Bible (Cogan 2001)	Garfinkel and Mumcuoglu (2013)
As regards his palace, Solomon spent thirteen years on it before the building was completed.	And it took Solomon thirteen years to build his house. Thus he completed his entire house.	
He built the Hall of the Forest of Lebanon, a hundred cubits long, fifty cubits wide, and thirty cubits high, on four rows of cedar wood pillars with cedar capitals on the pillars.	He built the House of the Forest of Lebanon, one hundred cubit long and fifty cubit wide and thirty cubit high, with four rows of cedar columns, and cedar beams on the columns;	
It was paneled in cedar on the upper part as far as the planks above the pillars. There were three rows of architraves, forty-five in all, that is fifteen in each row, facing one another from three sides.	and it was roofed with cedar from above, over the planks that were on the columns, forty-five (in number), fifteen to a row;	and it was roofed with cedar above the planks, which were placed on top of pillars, 45 planks in 15 groups (3 in each group, like triglyphs).
	And splayed (windows), (in) three rows, facing each other, three times;	And triple-recessed doorframe.
All the doors and uprights were of rectangular design, facing one another from three sides.	And all the entrances and doorposts had squared frames, and opposite, facing each other, three times.	And all the openings and the side door were square in shape (not rounded) with triple-recessed doors.
And he made the Hall of Pillars, fifty cubits long and thirty cubits wide ... with a porch in front.	He made the porch of columns, fifty cubits long and thirty cubits wide, and a porch was in front of them, and columns with a canopy was in front of them.	

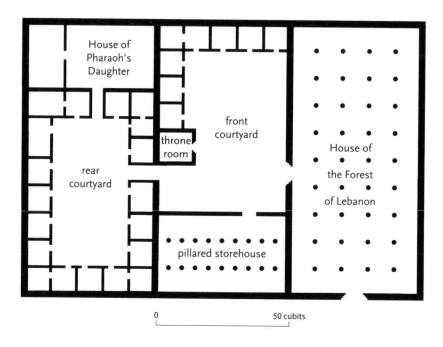

Fig. 69 Solomon's Palace: a proposed reconstruction incorporating the various elements mentioned by the biblical tradition into a single structure, with a number of wings organized around courtyards.

In verse 2 it is stated that the house had four rows of columns. Verse 3 speaks of an element that includes 45 components of some sort, arranged in 15 groups. Here the various Bible commentators faced a problem. Does the number 45 relate to the columns or to the planks mentioned in the first part of that sentence? According to one interpretation, the cedar planks that cover the roof are placed on 45 pillars arranged in three rows with 15 pillars in each row. Another interpretation states that the cedar planks are placed on 45 planks (subsidiary supporting planks) arranged in 15 groups, with three such planks in each group. In many English translations the text is understood as describing 45 pillars arranged in three rows. But in the previous verse it is clearly stated that the palace had four rows of columns, and 45 is not evenly divisible by 4.[2] Despite this, it is clear that the number 45 creates 15 rows, in other words, it is divided by 3. From what is written we can understand that the number 45 refers to the planks rather than to the columns. And it is precisely this architectural element that appears in the stone model from Khirbet Qeiyafa—the triglyphs that appear under the roof and are arranged in groups of three planks. Thus, the expression *"and it was roofed with cedar above the planks, which were placed on top of pillars, 45 planks in 15 groups* [3 in each group, as in the depiction of triglyphs]" describes three architectural elements placed one upon the other: first the pillar, above it the triglyph, and above that the planks of the palace roof.

Following on from these conclusions, we can then compare the prophet Ezekiel's description of the roof of the Temple (41:6) (Table 5). This technical description is also difficult to understand, but in our interpretation we suggest: *"and the planks were organized three together."* In other words, the planks are arranged in groups of three, like the triglyphs in the stone model from Khirbet Qeiyafa and in the description of Solomon's palace. It then continues: *"... as thirty triglyph-like groups, placed on top of the wall, around all the building,"* which we can understand as meaning that around the building were 30 triglyphs (a total of 90 planks). The

	Hebrew Massoretic Text	King James Version (1611)	Revised Standard Version (1901)	The Jerusalem Bible (Jones 1966)	Garfinkel and Mumcuoglu (2013)
6	והצלעות צלע אל צלע שלוש ושלושים פעמים ובאות בקיר אשר לבית לצלעות סביב סביב להיות אחוזים ולא יהיו אחוזים בקיר הבית	And the side chambers were three, one over another, and thirty in order; and they entered into the wall which was of the house for the side chambers round about, that they might have hold, but they had not hold in the wall of the house.	And the side chambers were in three stories, one over another, thirty in each story. There were offsets all around the wall of the temple to serve as supports for the side chambers, so that they should not be supported by the wall of the temple.	The cells were one above the other, thirty of them in three stories. The supports for the surrounding cells were fixed into the Temple wall, so that the cells were not recessed into the wall of the Temple.	And the planks were organized three together, as thirty triglyph-like groups, placed on top of the wall, around all the building, without being integrated into the walls of the building.

Table 5: The Hebrew text and various translations of Ezekiel 41:6.

description ends stating that the latter were not *"integrated into the walls of the building,"* which we interpret to mean that the triglyphs, as part of the roofing, were not built into the walls of the building, but instead rested on top of the walls.

There is a further problem in understanding 1 Kings 7:4–5 (Table 4). Two widely accepted interpretations have been proposed for the Hebrew term *shequfim* as either a window or a window frame. The translation as window is certainly influenced by the appearance of the word in the previous chapter, which outlines the building of the Temple, and its windows (1 Kings 6:4). However, here again interpretation is problematic because these windows are described as being both transparent and opaque. How is it possible that the Temple's windows could have these two opposite qualities? The second interpretation of the word *shequfim*, as door or window frame, appears in the Septuagint, the Greek translation of the Bible dating to the Hellenistic period, as well as in the commentary of the French Rabbi Rashi of the 11th century. This form of the word, *mashkof*, also appears in an inscription engraved on the doorframe of the Baram synagogue in northern Israel, which reads: "Yosi son of Levi the Levite made this *shaquf*."[3] The model of the building from Khirbet Qeiyafa supports this interpretation. It is noteworthy that the following passage includes a pair of words difficult to understand: *reva'im sheqef*. This would appear to refer to square frames, and therefore the opposite of openings in the form of an arch, such as are known for example in clay temple models from Tel Rehov, which have an opening with a rounded upper part (see Fig. 53). In what follows in 1 Kings 7, describing the casting of cult objects for the Temple, the Bible clearly notes that "their frames are square and not rounded" (1 Kings 7:31). Thus, the author attributed great importance to the precise description of the forms of the house and its contents.

The word *mahazeh* appears four times in the two passages under consideration and is also not easy to comprehend. It may be interpreted in several different ways. The likely literal translation would relate to the root "to see" or "to observe," hence the passage can be understood as saying: "the triple frame would be visible three times [from each side of the opening and from above]." Another possibility is that the root of the word is *ahaz* ("to grasp," "to attach"), thus the meaning would be that the frames are gripped by one another three times. To summarize, the biblical description of Solomon's palace can be visualized as follows: the entrance has a triple frame visible on the left and right sides and the top; all of the openings have triple square posts and lintels (and are not surmounted by rounded arches).

Despite the problems in the precise understanding of many of the words in the passages considered, the context is quite clear: it is a description of openings in the palace that are of outstanding richness. The archaeological examples discussed in Chapter 6 come from similar contexts and are all examples of luxury production: the Khirbet Qeiyafa temple model; carved ivories, a rare and costly raw material found in the palaces of Assyria and Samaria; a carved stone stela from the vicinity of Kourion and royal tombs at Tamassos, both in Cyprus (Figs 61–63). These do not depict architecture intended for the common person, but form part of the royal building style of the biblical period, in the 10th–7th centuries BCE. Evidence that this architectural concept already existed at the end of the 11th and the beginning of the 10th century BCE is provided by the stone model from Khirbet Qeiyafa. As such, it sheds light on descriptions detailed in the Bible, including certain technical terms whose significance was lost over the course of the centuries.

The finds from Khirbet Qeiyafa pre-date the days of King Solomon and were found in a border city, but it is possible that buildings in the capital were constructed in the same style at this early phase of the Iron Age. If so, the biblical descriptions of luxury construction in 10th-century Jerusalem could preserve historical memories. In this context it is interesting to read the Bible's description of the construction of David's palace: "Now Hiram king of Tyre sent messengers to David, along with cedar logs and carpenters and stonemasons, and they built a palace for David" (2 Samuel 5:11). What is the significance of the fact that the construction was directed by experts from the city of Tyre, today in Lebanon? It surely means that the building was executed in the royal international style of the biblical period, as is seen in the Khirbet Qeiyafa model.

A further interesting aspect is that the stone model from Khirbet Qeiyafa was painted red. This, along with the presence of wooden planks below the roof (the triglyphs), recalls the description of the palace of Jehoiakim at the end of the First Temple period, which appears in the context of harsh criticism voiced by the prophet Jeremiah: "Woe to him who builds his palace by unrighteousness, his upper rooms by injustice, making his own people work for nothing, not paying them for their labor. He says, 'I will build myself a great palace with spacious upper rooms.' So he makes large windows in it, panels it with cedar and decorates it in red." (Jeremiah 22:13–14)

The expression "panels it with cedar and decorates it in red" shows that the building was paneled with expensive cedar wood and painted in a color termed *shashar* in Hebrew. This word occurs only once in the Bible and its meaning is unclear, but it is generally translated as red. Thus, based on the description of Jehoiakim's palace and the appearance of our stone model, it seems that it was customary to paint elaborate buildings in the Kingdom of Judah red. It is noteworthy in this connection that remains of red paint were also found upon the carved stone windowsill from Ramat Rachel.

THE FIRST TEMPLE

As well as the description of Solomon's palace, 1 Kings 6–7 preserves a longstanding and detailed tradition concerning the construction of the First Temple by him. The first generation of modern scholars accepted this as a reflection of historical reality and attempted to reconstruct the building, based

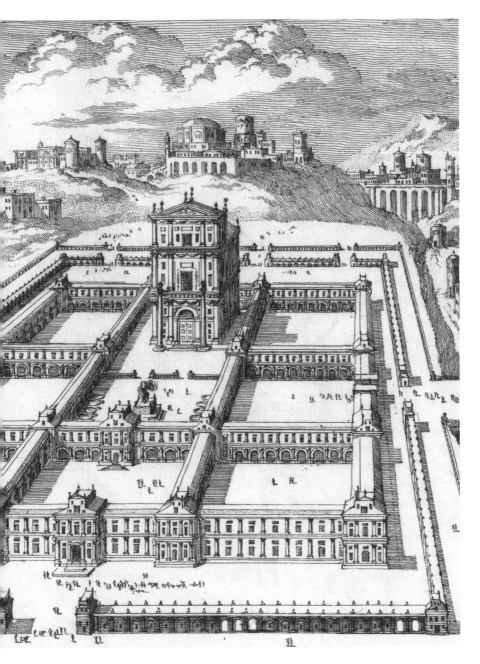

Fig. 70 An engraving of the Temple of Solomon in Jerusalem as imagined by the seventeenth-century Dutch artist Jan Juyken.

also on discoveries at temples uncovered in archaeological excavations. The parallels generally turned to are the temple at Arad, that at Ain Dara in northern Syria, and a temple from Tell Tayinat in southern Turkey. Scholars of the minimalist school, however, claimed that a temple was not built in Jerusalem in the time of King Solomon. In their view, the description in the Bible was composed only in the Hellenistic or Roman period, and therefore relates to the Second Temple. Other theorists dated the writing of the description of the temple to the 8th century BCE or even to the end of the First Temple period in the 7th century BCE, and could therefore not discern any reliable historical evidence in the text for the existence of an actual building in the mid-10th century BCE.

The Temple Mount has experienced numerous upheavals over the centuries, from the destruction of the First Temple by the Babylonians in 586 BCE, its reconstruction as the Second Temple after the return from the Babylonian exile, the building of a new temple by Herod, the raising of a pagan temple in the Roman city of Aelia Capitolina around 130 CE, and finally the construction of the Islamic shrine of the Dome of the Rock. Thus, no archaeological remains of the First Temple exist, and archaeology cannot provide any direct evidence. The detailed description in the Bible of the Solomonic temple has been debated by many scholars, and this is not the place to recapitulate all the various opinions.[4] However, similarities between the temple models from Khirbet Qeiyafa and the Bible's description should be noted. While not a direct and complete parallel, or even a close one, there are several shared architectural motifs. It should be remembered that the finds from Khirbet Qeiyafa are older by several decades than the period of King Solomon and therefore a direct correlation cannot be drawn between these finds and the biblical tradition. But the existence of similar and even identical elements is not coincidental, and is evidence that the Bible's description is based on the realities of 10th-century BCE Judah.

According to the Bible, the central temple structure consisted of three rooms arranged in sequential order: forecourt; outer sanctuary; Holy of Holies. Around them was the side chamber, a further envelope that prevented direct access to the walls of the temple (Fig. 71). Two columns, named Jachin and Boaz (1 Kings 7:21), stood at the front of the temple. Describing the entrance from the forecourt into the outer sanctuary, the Bible states: "He also made four-sided doorposts of olive wood for

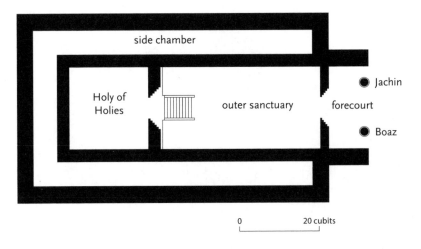

Fig. 71 Proposed reconstructed ground plan of Solomon's Temple (drawing by Roy Albag).

the entrance" (1 Kings 6:33), and concerning the doorway between the outer sanctuary and the Holy of Holies it says: "he made doors of olive wood with five-sided doorposts" (1 Kings 6:31). The description of the temple in 2 Chronicles 3:14 refers to the *parochet*, a curtain separating the outer sanctuary and the Holy of Holies. This is not mentioned in 1 Kings, but appears numerous times in traditions relating to the Tent of Assembly.

Elements of Solomon's Temple described in the Bible can be found in both the temple models from Khirbet Qeiyafa. The clay model has two columns on the façade and a *parochet*. This model also has ropes wrapped around the columns; these are not referred to in the Bible and we are not certain what their function was. The stone model, particularly its elaborate façade, provides us with an understanding of such technical aspects as four- and five-sided doorposts. Rabbi David Kimchi (RaDak), the medieval commentator on the Bible, explained this saying "the doorpost had five ribs, one in front of the other." In the 20th century the archaeologist Shmuel Yeivin noted that it is possible to understand this expression in one of two ways.[5] In the first interpretation, the front of the opening had five consecutive doorframes receding inward. This is how Michael Avi-Yonah designed the entrance to the Holyland model of the Second Temple (today at the Israel Museum in Jerusalem), and it appears like this in all books discussing the Second Temple. According

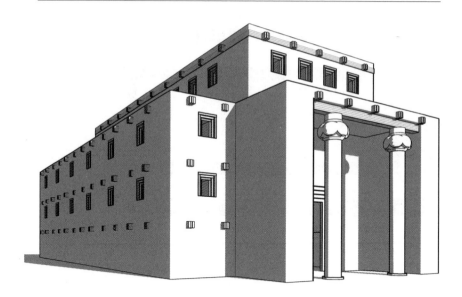

Fig. 72 Solomon's Temple: a new proposal by Roy Albag, based on a better understanding of the biblical text supported by the Khirbet Qeiyafa stone model.

to the second interpretation, the entrance had three receding doorframes on the outside and three receding doorframes on the inside, together forming five doorframes. However, there are no archaeological examples to support this hypothesis.

If we understand the term *shequfim* to mean doorframes, a further aspect of the temple building as found in the phrase "and for the house he made windows of *shequfim atumim*" (1 Kings 6:4) can be addressed. Rivers of ink have been expended in efforts to understand the term *shequfim atumim*. Numerous scholars have understood the term *shequfim* as meaning transparent windows that allow light to enter, and *atumim* as describing opaque windows that light cannot penetrate. But as noted above, this seems contradictory. In our view, *shequfim* does not describe light penetrating the windows, but rather the window frames that we interpret as being arranged in receding planes, similar to those seen in the ivories depicting the woman in the window and in the schematic stone window found near Kourion in Cyprus.

As discussed above, in the description of the palace, wooden planks were organized in threes as triglyphs; the same term is also used in the description of the temple.[6] Our understanding of the term as relating to wooden planks, together with the other terms discussed above, enable us to present a new reconstruction for the First Temple (Fig. 72).

The Khirbet Qeiyafa temple model provides evidence that openings decorated with receding frames and triglyph-like wooden beams were known in Judah as early as the beginning of the 10th century BCE. This is of tremendous importance, for until the excavation of the site, this style of building was known for the biblical period only from the ivories that are dated some 150 years later, to the mid-9th century BCE, or the Cypriot royal tombs of Tamassos dated some 200 years later. On this basis, it could then be maintained that the biblical tradition relating to the building activities of Solomon was describing later activity and was an anachronism with no historical basis. Now, for the first time, we have data from extra-biblical finds that challenge this interpretation. Moreover, the biblical description notes that the temple was built with the assistance of expert builders sent from Tyre (1 Kings 5). This information is surely significant in understanding how the tradition of entrances with receding frames, known from temples at Mari in Syria and Alalakh in Turkey in the Middle Bronze Age, reached Iron Age Jerusalem. The style could have been preserved in the northern Levant through the Middle and perhaps also the Late Bronze Age, was then diffused to the early Iron Age cities of the Lebanese coast, and from there reached Jerusalem with the builders who brought their expertise to the city.

9

LINKING BIBLE, ARCHAEOLOGY, AND HISTORY

A popular view of archaeology might imagine that it is possible to look for direct evidence for the biblical tradition, for example hoping to find Goliath's sword. Archaeological science cannot possibly satisfy such unrealistic expectations. The level of resolution is not that high and, in general, we cannot deal with questions related to specific individuals, however important they might have been. The power of archaeology lies in two main areas: first, it is able to examine political, social, and economic change over decades and centuries. Second, it allows us to point to models of behavior during given periods. From the abundance of data discussed in this book, we have chosen several examples to highlight how research at Khirbet Qeiyafa contributes to each of these points.

With regard to political, social, or economic change, the excavations at Khirbet Qeiyafa allow us to examine the processes that took place during the transition from Iron Age I (the period of the Judges in biblical terms) to Iron Age II (the period of the monarchy in the Bible). This transition finds expression in the abandonment of the settlement pattern of hundreds of small, unfortified villages that characterizes Iron Age I and the appearance of concentrations of population in large fortified cities. At Khirbet Qeiyafa, radiocarbon dating of olive pits and the character of its urban planning attest to this process having begun by the end of the 11th century BCE in the Kingdom of Judah. Thus, the archaeological data fit the biblical tradition. This does not involve circular argumentation, assumptions, or historical considerations. The dating has been established scientifically, by the Oxford University laboratory, and independent of the Bible. Khirbet Qeiyafa is located in the Elah Valley, a day's walk from Jerusalem. The urban planning at the site has been uncovered over an

Fig. 73 Excavations in Area C at Khirbet Qeiyafa, with the Elah Valley beyond.

extensive horizontal exposure, and similar urban planning is found at four other sites, all in the area of the Kingdom of Judah. Indeed, the biblical tradition itself appears to recognize this development of settlements and indicates a transition from a rural to an urban society, and that this process began in the south of the country, in Judah, rather than in the northern Kingdom of Israel.

Archaeological research has also illuminated the change in the settlement pattern in the wider region of the Sorek and Elah valleys over the course of some 400 years, from the 12th to the 9th century BCE. In the first 200 years, the Philistine city of Ekron (Tel Miqne) was an important center of settlement. During the following 200 years, it was supplanted by Gath (Tell es-Safi) as the major site. This has been clearly revealed in archaeological excavations, but the biblical tradition relating to these periods also indicates changes in the relative importance of the two Philistine centers: the earlier accounts concerning Samson and the Ark of the Covenant take place around the Sorek Valley, while the later events, including the story of David and Goliath, move to the Elah Valley.

Other patterns of human behavior during the period from the end of the 11th century to the beginning of the 10th century BCE, when Khirbet Qeiyafa was inhabited, are also illuminated by our excavations. Three cult rooms, single rooms located within houses rather than independent temple structures, were uncovered at the site. A similar phenomenon is known from the 11th–10th centuries at three other sites: Tel Qiri, Megiddo, and Lachish. The biblical tradition speaks of cult rooms in private houses at Mount Ephraim, Kiriath-jearim, and Jerusalem, precisely during the period of the Judges and the days of King David.

Cult practices were also represented archaeologically by the discovery at Khirbet Qeiyafa of three large iron swords, found together in the Area D cult room. Describing events in the same time period, the Bible tells us that the sword of Goliath the Philistine was preserved in a cult place (1 Samuel 21:10), and that at Saul's death his armor was taken by the Philistines and placed in the temple of their gods (1 Samuel 31:10). Three sources, one archaeological and two literary, point to an identical pattern of behavior consisting of the deposition of weapons in a cult place. Underlying this behavior there seems to be a theological concept: the deity participates in combat alongside his people, and weapons captured as booty following a successful battle are brought to the cult place as a thanks offering to that deity. Historical processes and cultural phenomena referred to in the Bible relating to the 10th century BCE thus find concrete expression at Khirbet Qeiyafa at the same time period.

Such clear examples of correspondence between archaeological finds and the biblical tradition stand in contrast to the theories of scholars advocating the minimalist approach, and their assertion that the Bible was written during the Hellenistic or Persian period, or at the end of the 7th century BCE, and contains no historical memory, but who have no data or finds to support such views. The extensive excavations at Khirbet Qeiyafa have brought to light an impressive Judahite administrative city of the 10th century BCE, dating to the first phase of the founding of a kingdom in Judah. This is a ground-breaking contribution to our knowledge of the period, for as noted, this initial phase has not previously been well understood because of problems involved in conducting archaeological excavations in Jerusalem and Hebron and also shortcomings in the identification of surface pottery in archaeological surveys. The difficulty in identifying this historical phase archaeologically led some schools of thought to question the existence of the Kingdom of Judah in the 10th to 8th centuries BCE. This in turn opened the way to casting doubt on the reliability of the historical traditions in the Bible regarding this period. While this scholarly approach can be credited with contributing to an understanding of the many limitations of the biblical tradition which had previously been accepted as historical truth, it went too far in its negative approach and rejected all sources equally.

The Khirbet Qeiyafa excavations have provided archaeological evidence corroborating historical memories from the time of King David and have prompted renewed debate among scholars concerning the quantity and quality of historical information preserved in the Bible. The excavations showed that at the end of the 11th century BCE an urban society and central monarchy began to take shape in the Kingdom of Judah. Khirbet Qeiyafa was a fortified city at the entrance to the Elah Valley, in a location that was of geopolitical importance for only a relatively limited period of time. This accords with biblical tradition, which also names one of the cities in this area as Shaaraim, which we identify with Khirbet Qeiyafa. We have also discovered that literacy during that period must have been far more widespread than had previously been thought. Consequently, historical events from the beginning of the 10th century BCE could have been recorded and passed down from one generation to the next until incorporated in the books of the Bible. The proposal that the Bible was written many hundreds of years after the events it describes, and that it reflects only the period in which it was written, is no longer sustainable. Evidence from the Khirbet Qeiyafa excavations also challenges the idea that the Kingdom of Israel developed first, in the 9th century BCE, while the Kingdom of Judah only emerged in the 8th century BCE.

The difficulties of excavating in Hebron and Jerusalem, the two main cities referred to in the Bible in relation to David's rule, mean that the scope for archaeological research to provide a clear picture of David's kingdom is limited. Thanks to the Khirbet Qeiyafa excavations, however, it is now possible to point to two fortified settlements, Khirbet Qeiyafa and Khirbet ed-Dawarra, that, together with Jerusalem and Hebron, constituted the urban core of the kingdom. There were in addition certainly small, unwalled sites, some between the urban centers and some farther south, as far south as Arad and Beersheba.

As early as the phase of its establishment, the Kingdom of Judah saw the construction of administrative centers following a standard plan consisting of a casemate wall with houses attached to it. This efficient model combined fortifications with dwellings, utilizing one external wall to separate two adjoining houses and allowing maximum use of the limited urban area within the walls, as well as economizing on building materials and labor. The large number of weapons at Khirbet Qeiyafa and the nearly 700 finger-impressed storage jar handles are evidence of a well-organized military and economic administration. Such finds had not previously been encountered at Iron Age I sites, and indicate the beginning of a new era, Iron Age II.

The stone temple model found in the excavation can also enlighten us about the architecture typical of elaborate public buildings during the biblical period in Judah, and demonstrates that the kingdom's inhabitants were familiar with this style as early as the time of David. It also elucidates obscure passages in the Bible relating to the doors and windows of the palace of Solomon and the First Temple. The scale and style of construction discovered at Khirbet Qeiyafa is testimony to the technical and economic capabilities of expert workmen during that period. They could undoubtedly also have been involved in the construction of fortifications and public buildings in Jerusalem, including the building projects known in the City of David that scholars date to the 10th century BCE, such as the Stepped Stone Structure and the Large Stone Structure (David's palace), as well as the fortifications in the Ophel. While structures in Jerusalem should be dated on the basis of finds from each specific building, our excavations have shown that it is no longer possible to state categorically, as some have done, that they cannot be attributed to the 10th century simply because a centralized kingdom and urban culture did not exist at that time.

Evidence provided by the excavations at Khirbet Qeiyafa supports the idea that at the end of the 11th century BCE a kingdom was founded that ruled over parts of the hill country and the Shephelah. At first organized over a relatively limited area, over the course of its history this kingdom became well established and expanded its territory. The great challenge of modern scholarship is to identify the processes in operation in the Kingdom of Judah during the 400 years of its existence: what was the pattern of development of settlements? What were the demographic trends? How can we characterize the economy of the kingdom? What technological means were available to its inhabitants? How did cult and writing traditions develop? Firm answers to these intriguing questions can be found only through further archaeological excavations in the area. We have deepened our understanding of the initial phase of the kingdom during the 10th century BCE; in future projects we hope to contribute to our knowledge of a more advanced phase in the life of the kingdom, which currently is also limited. In combination, such work will form a scientific basis for a fuller picture of the history of the early Kingdom of Judah.

APPENDIX
THE LATE PERSIAN–EARLY HELLENISTIC
PERIOD AT KHIRBET QEIYAFA

In 539 BCE Cyrus the Great of Persia defeated the Babylonian army and went on to take the city of Babylon, creating a vast empire that ruled over large areas of the ancient Near East. Cyrus allowed populations previously exiled by the Babylonian empire to return to their homelands. An expression of this policy is preserved in the Bible in Cyrus' declaration allowing the return of the Israelites to Zion and the establishment of the Second Temple (Ezra 1:2–4; 2 Chronicles 36:23). Following the conquest of Egypt by Cambyses II in 525 BCE, the Persian Empire began to cast its gaze towards Greece. In 490 BCE, the battle of Marathon was waged on Greece's eastern shore, 42 km (26 miles) from Athens, and the invading Persian army under Darius I was defeated. But the Persians returned under Xerxes, capturing and burning Athens, only withdrawing following their defeat at the naval battle of Salamis in 480 BCE and the battle of Plataea in 479 BCE. Around 334 BCE, a 22-year-old king named Alexander left Macedon in northern Greece and in two years conquered the mighty Persian Empire, including an outstanding victory over the Persian king Darius III at the battle of Issus in 333 BCE. Alexander the Great became a legend during his own brief lifetime and died in Mesopotamia aged 32. His death in 323 BCE marks the beginning of the Hellenistic period.

The Hellenistic period is generally divided into three main phases in Israel. Initially, the country was ruled by the Ptolemaic dynasty, whose capital was at Alexandria in Egypt. Then, around 200 BCE, Antiochus III of the Seleucid dynasty defeated Ptolemy VII and the territory passed under the rule of the Seleucids, with their capital at Antioch (today Antakya in Turkey). The Seleucid kings ruled for nearly 100 years, with the second half of this period being characterized by conflict and fierce battles with the Jews under the leadership of Mattathias the Hasmonean, his five sons and his grandsons. In the third Hellenistic phase, Judea was independently ruled by the Hasmonean dynasty, whose outstanding monarchs were John Hyrcanus, Alexander Jannaeus, and Queen

Shlomtzion (Salome Alexandra). In 63 BCE, the Roman general Pompey conquered Jerusalem and defeated the Hasmoneans, which marked the beginning of Roman rule.

During this turbulent period a settlement was built on the ruins of the city of the time of King David at Khirbet Qeiyafa.¹ The dating of this late phase was based on coins uncovered in the excavation. While pottery was found, and olive pits could have been dated by the radio-carbon method, the coins provide accurate dating. They were analyzed by Yoav Farhi, a specialist in numismatics, the study of ancient coins. A large number of coins were found, which fall into three different groups. The earliest date to the end of the Persian period, from around 350 BCE onward. Made of silver, they belong to the types known as *yhd* and *plšt* coins based on where they were minted: the former originate in Jerusalem, while the latter come from Ashdod or Ashkelon in ancient Philistia. In terms of administration, the region of Judah was known at this time as Yehud province, and so the name *yhd* (Yehud) appeared on its coins, occasionally with the addition of the name of the governor. One small silver coin of the province of Yehud bears the inscription: "Yehezekiah the governor" (Fig. 74). The second group of coins consists of those of Alexander the Great and his successors. Among this group are some large and particularly impressive silver coins, including ones bearing

Fig. 74 Obverse and reverse of a small silver coin found at Khirbet Qeiyafa, dated to the end of the Persian period. One side of the coin depicts a bird (owl) and the inscription "Yehezekiah the Peha" or "Yehezekiah the governor." The reverse is blank. Diameter: 6 mm.

Fig 75 Obverse and reverse of a large silver coin found at Khirbet Qeiyafa portraying Alexander the Great. On the obverse is the profile face of the king and on the reverse he is shown sitting on a throne and holding a scepter in one hand as a bird perches on the other. Diameter: 3 cm.

the portrait and name of Alexander himself (Fig. 75). The third group originates in Egypt and is dated to the time of Ptolemy I and Ptolemy II, who ruled from 285 to 246 BCE.[2]

The assemblage of coins found at Khirbet Qeiyafa provide evidence of the date of the level of the city they were found in. This begins in the second half of the 4th century BCE, at the end of the Persian period, and continues into the time of Alexander the Great, with the city apparently unscathed by the transition from Persian to Hellenistic rule. This stratum then continued through the reigns of two of the eight Ptolemaic rulers at the beginning of the Hellenistic period. Yoav Farhi therefore concluded that the stratum ranges in date from 350 to 270 BCE, leading to the rather awkward designation used here: late Persian–early Hellenistic period.

Beyond their importance as a means of dating, from a numismatic perspective the coins are a great source of information. A previously unknown coin type was recovered at the site, in addition to a large number of very rare types, some never before found in scientific excavations and otherwise known only in collections of antiquities resulting from looting. The coins also provide evidence of trade relations and economic development.

Our experience has taught us that when we begin to excavate anywhere at Khirbet Qeiyafa we generally find late Persian–early Hellenistic period remains immediately below the surface. The thickness of the accumulation of remains and the nature of human activity they reflect change from one area to another: a thin layer of soil with a scatter of sherds indicates an open area between buildings, elsewhere scant remains of walls apparently reflect simple houses. In two areas we excavated substantial buildings, the dwellings of particularly important families (Fig. 76). As it was near the surface, this stratum was largely destroyed over the years. In addition, the presence of lime kilns at the site and in the immediate vicinity suggests the fate of the later structures—large parts of the walls were probably dismantled and burnt to produce lime.

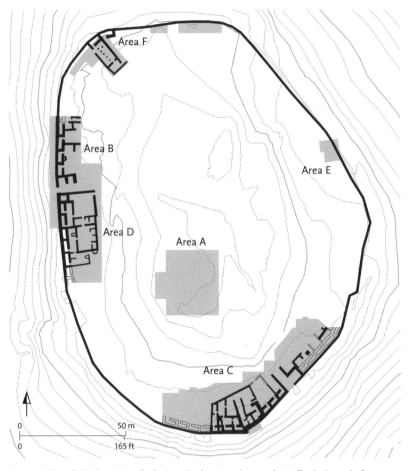

Fig 76 Plan of Khirbet Qeiyafa during the late Persian–early Hellenistic period.

What follows is a summary of the elements of the settlement of this period uncovered in our excavation.

The western gate: During this period, as in the biblical period, the settlement had two gates, one on the west and the other on the south. The western gate was constructed on the Iron Age gate, but as the inhabitants of the later period did not need such a broad gate they blocked half the entrance, reducing it to a width of only 2 m (6½ ft). On top of the large stone threshold of the Iron Age, a higher threshold was now constructed, composed of three large flat stones. On the southern side of the gate a new drainage channel was created, so that today's visitor sees two drainage channels: the northern Iron Age one and the southern one from the late Persian–early Hellenistic period. Of the four Iron Age gate chambers, two on each side of the passageway, the two southern ones were blocked by a wall and incorporated in a large administrative building. One chamber became a storage silo and the other was dismantled and turned into an open courtyard with an oven (*tabun*) built on the remains of the wall of the original chamber. Little evidence of activity was found in the two northern chambers.

The reuse of the gate in this later period entirely destroyed the biblical period living surfaces, but we could recover the outline of the foundations of the original gate and its chambers. At a certain point in the late Persian–early Hellenistic period, this gate went out of use and a large installation was constructed on the road leading to it, obstructing access. The gate area, lower than its surroundings, was used for the disposal of rubbish, and was blocked by a considerable quantity of sherds and a few animal bones.

The southern gate: The southern entrance was not located in the Iron Age gate structure but 20 m (65 ft) east of it. A new opening to the Elah Valley was created in the fourth casemate of the biblical wall. An access corridor was built, leading from west to east, about 10 m (33 ft) long and 3 m (10 ft) wide, almost completely destroying the biblical period construction here. Since the surface inside the settlement was some 3 m (10 ft) higher than that outside the gate, the corridor was sunk into the biblical period stratum and it was necessary to support its sides to prevent collapse. Stone supporting walls were therefore constructed on each side of the corridor, which we dismantled in the course of excavation and so they are no longer visible.

The question arose of when precisely each of these later gates was built. From the data obtained in the excavation, it appears that they were not in use simultaneously. The western gate was built first, on top of the Iron Age gate. At this stage there was no need for an additional gate, and the southern gate of the Iron Age was blocked and a large dwelling built in it. The western gate then became blocked and it was no longer possible to use it. It was around that time, we believe, or slightly earlier, that the new southern gate was created. The change in location of the gates perhaps reflects a change in the settlement's orientation, from the west (the Coastal Plain) to the east (Judah), creating the need for a gate descending to the Elah Valley. Since it was not possible to use the original Iron Age southern gate as it was by now incorporated into a large dwelling, a new opening was created in the southern city wall. At this phase the western gate was blocked and was no longer in use.

The city wall: A relatively thin wall was now constructed around the city, approximately 1.5 m (5 ft) thick, in contrast to the ancient wall, which has a total width of 4 m (13 ft). This later wall, clearly seen in aerial photographs of Khirbet Qeiyafa, is constructed of small- and medium-sized limestone stones and rests on the outer face of the biblical casemate wall, with the western gate attached to it. During the Hellenistic period, the site was abandoned, but despite this, the wall remains exposed to the present day. It seems that farmers living in the vicinity continued to maintain it over the generations as a terrace wall to enclose an area used as an orchard and for growing field crops over thousands of years.

The administrative building in the west: For three seasons of excavation a large group from Southern Adventist University worked in Area D under the direction of Michael G. Hasel. The members of the group excavated a building (Fig. 77) with an area of some 700 sq. m (7,535 sq. ft) attached to the western gate and consisting of three adjacent units. Each of the two northern units includes a large courtyard with a number of surrounding rooms. In the northern courtyard a large cave is quarried into

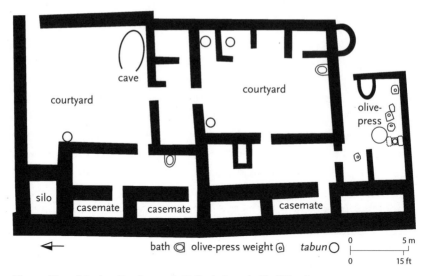

Fig. 77 Plan of the late Persian–early Hellenistic period building in Area D.

bedrock, which remained in use until the Islamic period, as revealed by sherds found in it. Various installations were uncovered in the building: numerous *tabun*, large silos, and even two plastered bathtubs. On the western side, each unit had a long corridor along the Iron Age casemate wall. Occasionally, the ancient casemates were incorporated into the later building, while others were blocked and not reused.

The third unit, in the south, is an olive oil press in which over 1,600 olive pits were found. The press included four stone weights in a row and four additional stone weights, some of which had later been incorporated into the walls. Analysis of the finds enables us to reconstruct how the oil was produced. First, the olives were crushed, perhaps in an installation in the eastern part of the room. The crushed olives were then put in flat baskets, which were stacked one on top of each other above a pit quarried in bedrock between two upright stones. Only one of these stones has been preserved, south of the pit, but a scar is visible on the other side, created when the second stone was removed for some later use. A large wooden beam was then positioned on the standing stones and heavy weights hung from it. The weights are still arranged in a row from west to east, recording the location of the beam when the installation was in use. The pressing produces a mixture of oil, water, and crushed olives, which drained into the pit between the stones and was then transferred to a large basin. The oil, which has a lower density than the other components, floats on top and can thus be separated. The builders of the olive press ensured cleanliness in the production process by plastering the floor of the room and its walls with a thick layer of white lime plaster. This is the only room in the entire late Persian–early Hellenistic stratum whose floor and walls were so carefully plastered.[3]

This building in Area D is unique in several respects: it is the largest structure known in the Shephelah of Judah in this period, it contained numerous silos and a particularly large number of coins were found in it,

Fig. 78 Aerial photograph showing the southern part of Area D. The large room visible in the upper right corner is a late Persian–early Hellenistic period oil press, constructed on bedrock, that has virtually obliterated earlier remains. In other areas, Iron Age IIA remains were better preserved and include several rooms and a hallway; to the right is a wall with a bench built against it.

as well as sherds of Attic pottery (imported from Greece) and a fragment of a stone vessel of schist. It appears to have been the most important structure at the site during this period. Was it a private house or did it also have an administrative function? The location of the building adjoining the entrance to the settlement, the many storage pits, and the coins certainly suggest an administrative function.

Large domestic dwelling in the south: Another notable structure, measuring approximately 370 sq. m (3,980 sq. ft), was built inside the Iron Age southern gate and gate piazza (Fig. 79). The house contained 20 different spaces, including a large courtyard with several cooking installations in front of the building. A glass seal in the form of a scarab bearing the image of a goddess with a spear in her hand and standing on a lion was found here. From this courtyard two casemates of the wall can be accessed, which were cleared of Iron Age collapse and found to contain late Persian–early Hellenistic-period living surfaces. An inner part of the

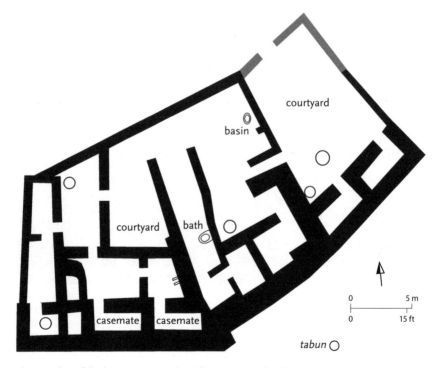

Fig. 79 Plan of the late Persian–early Hellenistic period building in Area C.

building is reached via a narrow entrance corridor. Here was an array of several more courtyards and numerous rooms, three of which were originally casemates of the Iron Age wall. In the westernmost casemate, a wall divided the space into two; in the eastern part a silo was created and a cooking stove in the western. This building is characterized by the large number of installations it contained, including a stone basin near the entrance, several *tabun*, a bathtub, and silos.

Additional building remains: Evidence for small and relatively simple structures was found in Area B, north of the large administrative building of Area D, and also in Area C, to the east of the large dwelling. A particular style of construction is observable in some of the walls of the late Persian–early Hellenistic level that is not found in other periods at the site: long, narrow stones were laid at an angle on their narrow sides, sometimes incorporated within walls, to create a sort of herringbone effect. These walls do not form parts of complete buildings or even complete rooms.

An interesting situation was found in Iron Age building C4, of which 12 rooms were excavated. The majority of the rooms contained a rich destruction layer associated with Iron Age vessels. In one room, however, room D, the picture was entirely different: only late Persian–early Hellenistic finds occurred down to bedrock. It appears that a basement was dug here in a later period that utilized the walls of the Iron Age room. This serves as an important warning in relation to archaeological excavation techniques: if archaeologists had arrived at Khirbet Qeiyafa and by chance excavated a single test probe in this room, they might conclude that the entire city had been built in the Hellenistic period. In this way, excavation in narrow trenches or test probes can run the risk of misleading conclusions regarding the date of buildings or strata.

ARTIFACTS AND VESSELS OF THE LATE PERSIAN–EARLY HELLENISTIC PERIOD

The late Persian–early Hellenistic period city was abandoned in an orderly fashion and the inhabitants took their household utensils with them. On the floors of the buildings we generally find only sherds and fragments of stone vessels that had been discarded. A number of bronze artifacts include fibulae (pins) for fastening clothing and kohl sticks for applying makeup. With the exception of several figurines of horses (Fig. 80), there is no evidence for cult or art during this period. There is some evidence for writing, including letters written in ink or engraved by potters on vessels before firing. The quantity and quality of coins from this phase, numbering nearly 100, make Khirbet Qeiyafa a very significant site for this period.

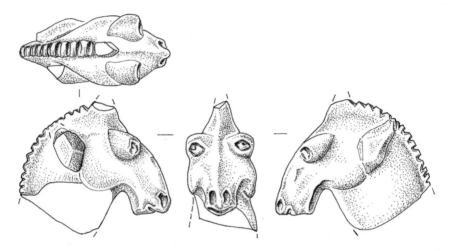

Fig. 80 Fired-clay figurine of a horse dated to the late Persian–early Hellenistic period.

NOTES

Chapter 1 (pp. 12–21)

1. Dothan 1982; Yasur-Landau 2010.
2. On this settlement pattern see Garfinkel 2007.
3. Adams 2009.
4. See Y. Yadin 1955; King 2007; Zorn 2010; Finkelstein 2002a; A. Yadin 2004. Zorn even takes this a step farther, claiming that Goliath was a chariot warrior, despite the fact that neither the Bible nor any historical source mentions chariots in Philistia, either in the time of Goliath, or in any other period.

Chapter 2 (pp. 22–51)

1. Many books have been written on the figure and life of David from the biblical perspective, see Zakovitz 1995, McKenzie 2000; Kirsch 2000; Halpern 2001; Brueggemann 2002; Van Seters 2009; Baden 2013; Blenkinsopp 2013; Wright 2014.
2. See, for example: Albright 1958; Y. Yadin 1958; Aharoni 1979; Bright 1981; Malamat 1984, B. Mazar 1986.
3. Thiele 1983; Galil 2001.
4. See, for example: Lemche 1988; Davies 1992; Thompson 1992; Jamieson-Drake 1991; Pfoh 2009; Van Seters 2009.
5. Fischer 1970, p. 62.
6. Biran and Naveh 1993, 1995.
7. Lemaire 1994.
8. Shiloh 1984, Stratum 14 in Area G.
9. E. Mazar 2006, 2007.
10. E. Mazar 2011.
11. Concerning these complex issues, see, for example: Ussishkin 2003; A. Mazar 2006.
12. Finkelstein 1996.
13. Additional archaeological data on sites mentioned in this book may be found in the *New Encyclopedia of Archaeological Excavations in the Holy Land*, Stern 1993.
14. See, for example, our survey at the biblical site of Socoh: Hasel, Garfinkel, and Weiss 2017.
15. Garfinkel and Ganor 2017.
16. See Lehman 2003 with references to various surveys.
17. See, for example, Tov 1985; Zakovitz 1995, pp. 96–105; Garsiel 2009.
18. I. Garfinkel 2016.
19. Hoffmeier 2011.
20. See proposed dates, from early to late: Halpern 2001; Garsiel 2009; Finkelstein 2002a; A. Yadin 2004; Tov 1985; Van Seters 2009.
21. Van Seters 2009, p. 32.
22. Römer and Brettler 2000, p. 417.
23. Aharoni 1979.
24. Cogan 2003, Inscription 1.
25. Ahituv 2008, pp. 389–418.
26. Biran and Naveh 1993; 1995.
27. Cogan 2003, Inscription 12.
28. Cogan 2003, Inscription 18.
29. See, for example, Cogan 2003, Inscription 27.
30. Cogan 2003, Inscription 39.
31. Cogan 2003, Inscription 40.

32. Cogan 2003, Inscription 41, year 7.
33. Garfinkel and Ganor 2009; Garfinkel, Ganor, and Hasel 2014.
34. Y. Yadin 1958.
35. See analysis in Hasel 2012.
36. Na'aman 2008a, 2010.
37. Lederman and Bunimovitz 2014.
38. Finkelstein and Fantalkin 2012.
39. Lehmann and Niemann 2014; see also Wright 2014.
40. Kehati 2009.
41. Ben-Shlomo 2010.
42. Gottlieb 2010.
43. Garfinkel 2011a.
44. Dagan 2009; see evaluation by Garfinkel, Kreimerman, and Zilberg 2016.
45. Na'aman 2008a.
46. Finkelstein and Piasetzky 2010.
47. Finkelstein 2002b; Finkelstein and Piasetzky 2010.
48. Zissu and Goren 2011.
49. Rollston 2011.

Chapter 3 (pp. 52–101)

1. Israel Map Coordinates 14595/12280.
2. Guerin 1868.
3. Conder and Kitchener 1883.
4. Dagan 1993.
5. Greenhut et al. 2001.
6. Garfinkel and Ganor 2008a, 2009; Garfinkel, Ganor, and Hasel 2014; Farhi 2016.
7. Shiloh 1978; Herzog 1997.
8. Kochavi 1998.
9. Begin 2000.
10. Keimer, Kreimermann, and Garfinkel 2015; Garfinkel, Ganor, and Hasel 2012.
11. Garfinkel, Streit, Ganor, and Hasel 2012; Garfinkel, Streit, Ganor, and Reimer 2015.

12. For earlier radiometric projects of the Iron Age see: Boaretto et al. 2005; Sharon et al. 2007; Levy et al. 2008; A. Mazar and Bronk Ramsey 2008.
13. Singer-Avitz 2010; Finkelstein and Piasetzky 2010.
14. For a detailed response to the claims of Singer-Avitz, Finkelstein, and Piasetzky, see Garfinkel and Kang 2011.
15. Garfinkel, Hasel, and Klingbeil 2013.
16. Garfinkel and Ganor 2017.

Chapter 4 (pp. 102–113)

1. Kang and Garfinkel 2009a, 2009b.
2. Gilboa 2012.
3. Cohen-Weinberger and Panitz-Cohen 2014.
4. Kang and Garfinkel 2015.
5. Ben-Shlomo 2009.
6. Ben-Shlomo et al. 2004.
7. Cohen-Klonymus 2014.
8. Cohen-Klonymus 2016.
9. Rabinovich 2016.
10. Gottlieb 2010.
11. Klingbeil 2016.
12. Schroer 2016.

Chapter 5 (pp. 114–127)

1. Bearman and Christens-Barry 2009.
2. Goldwasser 2010.
3. Misgav, Garfinkel, and Ganor 2009; Ahituv 2009; Demsky 2009; Yardeni 2009.
4. Galil 2009.
5. Levy and Pluquet 2016.
6. Yardeni 2009.
7. As in [אה]ר (א)ל and כל(א)י (א)ל. Ahituv 2008, p. 438. Our thanks to Shmuel Ahituv for this information.
8. Ahituv 2009.
9. Malamat 1987.

10. Ahituv 2008, Ostracon 3 from Lachish, on p. 63 and the Deir Allah inscription on pp. 435–38.
11. Garfinkel, Golub, Misgav, and Ganor 2015.
12. McCarter, Bunimovitz, and Lederman 2011; E. Mazar, Ben-Shlomo, and Ahituv 2013.

Chapter 6 (pp. 128–161)

1. Regarding these finds see, for example: Kletter 1996; Moorey 2003.
2. On Iron Age I cult, see A. Mazar 1990, pp. 348–52.
3. Aharoni 1975.
4. Kisilewitz 2015.
5. Ornan 2005; Van der Torn 1997.
6. Ben Ami 2004.
7. See, for example: Graesser 1972; Mettinger 1995; Blomquist 1999.
8. Weinberg 1979.
9. Ben-Tor and Portugali 1987, pp. 82–90, plan 29.
10. Loud 1948, pp. 44–46.
11. Aharoni 1975, pp. 26–32.
12. Garfinkel and Mumcuoglu 2016; Katz 2016.
13. Muller 2002, Figs 57, 60, 64, 73, 83, 88, 116–18.
14. Kletter et al. 2010.
15. A. Mazar 1980, pp. 82–84.
16. Barnett 1975, pp. 98–99, 145–51.
17. Shiloh 1979, Pl. 19.
18. Shiloh 1979, Pl. 18, no. 1.
19. Haines 1971, Pl. 86.
20. Our thanks to Ruhama Bonfil for bringing these two examples to our attention.
21. Shiloh 1979, Figs 37–38; Kletter et al. 2010.
22. Stager 2008.
23. Münger et al. 2011, Fig. 23.
24. Ucko 1968.
25. Kisilewitz 2015.

Chapter 7 (pp. 162–183)

1. Garfinkel and Ganor 2008b.
2. Na'aman 2008b.
3. Our thanks to Edith Doron for this insight.
4. Kang and Garfinkel 2015.
5. Finkelstein 1990.
6. Stern 1993, p. 344.
7. Garfinkel 2011b, 2012.
8. Christaller 1933.
9. Maeir and Uziel 2007.
10. Garfinkel 2007.
11. Garfinkel 1984.
12. For a possible reconstruction of the casemate wall at Gezer, see Herzog 1997, Fig. 5.17.
13. Bunimovitz and Lederman 2001, 2006.
14. Kang and Garfinkel 2015.
15. Ahituv 2008.
16. Barkay 1994.

Chapter 8 (pp. 184–197)

1. Garfinkel and Mumcuoglu 2013, 2016.
2. It is noteworthy that in the 1901 English Bible translation known as the Revised Standard Version, the number four was "corrected" to three.
3. Naveh 1978, p. 19, inscription no. 1.
4. For a detailed discussion, see Hurowitz 2009.
5. Yeivin 1965.
6. Garfinkel and Mumcuoglu 2013, 2016.

Appendix (pp. 204–215)

1. For a discussion on the later periods at the site see Stiebel 2010; Sandhaus and Kreimerman 2015; Farhi 2016.
2. Farhi 2016.
3. Hasel 2014a, 2014b.

BIBLIOGRAPHY

Adams, D. L. 2009. "Between Socoh and Azekah: The Role of the Elah Valley in Biblical History and the Identification of Khirbet Qeiyafa." In Garfinkel, Y. and Ganor, S. (eds.), *Khirbet Qeiyafa Vol. 1*, pp. 47–66. Jerusalem.

Aharoni, Y. 1975. *Investigations at Lachish: The Sanctuary and the Residency.* Tel Aviv.

Aharoni, Y. 1979. *The Land of the Bible: A Historical Geography.* Philadelphia.

Ahituv, S. 2008. *Echoes from the Past: Hebrew and Cognate Inscriptions from the Biblical Period.* Jerusalem.

Ahituv, S. 2009. "The Khirbet Qeiyafa Inscription – Response C." *New Studies in the Archaeology of Jerusalem and Its Region* 3, pp. 130–32 (Hebrew).

Albright, W. F. 1958. "Was the Age of Solomon Without Monumental Art?" *Eretz-Israel* 5, pp. 1–9.

Baden, J. 2013. *The Historical David. The Real Life of an Invented Hero.* London.

Barkay, G. 1994. "Excavations at Ketef Hinnom in Jerusalem." In Geva, H. (ed.), *Ancient Jerusalem Revealed.* Jerusalem.

Barnett, R. D. 1975. *A Catalogue of the Nimrud Ivories.* London.

Bearman, G. and Christens-Barry, W. A. 2009. "Imaging the Ostracon." In Garfinkel, Y. and Ganor, S. *Khirbet Qeiyafa Vol. 1*, pp. 261–70. Jerusalem.

Begin, Z. B. 2000. *As We do Not See Azeqa. The Source of the Lachish Letters.* Jerusalem (Hebrew).

Ben-Ami, D. 2004. "A Middle Bronze Age Cultic Enclosure at Tel Hazor." *Qadmoniot* 37, pp. 34–39 (Hebrew).

Ben-Shlomo, D. 2009. "Petrographic Analysis of Iron Age Pottery". In Garfinkel, Y., and Ganor, S. *Khirbet Qeiyafa Vol. 1*, pp. 161–74. Jerusalem.

Ben-Shlomo, D. 2010. *Philistine Iconography: A Wealth of Style and Symbolism.* Fribourg.

Ben-Shlomo, D., Shai, I., and Maier, A. M. 2004. "Late Philistine Decorated Ware ("Ashdod Ware"): Typology, Chronology, and Production Centers." *Bulletin of the American Schools of Oriental Research* 335, pp. 1–34.

Ben-Tor, A. and Portugali, Y. 1987. *Tell Qiri: A Village in the Jezreel Valley*. Jerusalem.

Biran, A. and Naveh, J. 1993. "An Aramaic Stele Fragment from Tel Dan." *Israel Exploration Journal* 43, pp. 81–98.

Biran, A. and Naveh, J. 1995. "The Tel Dan Inscription, A New Fragment." *Israel Exploration Journal* 45, pp. 1–18.

Blenkinsopp, J. 2013. *David Remembered: Kingship and National Identity in Ancient Israel*. Grand Rapids, MI.

Blomquist, T. H. 1999. *Gates and Gods: Cult in the City Gate of Iron Age Palestine. An Investigation of the Archaeological and Biblical Sources*. Stockholm.

Boaretto, E., Jull, A., Gilboa, A., and Sharon, I. 2005. "Dating the Iron Age I/II Transition in Israel: First Intercomparison Results." *Radiocarbon* 47, pp. 39–55.

Bright, J. 1981. *A History of Israel*. Philadelphia.

Brueggemann, W. 2002. *David's Truth in Imagination and Memory*. Minneapolis.

Bunimovitz, S. and Lederman, Z. 2001. "The Iron Age Fortifications of Tel Beth-Shemesh: A 1990–2000 Perspective." *Israel Exploration Journal* 51, pp. 121–47.

Bunimovitz, S. and Lederman, Z. 2006. "The Early Israelite Monarchy in the Sorek Valley: Tel Beth-Shemesh and Tel Batash (Timnah) in the Tenth and Ninth Centuries BCE." In Maeir, A. M. and de Miroschedji, P. (eds.), *"I Will Speak the Riddle of Ancient Times": Archaeological and Historical Studies in Honor of Amihai Mazar On the Occasion of His Sixtieth Birthday*, pp. 407–27. Winona Lake, IN.

Christaller, W. 1933. *Die zentralen Örte in Süddeutschland*. Translated by C. Baskin, *Central Places in Southern Germany*. Englewood Cliffs, N.J.

Cogan, M. 2003. *Historical Texts from Assyria and Babylonia: 9th–6th Centuries BCE*. Jerusalem (Hebrew).

Cohen Klonymus, H. 2014. *The Iron Age Groundstone Tools Assemblage of Khirbet Qeiyafa: Typology, Spatial Analysis and Sociological Aspects*. Unpublished M.A. thesis, Hebrew University. Jerusalem.

Cohen Klonymus, H. 2016. "The Iron Age IIA Judahite Weight System at Khirbet Qeiyafa". In Ganor, S. et al. (eds.), *From Sha'ar Hagolan to Shaaraim. Essays in Honor of Prof. Yosef Garfinkel*, pp. 33–59. Jerusalem (Hebrew).

Cohen-Weinberger, A. and Panitz-Cohen, N. 2014. "The Black Juglets". In Garfinkel, Y. et al. (eds.), *Khirbet Qeiyafa Vol. 2*, pp. 403–14. Jerusalem.

Conder, C. R. and Kitchener, H. H. 1883. *The Survey of Western Palestine, Vol. III.* London.

Dagan, Y. 1993. "Bet Shemesh and Nes Harim Maps Survey," *Excavations and Surveys in Israel* 13, pp. 94–95.

Dagan, Y. 2009. "Khirbet Qeiyafa in the Judean Shephelah: Some Considerations." *Tel Aviv* 36, pp. 68–81.

Davies, P. R. 1992. *In Search of "Ancient Israel."* Sheffield.

Demsky, A. 2009. "The Enigmatic Inscription from Khirbet Qeiyafa—Response B." *New Studies in the Archaeology of Jerusalem and Its Region* 3, pp. 126–29 (Hebrew).

Dothan, T. 1982. *The Philistines and Their Material Culture.* Jerusalem.

Farhi, Y. 2016. *Khirbet Qeiyafa Vol. 5: Excavation Report 2007–2013. The Numismatic Finds: Coins and Related Objects.* Jerusalem.

Finkelstein, I. 1990. "Excavations at Khirbet ed-Dawwara, An Iron Age Site Northeast of Jerusalem." *Tel Aviv* 17, pp. 163–208.

Finkelstein, I. 1996. "The Archaeology of the United Monarchy: An Alternative View." *Levant* 28, pp. 177–87.

Finkelstein, I. 2002a. "The Philistines in the Bible: A Late Monarchic Perspective." *Journal for the Study of the Old Testament* 27, pp. 131–67.

Finkelstein, I. 2002b. "Archaeology and Text in the Third Millennium: A View from the Center." In Lemaire, A. (ed.), *International Organization for the Study of the Old Testament. Congress Volume Basel 2001*, pp. 323–42. Leiden.

Finkelstein, I. and Fantalkin, A. 2012. "Khirbet Qeiyafa: An Unsensational Archaeological and Historical Interpretation." *Tel Aviv* 39, pp. 38–63.

Finkelstein, I. and Piasetzky, E. 2010. "Khirbet Qeiyafa: Absolute Chronology." *Tel Aviv* 37, pp. 84–88.

Fischer, D. H. 1970. *Historians' Fallacies: Toward a Logic of Historical Thought.* New York.

Galil, G. 2001. *The Chronology of the Kings of Israel and Judah.* Leiden.

Galil, G. 2009. "The Hebrew Inscription from Khirbet Qeiyafa/Neta'im: Script, Language, Literature and History." *Ugarit Forschungen* 41, pp. 193–242.

Garfinkel, I. 2016. "The Shaft of Whose Spear Was Like a Weaver's Beam? Another Suggestion." *Zeitschrift für die alttestamentliche Wissenschaft* 128, pp. 688–94.

Garfinkel, Y. 1984. "The Distribution of Identical Seal Impressions and the Settlement Pattern in Judea before Sennacherib's Campaign." *Cathedra* 32, pp. 35–53 (Hebrew).

Garfinkel, Y. 2007. "The Dynamic Settlement History of Philistine Ekron: A Case Study of Central Place Theory." In Ben-Tor, A. et al. (eds.), *Up to the Gates of Ekron. Essays on the Archaeology and History of the Eastern Mediterranean in Honor of Seymour Gitin*, pp. 17–24. Jerusalem.

Garfinkel, Y. 2011a. "The Birth and Death of Biblical Minimalism." *Biblical Archaeology Review* 37/3, pp. 46–53.

Garfinkel, Y. 2011b. "The Davidic Kingdom in Light of the Finds at Khirbet Qeiyafa." *City of David Studies of Ancient Jerusalem* 6, pp. 13–35.

Garfinkel, Y. 2012. "The Settlement History of the Kingdom of Judah from Its Establishment to Its Destruction." *Cathedra* 143, pp. 7–44 (Hebrew).

Garfinkel, Y. and Ganor, S. 2008a. "Khirbet Qeiyafa: A Fortified Border City between Judah and Philistia." *New Studies in the Archaeology of Jerusalem and its Region* 2, pp. 122–33 (Hebrew).

Garfinkel, Y. and Ganor, S. 2008b "Khirbet Qeiyafa: Sha'arayim." *Journal of Hebrew Scriptures* 8, Article 22.

Garfinkel, Y. and Ganor, S. 2009. *Khirbet Qeiyafa Vol. 1. Excavation Report 2007–2008*. Jerusalem.

Garfinkel, Y. and Ganor, S. 2017. "Khirbet er-Rai: An Iron Age Site in the Judean Shephelah." *New Studies on Jerusalem* 22, pp. 53–66 (Hebrew).

Garfinkel, Y. and Kang, H.-G. 2011. "The Relative and Absolute Chronology of Khirbet Qeiyafa: Very Late Iron Age I or Very Early Iron Age IIA?" *Israel Exploration Journal* 61, pp. 171–83.

Garfinkel, Y. and Mumcuoglu, M. 2013. "Triglyphs and Recessed Doorframes on a Building Model from Khirbet Qeiyafa: New Light on Two Technical Terms in the Biblical Descriptions of Solomon's Palace and Temple." *Israel Exploration Journal* 63, pp. 135–63.

Garfinkel, Y. and Mumcuoglu, M. 2016. *Solomon's Temple and Palace: New Archaeological Discoveries*. Jerusalem.

Garfinkel, Y., Ganor, S., and Hasel, M. G. 2012. "The Iron Age City of Khirbet Qeiyafa after Four Seasons of Excavations." In Galil, G. et al. (eds.), *The Ancient Near East in the 12th–10th Centuries BCE: Culture and History*, pp. 149–74. Münster.

Garfinkel, Y., Ganor, S., and Hasel, M. G. 2014. *Khirbet Qeiyafa Vol. 2. Excavation Report 2009–2013: Stratigraphy and Architecture (Areas B, C, D, E)*. Jerusalem.

Garfinkel, Y., Ganor, S., Silver, J. B. 2017. "Did the Ancient City of Khirbet Qeiyafa/Sha'arim Have Two Gates?" *Biblical Archaeology Review* 51/1, pp. 37–42.

Garfinkel, Y., Hasel, M. G., and Klingbeil, M. 2013. "An Ending and a Beginning: Why We're Leaving Qeiyafa and Going to Lachish." *Biblical Archaeology Review* 39/6, pp. 44–51.

Garfkinkel, Y., Kreimerman, I., and Zilberg, P. 2016. *Debating Khirbet Qeiyafa: A Fortified City in Judah from the Time of King David.* Jerusalem.

Garfinkel, Y., Ganor, S., Hasel, M., and Stiebel, G. 2009. "Khirbet Qeiyafa 2009 (Notes and News)." *Israel Exploration Journal* 59, pp. 214–20.

Garfinkel, Y., Golub, M. R., Misgav, H., and Ganor, S. 2015. "The ʾIšbaʿal Inscription from Khirbet Qeiyafa." *Bulletin of the American Schools of Oriental Research* 373, pp. 217–33.

Garfinkel, Y., Streit, K., Ganor, S., and Hasel, M. G. 2012. "State Formation in Judah: Biblical Tradition, Modern Historical Theories and Radiometric Dates at Khirbet Qeiyafa." *Radiocarbon* 54, pp. 359–69.

Garfinkel, Y., Streit, K., Ganor, S., and Reimer, P. J. 2015. "King David's City at Khirbet Qeiyafa: Results of the Second Radiocarbon Dating Project." *Radiocarbon* 57, pp. 881–90.

Garsiel, M. 2009. "The Valley of Elah Battle and the Duel of David with Goliath: Between History and Artistic Theological Historiography." In Galil, G., Geller, M., and Millard, A. (eds.), *Homeland and Exile. Biblical and Ancient Near Eastern Studies in Honour of Bustenay Oded,* pp. 391–426. Leiden.

Gilboa, A. 2012. "Cypriot Barrel Juglets at Khirbet Qeiyafa and Other Sites in the Levant: Cultural Aspects and Chronological Implications." *Tel Aviv* 39, pp. 133–49.

Goldwasser, O. 2010. "How the Alphabet was Born from Hieroglyphs." *Biblical Archaeology Review* 36/2, pp. 36–54.

Gottlieb, Y. 2010. "The Advent of the Age of Iron in the Land of Israel: A Review and Reassessment." *Tel Aviv* 37, pp. 89–110.

Graesser, C. F. 1972. "Standing Stones in Ancient Palestine." *Biblical Archaeology* 35, pp. 34–63.

Greenhut, Z., Strul, L., Bardah, L., and Weiss, D. 2001. *Ministry of the Interior Jerusalem District Master Plan 30/1, Archaeological Appendix.* Jerusalem (Hebrew).

Guerin, V. 1868. *Description géographique, historique et archéologique de la Palestine.* Paris.

Haines, R. C. 1971. *Excavations in the Plain of Antioch II. The Structural Remains of the Later Phases.* Chicago.

Halpern, B. 2001. *David's Secret Demons: Messiah, Murderer, Traitor, King.* Grand Rapids, MI.

Hasel, M. G. 2012. "New Excavations at Khirbet Qeiyafa and the Early History of Judah." In Hoffmeier, J. K. and Magery, D. R, (eds.), *Do Historical Matters Matter to Faith?* pp. 477–96. Wheaton, IL.

Hasel, M. G. 2014a. "Area D." In Garfinkel, Y., Ganor, S., and Hasel, M. G., *Khirbet Qeiyafa Vol. 2,* pp. 227–338. Jerusalem.

Hasel, M. G. 2014b. "The Olive Press Installation." In Garfinkel, Y., Ganor, S., and Hasel, M. G., *Khirbet Qeiyafa Vol. 2,* pp. 319–32. Jerusalem.

Hasel, M. G., Garfinkel, Y., and Weiss, S. 2017. *Socoh of the Judean Shephelah: The 2010 Survey.* Winona Lake, IN.

Herrmann G. 2017. *Ancient Ivory. Masterpieces of the Assyrian Empire.* London and New York.

Herzog, Z. 1997. *Archaeology of the City: Urban Planning in Ancient Israel and Its Social Implications.* Tel Aviv.

Herzog, Z. and Singer-Avitz, L. 2004. "Redefining the Centre: the Emergence of State in Judah." *Tel Aviv* 31, pp. 209–44.

Hoffmeier, J. K. 2011. "David's Triumph Over Goliath: 1 Samuel 17:54 and Ancient Near Eastern Analogues." In Bar, S., Kahn, D., and Shirley, J. J. (eds.), *Egypt, Canaan and Israel: History, Imperialism, Ideology and Literature. Proceedings of a Conference at the University of Haifa, 3–7 May 2009,* pp. 87–114. Leiden.

Hurowitz, V. A. 2009. "Tenth Century BCE to 586 BCE: The House of the Lord (Beyt YHWH)." In Grabar, O. and Kedar, B. Z. (eds.), *When Heaven and Earth Meet: Jerusalem Sacred Esplanade,* pp. 15–35. Jerusalem.

Jamieson-Drake, D. W. 1991. *Scribes and Schools in Monarchic Judah.* Sheffield.

Kallai, Z. 1971. "The Kingdom of Rehoboam." *Eretz Israel* 10: 245–54 (Hebrew).

Kang, H.-G. and Garfinkel, Y. 2009a. "The Early Iron Age II Pottery." In Garfinkel, Y. and Ganor, S., *Khirbet Qeiyafa Vol. 1,* pp. 119–49. Jerusalem.

Kang, H.-G. and Garfinkel, Y. 2009b "Ashdod Ware I: Middle Philistine Decorated Ware." In Garfinkel, Y. and Ganor, S. (eds.), *Khirbet Qeiyafa Vol. 1,* pp. 151–60. Jerusalem.

Kang, H.-G. and Garfinkel, Y. 2015. "Finger-impressed Jar Handles at Khirbet Qeiyafa: New Light on Administration in the Kingdom of Judah." *Levant* 47, pp. 186–205.

Katz, H. 2016. *Portable Shrine Models. Ancient Architectural Clay Models from the Levant.* Oxford.

Kehati, R. 2009, "The Faunal Assemblage." In Garfinkel, Y. and Ganor, S. (eds.), *Khirbet Qeiyafa Vol. 1,* pp. 201–08. Jerusalem.

Keimer, K. H., Kreimermann, I., and Garfinkel, Y. 2015. "From Quarry to Completion: *Hirbet Qēyafa* as a Case Study in Building Ancient Near Eastern Settlements." *Zeitschrift des Deutschen Palästina-Vereins* 131, pp. 109–28.

King, P. J. 2007. "David Defeats Goliath." In Ben-Tor, A. et al. (eds.), *Up to the Gates of Ekron. Essays on the Archaeology and History of the Eastern Mediterranean in Honor of Seymour Gitin*, pp. 350–57. Jerusalem.

Kirsch, J. 2000. *King David: The Real Life of the Man Who Ruled Israel.* New York.

Kisilewitz, S. 2015. "The Iron IIA Judahite Temple at Tel Moza." *Tel Aviv* 42, pp. 147–64.

Kletter, R. 1996. *The Judaean Pillar Figurines and the Archaeology of Asherah.* Oxford.

Kletter, R., Ziffer, I., and Zwickel, W. 2010. *Yavneh I. The Excavation of the 'Temple Hill' Repository Pit and the Cult Stands.* Fribourg.

Klingbeil, M. G. 2016. "Four Egyptian Seals from Khirbet Qeiyafa." In Ganor, S. et al. (eds.), *From Sha'ar Hagolan to Shaaraim. Essays in Honor of Prof. Yosef Garfinkel*, pp. 265–82. Jerusalem.

Kochavi, M. 1998. "The Eleventh Century BCE Tripartite Pillar Building at Tel Hadar." In Gitin, S. et al. (eds.) *Mediterranean Peoples in Transition: Thirteenth to Early Tenth Centuries BCE*, pp. 468–78. Jerusalem.

Lederman, Z. and Bunimovitz, S. 2014. "Canaanites, 'Shephelites' and those who will Become Judahites." *New Studies in the Archaeology of Jerusalem and its Region* 8, pp. 61–71 (Hebrew).

Lehmann, G. 2003. "The United Monarchy in the Countryside: Jerusalem, Judah and the Shephelah during the 10th Century B.C.E." In Vaughn, A. G. and Killebrew, A. E. (eds.), *Jerusalem in Bible and Archaeology*, pp. 117–164. Atlanta, GA.

Lehmann, G. and Niemann, H. M. 2014. "When Did the Shephelah Become Judahite?" *Tel Aviv* 41, pp. 77–94.

Lemaire, A. 1994. "'House of David' Restored in Moabite Inscription." *Biblical Archaeology Review* 20/3, pp. 30–37.

Lemche, N. P. 1988. *Ancient Israel: A New History of Israelite Society.* Sheffield.

Levy, E. and Pluquet, F. 2016. "Computer Experiments on the Khirbet Qeiyafa Ostracon." In *Digital Scholarship in the Humanities Advance Access*, published August 31, 2016.

Levy, T. E. et al. 2008. "High-precision Radiocarbon Dating and Historical Biblical Archaeology in Southern Jordan." *Proceedings of the National Academy of Science* Vol. 105, No. 43, pp. 16460–65.

Loud, G. 1948. *Megiddo II. Seasons of 1935–39*. Chicago.

McCarter, P. K., Bunimovitz, S.. and Lederman, Z. 2011. "An Archaic Baal Inscription from Tel Beth-Shemesh." *Tel Aviv* 38, pp. 179–93.

McKenzie, S. L. 2000. *King David: A Biography*. New York.

Maeir A. M. and Uziel, J. 2007. "A Tale of Two Tells: A Comparative Perspective on Tel Miqne-Ekron and Tell es-Safi/Gath in Light of Recent Archaeological Research." In Ben-Tor, A. et al. (eds.), *Up to the Gates of Ekron. Essays on the Archaeology and History of the Eastern Mediterranean in Honor of Seymour Gitin*, pp. 29–42. Jerusalem.

Malamat, A. 1984. "The Monarchy of David and Solomon." In Shanks, H. (ed.) *Recent Archaeology in the Land of Israel*, pp. 161–72. Washington andJerusalem.

Malamat, A. 1987. "A Forerunner of Biblical Prophecy: The Mari Documents." In Miller, P. D. et al. (eds.), *Ancient Israelite Religion: Essays in Honor of F. M. Cross*, pp. 33–52. Philadelphia, PA.

Mazar, A. 1980. *Excavations at Tell Qasile, Part 1*. Jerusalem.

Mazar, A. 1990. *Archaeology of the Land of the Bible, 10,000 to 586 B.C.E.* New York.

Mazar, A. 2006. "Jerusalem in the 10th Century B.C.E.: The Glass Half Full." In Amit, Y. et al. (eds.), *Essays on Ancient Israel in Its Near Eastern Context: A Tribute to Nadav Na'aman*, pp. 255–72. Winona Lake, IN.

Mazar, A. and Bronk Ramsey, C. 2008. "14C Dates and the Iron Age Chronology of Israel: A Response." *Radiocarbon* 50, pp. 159–80.

Mazar, B. 1986. "The Philistines and the Rise of Israel and Tyre." In *The Early Biblical Period, Historical Studies*, pp. 63–82. Jerusalem.

Mazar, E. 2006. "Did I Find King David's Palace?" *Biblical Archaeology Review* 32/1, pp. 16–27, 70.

Mazar, E. 2007. *The Excavations in the City of David in 2005 (the Visitor Center)*. Jerusalem.

Mazar, E. 2011. *Discovering the Solomonic Wall in Jerusalem*. Jerusalem.

Mazar, E., Ben-Shlomo, D., and Ahituv, S. 2013. "An Inscribed Pithos from the Ophel, Jerusalem. *Israel*." *Exploration Journal* 63, pp. 39–49.

Mettinger, T. N. D. 1971. *Solomonic State Officials*. Lund.

Mettinger, T. N. D. 1995. *No Graven Image? Israelite Aniconism in Its Ancient Near Eastern Context*. Stockholm.

Misgav, H., Garfinkel, Y., and Ganor, S. 2009. "The Khirbet Qeiyafa Ostracon." *New Studies in the Archaeology of Jerusalem and Its Region* 3, pp. 111–23 (Hebrew).

Moorey, P. R. S. 2003. *Idols of the People. Miniature Images of Clay in the Ancient Near East.* Oxford.

Muller, B. 2002. *Les "Maquettes Architecturales" du proche-orient ancien.* Beirut.

Münger, S., Zangenberg, J., and Pakkala, J. 2011. "Kinneret—An Urban Center at the Crossroads." *Near Eastern Archaeology* 74:2, pp. 68–90.

Na'aman, N. 1986. "Hezekiah's Fortified Cities and the *Lmlk* Stamps." *Bulletin of the American Schools of Oriental Research* 261, pp. 5–21.

Na'aman, N. 2008a. "In Search of the Ancient Name of Khirbet Qeiyafa." *Journal of Hebrew Scriptures* 8: Article 21.

Na'aman, N. 2008b. "Sha'arim—The Gateway to the Kingdom of Judah." *Journal of Hebrew Scriptures* 8: Article 24.

Na'aman, N. 2010. "Khirbet Qeiyafa in Context." *Ugarit-Forschungen* 42, pp. 497–526.

Naveh, J. 1978. *On Stone and Mosaic.* Jerusalem (Hebrew).

Ornan, T. 2005. *The Triumph of the Symbol: Pictorial Representation of Deities in Mesopotamia and the Biblical Image Ban.* Fribourg.

Pfoh, E. 2009. *The Emergence of Israel in Ancient Palestine.* London.

Rabinovich, A. R. 2016. *The Iron Age Metal Assemblage of Khirbet Qeiyafa: A Glimpse into the Transition from Bronze to Iron in the Early Iron IIA.* Unpublished M.A. thesis, Hebrew University. Jerusalem.

Rollston, C. A. 2011. "The Ossuary of Mariam Daughter of Yeshua in Context: Limning the Broad Tableau of the Epigraphic and Literary Data." www.rollstonepigraphy.com. 6 July, 2011. Accessed 7/3/2018.

Römer, T. and Brettler, M. Z. 2000. "Deuteronomy 34 and the Case for a Persian Hexateuch." *Journal of Biblical Literature* 111, pp. 401–19.

Sandhaus, D. and Kreimermann, I. 2015. "The Late 4th/3rd Century BCE Transition in the Judean Hinterland in Light of the Pottery from Khirbet Qeiyafa." *Tel Aviv* 42, pp. 151–71.

Schroer, S. 2016. "Drei Stempelsiegelamulette aus Ḥirbet Qēyafa." *Zeitschrift des Deutschen Palästina-Vereins* 132, pp. 134–45.

Schroer, S. and Münger, S. (eds.). 2017. *Khirbet Qeiyafa in the Shephelah.* Fribourg.

Sharon, I., Gilboa, A., Jull, T., and Boaretto, E. 2007 "Report on the First Stage of the Iron Age Dating Project in Israel: Supporting the Low Chronology." *Radiocarbon* 49, pp. 1–46.

Shiloh, Y. 1978. "Elements in the Development of Town Planning in the Israelite City." *Israel Exploration Society* 28, pp. 36–51.

Shiloh, Y. 1979. *The Proto-Aeolic Capital and Israelite Ashlar Masonry.* Jerusalem.

Shiloh, Y. 1984. *Excavations at the City of David, Vol. I. Interim Report of the First Five Seasons.* Jerusalem.

Singer-Avitz, L. 2010. "The Relative Chronology of Khirbet Qeiyafa." *Tel Aviv* 37, pp. 79–83.

Stager, L. E. 2003. "The Patrimonial Kingdom of Solomon." In Dever, W. G. and Gitin, S. (eds.), *Symbiosis, Symbolism, and the Power of the Past: Canaan, Ancient Israel and their Neighbors from the Late Bronze Age through Roman Palaestina,* pp. 63–74. Winona Lake, IN.

Stager, L. E. 2008. "The Canaanite Silver Calf." In Stager, L. E. et al. (eds.), *Ashkelon 1,* pp. 577–80. Winona Lake, IN.

Stern, E. (ed.). 1993. *The New Encyclopedia of Archaeological Excavations in the Holy Land.* Jerusalem.

Stiebel, G. D. 2010. "By the Way—Khirbet Qeiyafa in the Classical and Late Periods." *New Studies in the Archaeology of Jerusalem and Its Region* 4, pp. 161–69 (Hebrew).

Thiele, E. R. 1983. *The Mysterious Numbers of the Hebrew Kings.* Grand Rapids, MI.

Thompson, T. L. 1992. *Early History of the Israelite People from the Written and Archaeological Sources.* Leiden.

Tov, E. 1985. "The Composition of 1 Samuel 16–18 in the light of the Septuagint Version." In Tigay, J. H. (ed.), *Empirical Models for Biblical Criticism,* pp. 98–130. Philadelphia, PA.

Ucko, P. J. 1968. *Anthropomorphic Figurines of Predynastic Egypt and Neolithic Crete.* London.

Ussishkin, D. 2003. "Solomon's Jerusalem: The Text and the Facts on the Ground." In Vaughn, A. G. and Killebrew, A. E. (eds.), *Jerusalem in Bible and Archaeology: The First Temple Period,* pp. 103–15. Atlanta, GA.

Van der Toorn, K. (ed.). 1997. *The Image and the Book: Iconic Cults, Aniconism, and the Rise of Book Religion in Israel and the Ancient Near East.* Leuven.

Van Seters, J. 2009. *The Biblical Saga of King David.* Winona Lake, IN.

Weinberg, S. S. 1979. "A Two-Storey Lamp from Palestine." *Israel Exploration Journal* 29, pp. 143–47.

Wright, J. L. 2014. *David, King of Israel, and Caleb in Biblical Memory.* Cambridge.

Yadin, A. 2004. "Goliath's Armor and Israelite Collective Memory." *Vetus Testamentum* 54, pp. 373–95.

Yadin, Y. 1955. "Goliath's Javelin and the *mnwr 'rgym*." *Palestine Exploration Quarterly* 57, pp. 58–69.

Yadin, Y. 1958. "Solomon's City Wall and Gate at Gezer." *Israel Exploration Journal* 8, pp. 80–86.

Yardeni, Y. 2009. "The Khirbet Qeiyafa Inscription—Response A." *New Studies in the Archaeology of Jerusalem and Its Region* 3, pp. 124–25 (Hebrew).

Yasur-Landau, A. 2010. *The Philistines and Aegean Migration at the End of the Late Bronze Age*. Cambridge.

Yeivin, S. 1965. *Encyclopaedia Miqra'it* 3. Jerusalem, cols. 191–92 (Hebrew).

Zakovitz, Y. 1995. *David: From Shepherd to Messiah*. Jerusalem (Hebrew).

Zissu, B. and Goren, Y. 2011. "The Ossuary of 'Miriam Daughter of Yeshua Son of Caiaphas, Priests [of] Ma'aziah' from Beth 'Imri." *Israel Exploration Journal* 61, pp. 74–95.

Zorn, J. R. 2010. "Reconsidering Goliath: An Iron Age I Philistine Chariot Warrior." *Bulletin of the American Schools of Oriental Research* 360, pp. 1–22.

SOURCES OF ILLUSTRATIONS

Frontispiece: Bildarchiv Monheim GmbH/Alamy Stock Photo.

Figures in text:

1, 2 Yosef Garfinkel; 3 J. Rosenberg, maps; 4 Lebrecht Music and Arts Photo Library/Alamy Stock Photo; 5 Rijksmuseum, Amsterdam; 6, 7 J. Rosenberg, maps; 8 Ada Yardeni; 9 Oriental Institute, The University of Chicago; 10 Musée du Louvre, Paris; 11 Yosef Garfinkel; 12, 13 Sky-view; 14 J. Rosenberg, maps; 15 Yosef Garfinkel; 16–23 J. Rosenberg, maps; 24 Yosef Garfinkel; 25–33 J. Rosenberg, maps; 34 Yosef Garfinkel; 35 Amir Biberman; 36 Clara Armit; 37–43 Olga Dobovsky; 44 Sky-view; 45 Courtesy of Ada Yardeni; 46 Tal Rogovskey; 47 Courtesy of Ada Yardeni; 48 Metropolitan Museum of Art, New York. Harris Brisbane Dick Fund, 1917 (17.3.3449.11); 49, 50 Yosef Garfinkel; 51 J. Rosenberg, maps; 52–54 Olga Dobovsky; 55–57 J. Rosenberg, maps; 58–65 Olga Dobovsky; 66 Musée des Arts Decoratifs, Paris/Archives Charmet/Bridgeman Images; 67 J. Rosenberg, maps; 68 Metropolitan Museum of Art, New York. The Elisha Whittelsey Collection, The Elisha Whittelsey Fund, 1966 (66.613.16); 69 J. Rosenberg, maps; 70 Rijksmuseum, Amsterdam; 71, 72 Roy Albag; 73 Yosef Garfinkel; 74, 75 Clara Armit; 76, 77 J. Rosenberg, maps; 78 Sky-view; 79 J. Rosenberg, maps; 80 Olga Dobovsky.

Plates:

i The Israel Museum, Jerusalem/Bridgeman Images; ii Hanan Isachar/Alamy Stock Photo; iii Duby Tal/Albatross/Alamy Stock Photo; iv Photo by Sky-view; v Research and Reconstruction of Archaeological Sites – Architect Roy Albag, Bible Lands Museum, Jerusalem; vi Yosef Garfinkel; vii, viii Photo by Sky-view; ix Yosef Garfinkel; x, xi Photo by Sky-view; xii–xvi Photo by Clara Amit, The Israel Antiquities Authority; xvii Yosef Garfinkel; xviii, xix Photo by Amir Biberman; xx Photo by Clara Amit, The Israel Antiquities Authority; xxi Yosef Garfinkel; xxii, xxiii Photo by Gabi Laron; xxiv British Museum, London (1848, 1104.314); xxv, xxvi Research and Reconstruction of Archaeological Sites – Architect Roy Albag, Bible Lands Museum, Jerusalem.

INDEX